MW01515064

# The
# Pennsylvania German
# Folklore Society

## VOLUME TWENTY-THREE

## 1958-1959

Printed MCMLXI

SCHLECHTER'S — ALLENTOWN, PENNA.

6

Initial Fraktur Letters
from The Ephrata ABC Book

II

# The Fraktur-Writings or Illuminated Manuscripts of the Pennsylvania Germans

by

## Donald A. Shelley

Executive Director

Henry Ford Museum and Greenfield Village

Dedicated to

WALTER W. S. COOK

Founder of the Institute of Fine Arts

New York University

Blessed are the Builders

its close connection to the other arts and crafts, it provides an excellent means for solving problems of dating in the general field of Pennsylvania Folk Art.

A third, and equally important, purpose of this monograph is the preservation of some adequate record of the Pennsylvania German Style of Illumination, certainly one of the most colorful Folk Art expressions to be found anywhere in our country. Today, as the 200-year-old barriers of the Pennsylvania German isolation gradually melt away, it is possible for the first time to examine these intimate and homely arts and crafts, and to appreciate more fully their richness of color and their vigor of design. Here is European 18th century Folk Art transplanted to colonial Pennsylvania, adapted, and rejuvenated in typical American fashion.

The manuscripts dealt with here under the name "Fraktur" — the generic term used to describe these illuminated manuscript pages employing letters based on the 16th century Gothic type-face of the same name — include not only the usual illuminated Birth-and-Baptismal Certificates, Vorschriften (writing specimens), and books, but also various printed religious broadsides with decorated borders, Haus-Segens, Irrgartens (labyrinths), and occasional watercolor portraits which are directly related to this technique.

Most of the material which follows is unrecorded, unpublished, and unillustrated. It has been gathered and studied over a period covering the last 20 years, during which the author has photographed some 2,000 manuscript pages in both public and private collections. This total probably constitutes only about one-fourth of those seen. Since such a large majority of the material has been in private collections, some of the largest of which have subsequently been dispersed, this study will bring together here important manuscripts which are no longer readily available to other scholars in the field, and will relate them to what is accessible in known public collections.

Inasmuch as most of the Pennsylvania German religious sects employed these illuminated documents as a means of preserving their genealogical record, it is easily understood that the thousands of certificates produced between 1750 and 1850 contain a vast store of information. Both artistically and technically these manuscripts provide a

# I. PREFACE

O other phase of early American arts and crafts is better characterized by the term "Folk Art" than that produced by the German-speaking immigrants who settled southeastern Pennsylvania. The same ties which bound these people together into one homogeneous social group in the 18th and early 19th centuries—their language, religion, customs, and their common geographical background — still exist today in spite of repeated invasions of modern American industrial life. So colorful and so decorative are the furniture, pottery, ironwork, glass and illuminated manuscript pages they produced, that for many years the term "Pennsylvania German" has been synonymous with "Folk Art." This typical regional art represents an important contribution to American culture, and as such offers an unusually rich field for investigation both to the art historian and to the student of Folk Art.

The Pennsylvania German Style of Illumination was chosen as the subject for this monograph, first, because it constitutes the most important single aspect of Pennsylvania German Folk Art. Transplanted from Europe to America about the middle of the 18th century, this lineal descendant of the medieval manuscript tradition enjoyed in this country for more than 100 years a period of revival and fruition. During this century it not only served as a "carrying stream" for preserving the typical designs and "dialect" of Pennsylvania German Folk Art, but also was employed upon the painted furniture, slipware and sgraffito pottery, decorated toleware, and numerous household utensils bearing the motifs so characteristic of this region.

A second reason for making this study of the history and development of the Pennsylvania German Style of Illumination is that it has not thus far received scholarly or sufficiently scientific treatment. Here is a vast body of material varying greatly in content, design, color, and size, which has never been adequately analyzed and classified. Because of the extended period over which the technique was practiced here and

# TABLE OF CONTENTS

most interesting link between Europe and America on the one hand, and between late medieval and modern times on the other — or, from an Art History point of view, a link between medieval manuscripts and the hand-illuminated manuscripts of the Ephrata Cloister, as well as between the Gutenberg Bible and the printed forms of the Reading, Pennsylvania, presses.

The reticence and modesty of the Pennsylvania German people have encouraged them to enjoy their treasures privately and to refrain, in their traditional manner, from ostentatious display. Thus, although it is now 63 years since Dr. Henry C. Mercer first called attention to these manuscripts, public interest in them is only now taking hold. Typical of this half century during which a few enthusiastic collectors quietly filled their portfolios with these illuminated documents, was the author's own accidental discovery of the existence of Fraktur in Macy's, the "World's largest Department Store" — after having lived right in the Pennsylvania German area some twenty years! Even after further investigation, the first inkling of the variety and extent of this field came only when the author's original estimate of some 500 to 1,000 examples had to be revised upwards to include between 8,000 and 10,000 Frakturs. And this total would be exclusive of numerous small bookplates, or the fully illuminated musical manuscripts such as were produced within the Ephrata Cloister itself.

While it is true that examples turn up throughout the 48 states from Maine to California, the segregation of the Pennsylvania Germans from the outside world due to language barriers and folk customs has kept the majority of these certificates in the eastern Pennsylvania area. Local Pennsylvania museums and historical societies usually have small groups of them, but the Metropolitan Museum of Art, The New-York Historical Society, and The Brooklyn Museum were the only out-of-state public museums which displayed them up to a decade ago. Hundreds of isolated pieces no doubt remain in the families of those persons for whom they originally were made. Others are still hidden in family bibles, pasted in dower chests, or have been carried to some out-of-way place where they continue to remain unnoticed even today.

Large numbers of these Pennsylvania German Illuminated Manuscripts have also been dispersed by auction in such famous sales as

3

those of Governor Samuel W. Pennypacker (1907-10, 1920), Jacob Paxson Temple (1922), Howard Reifsnyder (1929), Schuyler B. Jackson (1933), Theodore Offerman (1937), George Horace Lorimer (1944), and Mrs. Albert K. Hostetter (1946). A large portion of the Elie Nadelman collection was sold privately during 1948 and 1949, and the Paul M. Auman collection in 1950. The most recent groups of moderate size to be dispersed appeared at Reading, Pa., in the William Keible (May, 1951), and Walter Himmelreich (May, 1958) auctions; also at Flushing, Long Island, the Clarence W. Brazer auction (Feb., 1959). The last of the major pioneer collections of top quality to be auctioned, the Arthur Sussel collection, established all-time records at the Parke-Bernet Gallery, New York, in October, 1958.

So avidly are these illuminated manuscripts collected today that, within a few months after the Hostetter, Lorimer, and Sussel auctions, hundreds of pieces had vanished into private collections all over the United States. Fortunately, the author had the opportunity to record all of these collections in toto before they were dispersed, as well as the Nadelman, Auman, Keible, Odenwelder, Renner, and Brazer groups. The Claude W. Unger-Harvey Bassler collection of important early imprint material, now on temporary loan to Franklin and Marshall College at Lancaster, Pa. was likewise completely photographed fifteen years ago.

In preparing this survey of the development of the Pennsylvania German Style of Illumination, it soon became apparent that Fraktur served a purpose much broader than mere record-keeping. In reality, it preserved for a period of more than 100 years both the motifs and the character of Pennsylvania German Folk Art. Like pottery, basketry, furniture decoration, and other Folk Arts, it has in some cases been practiced down to the present day, although the twilight of the Industrial Revolution has long since obscured the existence of any large-scale production.

Since the time the present study was begun 20 years ago, some 65 collections, both public and private, have been studied and photographed, with a total of more than 3,000 photographs to work from. It is due to the generosity of the curators of the various public museums and numerous private collectors that most of the works of art, and much

4

of the information contained in this monograph, became available. All of the private collectors of Pennsylvania German Illuminated Manuscripts approached by the author, excepting' two, cooperated fully in making their collections available for study.

Grateful acknowledgment is made here to the American Association of Museums which, by means of a Fellowship, made it possible for the writer to spend the summer of 1938 in the Rhineland where he gathered the unpublished material included here in the European chapters. While there he also procured a collection of photographs of related Folk Art objects, many of which have undoubtedly since that time been destroyed during World War II.

## II.  INTRODUCTION TO FOLK ART

HE chief result of the intensive study made in recent years of the progress and development of the arts in America has been to disprove the old cliche which appeared in every book on early American Art, namely, that there was very little of it.  Now that the first enthusiastic collectors and antiquarians have cleared the way, students and research workers are busily engaged in analyzing and classifying the available material.  It is already quite evident that the richness of the field of early American Art goes far beyond our fondest expectations.

With scientific study of our early arts — painting, sculpture, architecture, prints, and the arts of decoration — already well under way, attention has now begun to turn more and more to related archaeological and sociological phases of American culture.

Following closely on the heels of the interest in the arts of the Near and Far East in the 19th century — which had a profound effect upon the artistic production of that period both here and abroad, — the eyes of our early 20th century painters and aestheticians turned to the "primitive" arts of Africa and the South Pacific, and thence to the works created by the American Indian and by the local artists and craftsmen who were active later in various rural sections of the United States.

The grouping of all these varied arts under the heading "primitive" soon brought the need for a definition of terms.  At first used to indicate early date, it soon became apparent that the term "primitive" had more to do with the state of mind of the people and with the limited ability and technical training of their artists.  It referred more to group psychology than to early date, and to a craft production rather than to an academic tradition.

While many substitutes have since been suggested for "primitive," such as popular,[1] pioneer,[2] amateur, industrial, etc., it continues to be used chiefly to describe the arts of Africa, the South Pacific, the Eskimos, and other such ethnological groups, as well as for the 19th century non-professional painting done throughout the countryside. For rural arts and crafts, however, the term Folk Art has been found fairly satisfactory. It describes quite well the "arts of the common man"[3] — combining utility and beauty — and those arts and crafts which border on folklore and customs, yet go beyond into the realm of true decorative arts.

Although *Folk Art* was first divorced from *Folklore* some 30 years ago,[4] much in the same way that the primitive arts of Africa and the South Pacific were divorced from Ethnology and from Anthropology, the acceptance of all these as subjects deserving special investigation by the art historian has only fairly recently been acknowledged. While 20th century painters have constantly delved into Primitive Art as well as into Folk Art for inspiration and for justification of their use of abstraction, distortion, and non-representational forms, full appreciation of Folk Art is yet to be seen.

In contrast to the scholarly treatment accorded Primitive Art during the past decade, the attitude toward American Folk Art continues to be chiefly non-scientific and antiquarian. The only major exhibitions were held at the Newark Museum in 1930[5] and 1931,[6] at the Museum of Modern Art in 1932,[7] and at the Brooklyn Museum in 1939;[8] small

---

[1] Brooklyn Museum exhibition catalogue, *Popular Art in America*. Brooklyn, N.Y.: Brooklyn Museum Press, 1939, p. 1.

[2] Drepperd, Carl W., *American Pioneer Arts and Artists*. Springfield, Mass.: The Pond-Ekberg Co., 1942, pp. 1-12, "What Is Primitive and What Is Not?"

[3] Museum of Modern Art exhibition catalogue, *American Folk Art: The Art of the Common Man in America, 1750-1900*. New York, N.Y.: Museum of Modern Art, 1932, pp. 5-8.

[4] Hahm, Konrad, *Deutsche Volkskunst*. Berlin: Deutsche Buch-Gemeinschaft, 1928.

[5] Newark Museum exhibition catalogue, *American Primitives*, edited by Holger Cahill and Elinor Robinson, November, 1930.

[6] Newark Museum exhibition catalogue, *American Folk Sculpture*, edited by Holger Cahill and Elinor Robinson, October, 1931.

[7] Museum of Modern Art, *op. cit.*

[8] Brooklyn Museum, *op. cit.*

gallery shows were more numerous.[9]  Yet at the London exhibition of American Art shown at the Tate Gallery during the summer of 1946, the so-called American "primitives" were most enthusiastically received by the British critics and public alike,[10] and were better appreciated than the paintings by more highly-rated artists like Copley, Bingham, and others we prize today.

But then, is it strange that arts which speak such a simple, universal language should be preferred to the more sophisticated schools of painting and sculpture?  Although accepted on the basis of a "certain kinship with modern art" and of their "quaintness," is there any reason why these homely but sincere expressions of the folk artists' love of beauty should not achieve aesthetic quality and importance equal to the "Fine Arts?"

The widespread interest in American Folk Art today stems originally from a tremendous activity abroad in the same field not so many years ago.  Starting shortly after World War I, and especially in the 1920's, the various European countries saw in Folk Art a powerful means for reviving interest in their nations' past.  Folk Art museums sprang up all over Europe.  Modern manufacturers of textiles, pottery, china, and household utensils of all sorts, turned to the old designs for inspiration.  There was a veritable flood of books on European Folk Art.

In 1928, the First Folk Art Congress met at Prag.[11]  Regional as well as national exhibitions were held,[12] visits to early production sites were encouraged, and small Folk Art museums were set up in every province and city.  Even in the schools, attempts were made to revive

---

[9] Whitney Studio Club Show of Primitives, 1924; Dudensing Gallery Exhibition, 1925; Whitney Studio Club Show of Mrs. Isabel Carleton Wilde's Collection, 1927; Harvard Society for Contemporary Art Exhibition of *American Folk Painting*, 1930; and the Downtown Gallery Exhibitions: *Vital Statistics*, 1936, *Children in American Folk Art, 1725 to 1865*, 1937, and *Folk Art Sculpture of the American Index of Design*, 1937.

[10] Winchester, Alice, 'American Painting in London,' *Antiques*, LI, 2 (February, 1947), pp. 100-108, 127.

[11] Prag, 1928; Antwerp, 1930; Berlin, 1938; Switzerland, 1940.

[12] *Süddeutsche Volkskunst*, Ausstellungspark, München (3, Juli bis 17. Oktober, 1937); *Ausstellung Deutsche Bauernkunst*, Stattliches Museum fur Deutsche Volkskunde, Berlin (1938).  Also, the Brooklyn Museum's series of exhibitions: Czechoslovakia, Hungary, Roumania, and Montenegro (1921), European costumes, textiles and ceramics (1923), Norwegian handicraft (1925), Peasant arts of Czechoslovakia (1926), Arts and crafts of Denmark (1927), Arts of Czechoslovakia (1935), Peasant costume (1937), Swedish folk art (1938), Polish arts and crafts (1939), Italian folk arts and crafts (1939), and Arts of Scandinavia (1944).

Folk Art artificially among the children, though with only moderate
success. In 1932, Konrad Hahm estimated that there were some 2,000
local Folk Art museums in Germany alone![13]

The flood of publications on Folk Art which ensued in Germany,
Switzerland, France, Italy, and in the Scandinavian countries, focused
attention upon certain basic concepts. Chief of these was the fact that
Folk Art, regardless of certain national and local characteristics, constituted a gigantic *common denominator* throughout Europe in the 18th
and 19th centuries. Whatever regional variations occur are within the
general framework of this universal folk expression. Such variations
are more apt to appear in the *interpretation* of the specific motif rather
than in the choice of that motif or design, or else in the *choice of certain
colors* rather than in the use of color itself. In spite of geographical,
political, or language borders, in other words, a great basic homogeneity
exists.

Small wonder then, that variations even within a country like Germany would be subordinated to the larger whole; that perfectly clear
distinctions between the Folk Art of the various German Provinces due
to materials, climate, soil, customs, religion, etc., are nevertheless only
small variations of the larger common theme.

And not so strange, then, is the realization that the arts which the
German, Swiss, and French Huguenot immigrants brought with them
to America, and especially to Pennsylvania, should echo the Province
from which each group came. As a matter of fact, what real differences
there were in the Fatherland seem to show up all the more as the art is
transplanted to the strange soil of colonial Pennsylvania and becomes a
"memory art."

Recent attempts to give the impression that the Pennsylvania German Folk Arts are based not upon what the immigrants *brought* with
them, but upon what they *found* already under way in Pennsylvania,
has little basis in fact. Drepperd's attempt to credit the entire development to Swedish and to Dutch prototypes,[14] none of which he actually
produces, is more clever than honest.

---

[13] Hahm, Konrad, *Deutsche Volkskunst*. Breslau: Ferdinand Hirt, Jedermanns
Bucherei, 1932, p 12
[14] Drepperd, Carl W., 'Origins of Pennsylvania Folk Art.' *Antiques*, XXXVII,
2 (February, 1940), 64-68. This attempt derives from a fundamental lack of understanding of Folk Art itself — which though somewhat similar in neighboring
countries, varies like a local dialect. Only a sufficient knowledge of these small
*nuances* enables one to differentiate between countries.

Intensive research has revealed little that survived in Pennsylvania from the earliest period of colonization by the Swedes and the Dutch. It has produced (1) no inscriptions on individual pieces in either of these languages, (2) no signatures of artists of these two nationalities and, (3) no specific forms which can definitely be proved to be Swedish or Dutch, but *not* German or Swiss. Miss Whitmore,[15] although occasionally incorrect in her dating, nevertheless has demonstrated the lack of sound reasoning in the arguments put forward by Drepperd. The chief argument of all is the interpretation of the individual forms themselves, which time and again is so closely allied to the South German and Swiss forms that it is difficult to distinguish between them.

Joseph Downs has cited instance after instance of this;[16] the forms, materials, and motifs are direct transplantations. What more fertile ground could there have been than this island of German peasant culture in the New World which, because it was composed of a different language group, was simply dismissed by the surrounding English and Scotch-Irish settlers as dumb, hopeless, and beyond possible improvement?

Folk Art, usually anonymous, represents a *group* tradition rather than *individual* accomplishment. Only occasionally when you get a Rousseau, a Hicks, Landis, or Pickett, does it get beyond the designation of a "school." This is entirely in keeping with the situation in German and Swiss Folk Art, where practically no names of individual artists have been handed down. Actually, in many cases, the technique used in a certain *region* is named after that region, and the individual craftsmen who employed it remain nameless.[17]

Folk Art, then, was a creation of the peasant to suit his own taste. Beyond mere utility, it expressed his joy in life, and his great love for the beauty of nature It reflected his pride in his home and his satisfaction in the small pleasures of everyday life. In the constant cycle of birth marriage, and death, in the succession of the seasons, and in the ever-changing years, he watched the unfolding of a great plan of which he felt he was himself an integral part.

---

[15] Whitmore, Eleanore M., 'Origins of Pennsylvania German Folk Art,' *Antiques.* XXXVIII, 3 (September, 1940), 106-110.

[16] Downs, Joseph, *The House of the Miller at Millbach.* Philadelphia: The Pennsylvania Museum of Art, 1929.

[17] "Marburger Stil," "Tolzer Art," etc.

Accepting the role he felt he was to play in this divine plan, he then set about making the home he was to occupy during his brief stay on this earth as attractive and as comfortable as possible. Beyond this, he must also remember his children for they would succeed him, and so he built "for the ages." His house and his barn, his furniture, his pottery, and his pewter, all had that solid and substantial look which proclaims their fundamentally utilitarian purpose.

## III. RHINE TO PENNSYLVANIA:

## VOLKSKUNST TO FOLK ART

HERE can be little doubt that the real reason our antiquarian and amateur attitude toward Pennsylvania German Folk Art has persisted so long is our lack of knowledge of the people and their background. Nor is this lack of knowledge of the Pennsylvania German people limited to their Folk Art alone, for its exists likewise with regard to their contributions to American agriculture, education, science, literature, and military history. The explanation for this, as it has been presented recently in great detail by Shryock,[18] is that "the Pennsylvania Germans simply were not seen by the historian. Or, to be more exact, they were not seen by the majority of professional historians over a long period."

Sensing this oversight, Pennsylvania German scholars during the past two decades have put forth special efforts to correct the situation. Further studies of the immigration itself have been made, general books enumerating and evaluating the contributions of the group such as Wood's *The Pennsylvania Germans* have been published, and an extensive bibliography of individual scientific works in all fields has been built up. To supplement and augment the work of the long-distinguished Pennsylvania German Society, a second organization known as the Pennsylvania German Folklore Society was formed in 1935[19] with the purpose of preserving for future generations the folklore of the Pennsylvania German past. This renewed activity in this field, it is significant to note, has been accompanied by an increased popular interest in the Pennsylvania Germans themselves, and will no doubt lead to a more accurate evaluation of their contributions to American life.

---

[18] Shryock, Richard H., 'The Pennsylvania German as Seen by the Historian,' from Ralph Wood, editor, *The Pennsylvania Germans*, IX, p. 239.
[19] May 4, 1935.

To understand more fully this people whose language, customs, art, and traditions have seemed so un-American to our early historians, only a fuller knowledge of their European background will suffice  As one writer has expressed it, "perhaps nowhere else in America have European customs been so faithfully perpetuated as among the Pennsylvania Germans."[20]  Two important factors which made such a perpetuation possible during the entire period of immigration were, first, that the settlers arrived in an almost *continuous stream* and, second, that the area which they settled was so *closely confined*.  As a result, even daily contact with other language groups failed to weaken the European traditions.

Although the earliest explorations and settlements in Pennsylvania were made first by the Dutch and then by the Swedes, it is the period after 1664 when the English took over all Dutch possessions that is of interest here.  The history of Pennsylvania as we know it today actually begins in 1681 when King Charles II, in payment of a debt of 16,000 pounds sterling which he owed William Penn's father, Admiral Penn, granted the former this vast tract of land in the New World.  This charter, which Penn received on March 4, 1681, not only specified the name "Pennsylvania" or Penn's Woods, but established the boundaries and outlined the various powers and duties of the new proprietor  Realizing that his only hope of securing any financial return for his investment lay in converting his wilderness into productive farm land, Penn thought at once of those enterprising peasant farmers he had seen in the rich and productive valley of the Rhine some years before.

Nor was he any the less familiar with their religious beliefs than their success in agriculture.  Their religious ideas, as he had found on three previous trips to the Rhineland between 1671 and 1677, were quite similar to those of the Quakers.  So much so, in fact, that he had himself made several converts before he returned to England.  Penn, therefore, was well aware of the religious persecutions and almost continuous wars which had plagued the inhabitants of the Rhenish Palatinate, and he was convinced of their innate ability to develop the soil.  He knew that his ideas for establishing democracy and tolerance as the basic principles of his "Holy Experiment" in Pennsylvania would, therefore, appeal to them.

---

[20] Downs, Joseph, *A Handbook of the Pennsylvania German Galleries in the American Wing.*  New York, N.Y.: The Metropolitan Museum of Art, 1934, p. 4.

Thus, soon after William Penn had arrived at New Castle on the
.Welcome in 1682 to take possession of his new province of Pennsylvania,
his humanitarian and democratic ideas became the law of the land.
Printed broadsides were circulated throughout the Rhineland offering the
oppressed people freedom from political and religious intolerance, and
raising for them the bright hope of unlimited economic opportunity in
the New Land. What more fortunate climax could possibly be imagined
for the endless political and religious wars which had ravaged their
homeland year after year? Why should anyone hesitate to accept such
a glowing future? Furthermore, letters received from friends and relatives already in the New World proclaimed that it far surpassed their
fondest expectations.

To the many different Sects and people who inhabited the Rhenish
Palatinate at that time, Penn's invitation must have had a familiar ring.
For it was that same hope of freedom from religious persecution, from
the constant scourge of wars, and for some semblance of economic independence which had brought all of them together in the Palatinate: the
Mennonites from Switzerland, Huguenots from France, Moravians from
Bohemia, Schwenkfelders from Silesia, and countless smaller groups
from other central European areas. While each of these differed in some
respects from the others, they were all bound together by a *common
language* and by their *Protestant religion;* such differences as existed
were relatively minor ones by comparison and were apt to involve custom, social practice, or dress. It was these similarities and differences
within this relatively homogeneous group which, once the stream of
immigration began to overflow its banks, were carried directly into the
southeastern counties of Pennsylvania, and which explain some of the
local differences which still exist today.

The Rhine Valley, in which these refugees from **religious and po-**
litical wars had congregated, was one of the richest agricultural areas in
Germany because of its mild climate and its extraordinarily fertile soil
Bordering this valley both to the east and to the west, moreover, are
heavily wooded mountainous areas which provided the inhabitants with
a superfluity of pine and other soft woods. So desirable was this land
that throughout the history of Europe from Roman times to the present
day, one war after another has been waged back and forth over this

territory. Not by accident has it been characterized as "the cock-pit of western civilization."[21]

In fact, the very people who for twelve centuries have retained possession of the Rhine Valley and the Palatinate Uplands, the "Palatines" themselves, are the product of two of the most warlike of the ancient Germanic tribes, according to Oscar Kuhns.[22] In their contest against the Romans for this area, the Alemanni finally were victorious and took both banks of the Rhine. The Alemanni were in turn attacked by the Franks under Clovis in the 5th century, and were finally conquered by them. Rather than yield to the victors, some of the staunch Alemanni moved into Switzerland while those who remained on the Rhine mingled with the Franks to form a new Frankish-Alemannic group — the ancestors of the Palatines who ultimately came to Pennsylvania. As century after century brought only more wars, more oppression, more violence, and as more refugees from other lands sought haven in the Rhenish Palatinate, the peasant began to study his station in life and to reflect upon how he might improve it.

The basic unit of economic and social organization in the Palatinate, as in other parts of Germany, was the *agricultural village*. The peasant's home, barn, and stable were in the village itself, whereas the land which he tilled (but did not own) was outside of town. Each morning he walked out to it, worked hard all day long, and returned home at night. While the individual farm was not characteristic of those regions sending the largest migrations to America, it was common in the areas to the south of the Palatinate, in Baden, Bavaria, and in Switzerland.

The once universally accepted idea that freedom of religious worship was the sole purpose of their immigration has long since been disproved. The quest for freedom itself and for ownership of land, encouraged by promotional advertising, also played a large part.[23] Glowing letters sent back to Europe likewise stimulated the immigration. Further, and more detailed, studies of this immigration are constantly being made.

---

[21] Frederick, J. George, *The Pennsylvania Dutch and Their Cookery.* New York, N.Y.: The Business Bourse, 1935, p. 13.

[22] Kuhns, Oscar, *The German and Swiss Settlements of Colonial Pennsylvania: A Study of the So-Called Pennsylvania Dutch.* New York, N.Y.: Henry Holt, 1900, p. 7.

[23] Knittle, Walter Allen, *Early Eighteenth Century Palatine Emigrations.* Philadelphia, Pa.: Dorrence and Company, 1937.

The initial flood of immigration from the Rhineland extended from about 1683 to the time of the Revolution, and has been divided by Faust into three distinct periods: 1683-1710, 1710-1727, and 1727-1776.[24] While records on the two earlier ones are not extant, from 1727 on — due to the new law requiring names and places of origin to be given on ship-lists — the provinces from which the immigrants came have been tabulated. Not only have these been published,[25] but from time to time new lists have been discovered which have added immeasurably to our knowledge.[26] Nor were these immigrations up to the time of the Revolution the only ones. On the contrary, there was a continual and substantial flow down into the 19th century, so that the influence of the Fatherland was constantly being renewed. As we shall find, this factor played a large part in maintaining the basically European character of Pennsylvania German Folk Art.[27]

As a result of all this, although certain aspects of Pennsylvania German frontier life were bound to alter the life of the immigrant, he did not fundamentally change. In contrast to other colonial language groups, he succeeded fairly well in resisting the "melting pot." "The German peasant fleeing to Pennsylvania, although he realized that he must transfer his allegiance to the English government, had no intention of surrendering his tongue, religion, art, customs, costume, even his superstitions."[28] And he was further encouraged in this respect by the constant arrival of more immigrants from his homeland who not only brought him news of his relatives, but also revived his memory of his former home and its furnishings.

So strong and so closely-knit was this Pennsylvania German group that Franklin feared they would outnumber the English. Even in

---

[24] Faust, A. B., *The German Element in the United States.* Boston, Mass.: Houghton Mifflin Company, 1909. 2 vols.

[25] Rupp, I. Daniel, *A Collection of Upwards of Thirty Thousand Names of German, Swiss, Dutch, French, and other Immigrants in Pennsylvania.* Philadelphia, Pa.· Ig. Kohler, 1876.

[26] Hinke, William J., and Stoudt, John B., 'A List of German Immigrants to the American Colonies from Zweibruecken in the Palatinate, 1728-1749.' Pennsylvania German Folklore Society *Publications*, I (1936), 101-124.

Yoder, Donald Herbert, 'Emigrants from Wuerttemberg, The Adolf Gerber Lists.' Pennsylvania German Folklore Society *Publications*, X (1945), 103-327.

See the same, editor and translator, 'Pennsylvania German Pioneers from the County of Wertheim' by Otto Langguth. Pennsylvania German Folklore Society *Publications*, XII (1947), 147-289.

[27] See figures 228-237.

[28] Wertenbaker, Thomas J., *The Founding of American Civilization: The Middle Colonies.* New York, N.Y.: Charles Scribner's Sons, 1938, p. 13.

Quaker Philadelphia, the street signs had to be printed in *two* languages.[29]   At one time German very nearly became the official language of the state!

Their fanaticism in preserving traditions is seen in the fact that although the Public School Law was passed in 1834, English did not become compulsory until 1911. [30]   As late as 1939, there were 2.000 school children in Pennsylvania who did not speak one word of English.

If we accept the limitations of a purely Protestant subject-matter and a slight "thinning out" of the style, due to the use of more primitive materials in a semi-pioneer Colonial setting than those available in Europe, it is possible to cite surprisingly direct continuations in Pennsylvania German Folk Art of virtually all of the forms common to Rhenish Palatinate Folk Art.

Local conditions and everyday needs naturally dictated the selection of certain objects for special development, but that important element of European folk life, the "Bauernstube," continued uninterrupted in the rolling countryside of Pennsylvania.   The chief events in the life of the peasant farmer, whether in the Rhineland or in the Oley Valley, Pa., naturally centered around the family kitchen.   Tables, chairs, and capacious dressers to house the family china, pottery, or pewter, received more attention than did bedroom pieces.   For example, the Pennsylvania Germans did not develop anything comparable to the elaborately decorated *Himmelsbett* or the Bavarian *bemalte Schrank,* although the painted and decorated dower chest benefited by more attention as a result of this.

The painted and decorated furniture style of South Germany, especially, has received considerable attention because of its extensive history. [31]   The schrank, the open dresser, the chest of drawers, the dower chest, down to the tiniest trinket box — all were painted, or grained, or stippled, or otherwise decorated from the 17th century down through the 19th.   Prior to that time, the decoration was either carved

---

29 Ibid., p. 292.

30 Downs, Joseph, *Pennsylvania German Arts and Crafts, a Picturebook.* New York, N.Y.: The Metropolitan Museum of Art, 1942, p. 4. For a more detailed account see also Wood, Ralph, editor, *The Pennsylvania Germans* (1942), pages 116 and 125.

31 Gephard, Torsten, *Möbelmalerei in Altbayern.* München: Verlag Georg D. W. Callwey, 1937. Ritz, J. M., *Alte bemalte Bauernmöbel.* München: Verlag D. W. Callwey, 1938.

in low relief (simulating Gothic prototypes) or was inlaid with intarsia work designs (stemming from the lovely and intricate patterns of Renaissance inspiration).

Examples of grisaille and stencil work appeared as early as the late Gothic period, [32] and in Canton Apanzell as early as 1745 a *Schrank* had an inscription panel identical with the Pennsylvania types. The elaborate panel decorations containing city views, pictures of the Saints or of other human figures, and historical or genre scenes, however, have no counterpart in the Pennsylvania German work.

The chief interest of the Pennsylvania German decorated style lies not so much in any slavish imitation of the European technique, but rather in the novel and original alterations it developed from this painted technique. [33]   As has been pointed out by various writers, it was after all a *memory art* and as such it departed from the original models.   It was far removed from the wellsprings of Gothic, Renaissance, and Baroque art, and its forms as well as its designs were more apt to be reminiscences than literal copies of the real thing.

On the other hand, in the writer's opinion at least, it is not fair to characterize the Pennsylvania German work as "crude," as has been done by Wertenbaker. [34]   There is a certain amount of crudity, no doubt, in all Folk Art, but piece for piece the Pennsylvania German creations — though far simpler and less sophisticated in their designs — are frequently the equal of (if not superior to) the European prototypes in form and in color, as well as in construction.

Parallel cases are now being made for the superiority of Philadelphia Chippendale over English-made pieces, as well as for such American creations as the Windsor chair and the Newport block-front furniture.   The assimilation of European details into American silver, glass, pewter, and paintings, and their simplification and improvement to produce an American shape, can also be pointed out.   One needs to mention only Stiegel glass, first published by Hunter in 1914, [35] or

---

[32] Ritz, *op. cit.*, 6-7, ill. 1 and 2

[33] The inlay technique (both wood and putty), grisaille painting (marbleizing and graining), and the painted techniques, were all carried over into Pennsylvania German decorated furniture.

[34] Wertenbaker, *op. cit.*, p. 327.

[35] Stiegel brought over European glass blowers, engravers, and enamellers.

Johann Christopher Heyne pewter,[36] as examples of this assimilation. Not only will Stiegel glass hold its own with the best glass of other nations and of better-known periods, but in beauty of form, richness of color, and originality of design, it will surpass most of its competitors. Its contemporaries, the fine Pennsylvania German sgraffito pottery, decorated furniture, and Fraktur illumination, are only now beginning to come into their own.

All of these so-called Folk Arts — products of a true craft tradition not unlike that which brought forth the finest Egyptian glass, Islamic pottery, and Persian manuscripts — in their best form approach, or actually enter, the sphere of the Fine Arts. As such they deserve the attention and careful consideration of the art historian. It is interesting in this connection to note that Dr. Rudolf M. Riefstahl, an *Islamic specialist,* should have been the person to write the Introduction to the Sale Catalogue of the Jacob Paxson Temple Collection in 1922, the first large general collection of Pennsylvania Folk Art to reach the auction room.

Fraktur, of all the Pennsylvania German Folk Arts, is especially rich in its European overtones, and as such provides an excellent demonstration of the continuation and transformation of European ideas. Even at the height of the remarkable revival it enjoyed here in Pennsylvania, when it virtually developed into a new and independent art form, the essentially Old World flavor is always present. The reasons for this close tie become apparent after closer examination of the European sources of the Fraktur style, and the constantly renewed strength it received from the Fatherland well down into the 19th century.

---

[36] Keyes, Homer Eaton, 'The German Strain in Pennsylvania Pewter,' *Antiques, XXVII,* 1 (January, 1935), 23-25; 7 ill.

## IV. THE HISTORY OF FRAKTUR ILLUMINATION

HE course of the development of **Penn**-sylvania German Fraktur Illumination, from its origin to flowering and decadence, follows a pattern that is similar in many respects to its predecessor in Europe, but with certain original and unfamiliar alterations due to the New World setting. While its European origin and subsequent history in America have been noted in a general way, no attempt has been made to fill in this outline with the fascinating details which provide a logical and continuous story of the development of this manuscript style. It is the story of the rise and development of Pennsylvania German Fraktur which will be reconstructed here and which, as a result of some new discoveries, will have important consequences in the dating of related material in other media.

As in the field of glass, where every new discovery was once attributed to "Baron" Stiegel, or in pewter where Johann Christopher Heyne and Colonel William Will were names to conjure with, the period of speculation and irresponsible attribution of Fraktur manuscripts is past. [37] It is time to specialize, to clear the ground of oft-repeated half-truths and errors, and to voice new conclusions based solely upon facts. Just as Ledlie Laughlin's *Pewter in America* and George and Helen McKearin's *American Glass* have done this, so the present study will attempt to present the story of the development of the Pennsylvania German Style of Illumination based on the evidence available today.

The human eye has always been fascinated by expert calligraphy in any form or in any medium whatsoever, and the German, Swiss, and French immigrants who settled in the southeastern counties of Penn-

---

[37] Many times, in absence of information or lack of ability to read either German print or German script, the citation "found in Ohio" or "found in Bucks County" is all that is given. A favorite origin, not limited to Fraktur by any means, was of course "found at Ephrata."

sylvania during the 18th and 19th centuries were no exception. Combining an angular 16th century Gothic letter type known as "Fraktur" — familiar to them through written and engraved copybooks, [38] letters of apprenticeship, [39] deeds, and official edicts — with the somewhat Oriental motifs of 18th century European hand-blocked and woven textile designs, the Pennsylvania Germans produced a new art form of such great richness, and in such great quantities, that it should be regarded more as a *revival*, than as a *survival* of Medieval illumination.

## DEFINITION OF FRAKTUR

The term *Fraktur*, derived from the 16th century printed type of the same name, was quite aptly chosen by Dr. Henry C. Mercer in his pioneer pamphlet on this subject published 63 years ago. [40] It very accurately characterizes the large Gothic initials which appear so prominently in the Pennsylvania German manuscripts and which frequently employ strapwork, interlace, or other ornamentation associated with this early type-face. [41] Also, "Fraktur" seems much more inclusive than some of the more recently suggested terms such as "pen drawings," "pen-paintings," [42] or "script hangings." [43] Very few indeed are those Vorschriften, Certificates, Haus-Segens, or simple Designs which do not include a few Fraktur letters, even if only the initials of the owner.

The German word, "Fraktur," by general usage over the past 63 years, has therefore been widely accepted as the most adequate to describe the Pennsylvania German illuminations which usually are drawn with pen and ink, and then embellished with vigorous colors. This does not mean that similar forms were unknown elsewhere in the thirteen Colonies. Our early ancestors had a lively sense of color and a strong feeling for design. Any lack of these factors in their churches or other public buildings was more than equalized by the constant use made of them in their homes and on virtually every object employed in everyday

---

[38] Figures 3-10.
[39] Figures 11-14.
[40] Mercer, Henry C., 'The Survival of the Medieval Art of Illuminative Writing Among the Pennsylvania Germans', American Philosophical Society *Proceedings*, XXXVI (September 17, 1897), 423-432.
[41] See figures 1, 5-6, 8, 10.
[42] Jackson, Schuyier B., sale catalogue, *Pennsylvania Furniture, Pen-Paintings, and Other Objects, 1780-1850.* American Art Association-Anderson Galleries (#4067), 1933, introduction.
[43] Drepperd, Carl W., *Primer of American Antiques.* New York, N.Y.: Doubleday, Doran & Co., 1944, p. 253.

living. Nor were family records of the other States neglected in this respect, for all along the eastern seaboard they assumed quite artistic forms and were executed in many different media.

In contrast to the term *Fraktur*, however, the New England family registers are more apt to be described as "watercolor drawings," and frequently employ Roman letters rather than Gothic ones. [44] Nowhere outside of Pennsylvania, in fact, was Fraktur writing practiced in quite the same manner, or with the same motifs and meanings. Nowhere else was it so homogeneous in style or in content.

Yet a qualification must be added at this point. The neighboring States to which Pennsylvania Germans moved soon after their arrival in the New World reflected their impact. As they moved downward through the Shenandoah Valley they carried Fraktur writing into Maryland [45] and Virginia, [46] and as they moved westward, into Ohio. [47] In contrast, again, to the New England genealogical registers with family names and dates arranged in columns beneath decorative arches extending across the top of the page, [48] those Frakturs from States bordering upon Pennsylvania follow the ornamental writing and motifs of the eastern counties closely, both in the interpretation of the designs and in color. In fact, the Shaker "spirit drawings" of New York State of the 1840's are also very close. [49] The similarity of all these goes back, no doubt, to the European prototypes and to their common origins, more than to any common influences in this country. Even German immigrants who settled in Canada, and in Brazil, developed there Folk Arts which are reminiscent of their homeland. [50]

## EUROPEAN ORIGINS OF FRAKTUR

To understand better the development and character of Fraktur work, we must trace it back to its various European sources. Like many early American Folk Arts which began with ideas firmly rooted in the homeland, Fraktur writing in its new environment developed into

---

[44] See figures 299, 300, 301 and 304.
[45] See figures 293-294.
[46] See figures 295-296.
[47] For handwritten examples, see Zehner, Olive G., 'Ohio Fractur', *The Dutchman*, VI, 3 (Winter, 1954), 13-15. Herein see figs. 297-298; for printed form, fig. 247.
[48] See figures 303 and 305.
[49] Ford, Alice, *Pictorial American Folk Art, New England to California*. New York and London: The Studio Publications, Inc., 1949, 144-145; 4 ill.
[50] Graeff, Arthur D., 'The Pennsylvania Germans in Ontario', Pennsylvania German Folklore Society *Publications*, XI (1946), 1-80.

something quite different, quite original — something truly characteristic of the southeastern counties of Pennsylvania. Once it had arrived here, it was so widely practiced that it lost some of its pure character, but the heritage of the 18th century *Schreibmusterbücher* can easily be detected. Thus, while essentially a "memory art," it nevertheless goes back to certain very definite prototypes which inspired the very earliest Pennsylvania pieces at least. While little in the way of major pieces of furniture and household utensils could be carried to this country from Europe, the knowledge of good Fraktur writing was a different matter.

The Folk Art museums of southwestern Germany, Alsace, and Switzerland provide ample proof of the existence of many types of Fraktur work. While not plentiful, those Fraktur pieces reveal almost all the types and techniques which appear later in Pennsylvania, even though the format and text of the documents may be slightly different. [51] In this connection it cannot be emphasized too strongly how homogeneous and how standardized the various local types became, due to the large quantities in which they were produced in Pennsylvania. This is true of both the texts and the designs.

While the various types do appear in the Rhineland and in neighboring territories, they do not seem to have been produced there in such great quantities, or to have achieved so high a level of artistic perfection as they did in America. Family records of all types, lettres de baptême, [52] Taufzettel or Tauff-wunsch, [53] Geburtsbriefe, Liebesbriefe, [54] Haus-Segens, [55] Irrgartens, [56] Andenken or memorials, Gift-pieces, are among the many forms found. [57] Illuminated prayerbooks, [58] and schoolbooks, [59] perfect prototypes for those which were found in Pennsylvania, likewise confront us here. All of these Fraktur types appear in the collection at the National Folk Art Museum in Berlin, as well as in the smaller provincial museums and historical societies of the Pfalz, Baden, Bayern,

---

[51] Baud-Bovy, Daniel, *Peasant Art in Switzerland*. London: "The Studio," 1924. Identified as 'Manuscrit rustiques" or rural manuscripts.
[52] See figure 23.
[53] See figures 19-22, 24-26; also unusual Lancaster County example, figure 230.
[54] See figure 30.
[55] See figure 28.
[56] See figures 27 and 29.
[57] Neujahrswunsche, Lehrersbriefe, Soldaten-errinerungsbriefe, etc.
[58] See figure 31.
[59] See figure 32.

PLATE  I.  Ephratá Illuminated Manuscript, The Turteltaube, 1746
*The Pennsylvania State Library, Harrisburg, Pa.*

and Hesse-Darmstadt. [60]    For our purposes here, only a few of the more important examples need to be cited.

From an artistic point of view, the European examples are rather incompetent, they vary in color greatly, and they lean heavily upon the medieval Christian iconographical motifs which are almost completely lacking in the Pennsylvania German examples. The German and Swiss pieces incline to a somewhat nervous quality in their drawing, with great emphasis upon a narrow, uniform, and somewhat tortuous line. [61] There is more suggestion of third dimension, modeling, and shadows such as one rarely encounters in the American pieces, as well as more frequent use of the human figure. The flower designs are also less varied and less distinctly conceived, most of them following a set pattern.

As has already been pointed out, Fraktur represents an almost equal balance of two elements: (1) *script* and, (2) *designs,* both of which were already present in the 18th century copybooks. These copybooks depend heavily upon involutions and intricate designs in the borders, so it is not surprising to find that the European Fraktur samples exhibit this same tendency. [62] The European copybooks also show considerable interest in interlocking capital letters for inscriptions and titles, so it is to be expected that both European Fraktur as well as the first Fraktur done in this country will follow this same interest. [63]

The early Pennsylvania Vorschriften, for example, copy some of the methods of interlace right out of these copybooks, which any penman worthy of the name must have been familiar with. Copybooks printed at Halle, Nuremberg, and other similar centers, occasionally turn up in local Pennsylvania sales where they seem to have been in the possession of families for many years. [64] Many of these date back into the early 18th century, so that they might easily have been carried over to this country and used here.

Nuremberg, Augsburg, Regensburg, Dresden, and Frankfort are commonly the locations from which these European copybooks come.

---

[60] Also in private collections such as F. Heitz, Colmar, from which two Lettres de Baptême were reproduced by Hansi (Jean Jacques Waltz), 'L'art populaire en Alsace', *L'Illustration,* CXCIV, 4864 (May 23, 1936), 151-158.
[61] See figures 15-19.
[62] See figures 4-6, 8.
[63] See figures 133, 136, 138, 161, and 165.
[64] Dillir family book, printed at Halle, 1751.

They are the products of professional penmen, and hence display a finished craftsmanship surpassing what we are apt to find in this country. While many of the late 17th century examples are handwritten books and still echo closely the earliest Fraktur forms which — as is explained below — were introduced at Augsburg in 1507, beginning about 1680-1700 there appears a whole new supply of engraved and block-printed copybooks which continues down to the end of the 18th century.[65] It is precisely this period which had most importance for the Pennsylvania German illuminator and which deserves careful study here.

Fraktur as a type-face had been supreme since the start of the 17th century, and by the beginning of the 18th it was without any competitor as the national type of Germany. Title-pages of the books of this period are loaded with heavily twisted Fraktur titles which have a completely Baroque feeling, already noted by Crous and Kirchner,[66] as opposed to the Renaissance feeling of the *Schwabacher* type. While it was Nuremberg which was the undisputed center for book publishing as well as for illuminated writing, and which introduced more refined and modern letters, it was at Augsburg in the first decade of the 16th century that Fraktur got its start.

The original designer of Fraktur type was a Benedictine Monk, Leonhard Wagner, who was attached to a cloister in Augsburg. An employee of King Maximilian, he created in 1507, a manuscript copybook consisting of one hundred different letters, no two of which took the same form. His manuscript, *Hundert schriften von ainer hand der kaine ist wie die ander,*[67] is still extant and in the layout of its pages as well as in the capital letters he designed, shows beyond any question Wagner's priority as the creator of Fraktur type. An examination of Bauer's brochure,[68] reproducing additional pages from Wagner's manuscript *copybook,* will further establish this connection with the later Pennsylvania German Fraktur illumination.

---

[65] An excellent collection of both hand-written and engraved Copybooks may be found in the Plimpton Library, Columbia University, New York.

[66] Crous, Ernst, and Kirchner, Joachim, *Die gotischen Schriftarten.* Leipzig: Klinkhardt & Biermann, 1928, p. 38.

[67] Proba centum scripturarum diversarum una manu exaratarum fratris Leonhardi Wagner: *Hundert schriften von ainer hand der kaine ist wie die under.* See figure 1.

[68] Bauer, Konrad F., *Leonhard Wagner, der Schöpfer der Fraktur.* Frankfurt-am-Main: Bauersche Giesserei, 1936.

Throughout the 16th and 17th centuries, manuscript copybooks such as Wagner's appeared in southwestern Germany and also in the Netherlands, along with printed books of instructions for illumination such as Boltzen's, 1566. [69]   Apparently the demand for these must have been great, for as early as 1601 we find Neudörffer at Nuremberg issuing a handsome engraved copybook containing a whole series of alphabets progressing from simple to very ornate designs. [70]   Here decorative borders begin to vie with the Fraktur letters for importance on the page.

By 1700, *Schreibmusterbücher* were being published in even larger quantities so that Michael Bauernfeind's *Schreib-kunst* (apparently one of the most popular of these books), had to be issued and reissued every few years down through the 18th century.   These engraved copybooks usually consisted of two parts: a set of Instructions or text, and a series of beautifully designed plates with a wide variety of alphabets.   These included "Fraktur," "Cantzley," "Current" (or Cursiv) types, and frequently "Latina Litera" and "Litera Antiqua" alphabets, such as are listed on Bauernfeind's 1716 *Title-page*. [71]   The resemblances to the Carl F. Egelmann *Instruction Book* published in Reading, Pa., in 1821 and 1831, over a hundred years later, are especially noticeable in the pages containing the smaller alphabets. [72]

In the larger and more ambitious *Schreibmusterbücher*, several sizes of capital letters are developed and demonstrated in religious or legal use, and it is here that the closest approximation to our American Fraktur takes place. [73]   In the borders of some of these pieces also appear many of the details which later take their place in Pennsylvania German Vorschriften, such as birds, angels, flowers, etc.   Most of these, it must be admitted, are executed in black-letter with no attempt at coloring whatsoever.   There are, however, some specimens to which color has been added, as well as original manuscript copybooks themselves, [74] where color is used more brightly and strongly than even in the Penn-

---

[69] Boltzen, Valentinum, von Ruiach, *Illuminir-Buch/ Kuenstlich alle Farben zumachen und bereyten/ Allen Schreibern, Brieffmalern, und andern solcher Künsten liebhabern* . . . 1566.   See figure 2.

[70] Neudorffer, Antonio, *Schreibkunst*, Nuremberg, 1601.   See figures 3-6.

[71] See figure 7.

[72] Compare figure 8 with 269.

[73] Compare figures 4, 5, 6, and 8 with figures 267-269.

[74] Numerous examples in Plimpton Library, Columbia University, New York.

sylvania German pieces. The tendency seems to be to mix the colors too strong or at least to use them too freshly, so that the impression of brilliance is much closer to the medieval originals than to the neutralized Pennsylvania German colors.

## SURVIVAL OF FRAKTUR IN PENNSYLVANIA

The expression, "intimate story" of the development of the Pennsylvania German Style of Illumination, was not casually chosen. For these Fraktur-schriften were very personal indeed. That they escaped the notice of historians as long as they did is a direct result of their *intimate* character, and of the manner in which they usually have been preserved.

Dr. Mercer spoke of "these glowing relics of the venerable stone farmhouses of eastern Pennsylvania, sometimes falling to pieces through carelessness, sometimes preserved with veneration between the leaves of large Lutheran Bibles . . ." [75] thus alluding to the most common method of preservation. About four out of every five Frakturs have a fold-line through the center and are of such large size that only the capacious Family Bible could conveniently contain them. As we shall find, however, smaller Vorschriften and Birth Certificates are also frequently found in octavo-size Testaments or Hymnbooks, duodecimo-size Music Books, and occasionally even in School exercise books.

The second chief method of preservation was *framing*. That Vorschriften and decorative designs were actually framed and hung is evidenced by the fact that many of them still turn up in pegged and dovetailed frames which obviously were made for them at the time the Frakturs were drawn. Quite frequently they seem never to have been removed from these frames, a fact which can be detected by the age-marks, handmade nails, etc. Vorschriften would naturally have been hung on the wall or otherwise prominently displayed, whereas the intimate nature of Birth and Baptismal Certificates would favor instead their preservation in the Family Bible. But framing itself was not sufficient to guarantee preservation, for many times the dampness of the early stone houses produced mold and mildew behind the glass, encouraged

---

[75] Mercer, Henry C., 'The Survival of the Medieval Art of Illuminative Writing Among the Pennsylvania Germans', American Philosophical Society *Proceedings*, XXXVI (September 17, 1897), p. 425.

silverfish to destroy the fine old paper, and frequently resulted in actual watersoaking. [76] These pitfalls were avoided if the Fraktur were inserted into the Family Bible.

The most distressing method of preservation, which very likely is the one Dr. Mercer was referring to when he spoke of their "sometimes falling to pieces through carelessness," was that of *rolling the manuscripts,* shoving them into an already crowded drawer, and then slamming the drawer shut. In this way they are curled too tightly, dry out, and sooner or later are ripped by being caught in the drawer as it closes. [77] It is safe to say that this happened more frequently after the certificates had passed into the hands of descendants, than while in the possession of the persons for whom they were made.

Most interesting of all methods of preservation was that of applying them to the *inside of the lids of dower chests.* Not as safe as some other methods, this nevertheless was fairly common, quite a few instances having come to the author's attention. On some occasions, the chest contained not one but several Frakturs and, in one case at least, none of them were Birth Certificates! [78] Illuminations preserved in this fashion, however, were usually heavily pasted along the edges only (which have since turned quite brown in color) and the body of the Frakturs themselves is quite wrinkled and drawn from expansion and contraction due to temperature and humidity changes. They have frequently been further defaced by contact with whatever other objects happened to be stored in the dower chest and thus are usually missing corners or large portions of the compositions. Frakturs are also reported to have been pasted in the lids of Bible Boxes as was the custom abroad, although no such instances have as yet come to the writer's attention in Pennsylvania. Perhaps the most interesting case reported to date is that of a large Schrank, or wardrobe, which was completely covered inside, both back and sides, with the Birth and Baptismal Certificates made for the various members of the family to which the Schrank belonged! [79]

---

[76] See figures 68, 69, 156, 190, 192, 217, and 219.

[77] See figure 203 with torn edges stitched with needle and thread !

[78] The Metropolitan Museum of Art has a *Lancaster County Chest* with both an Otto Printed Haus-Segen and Otto Parrot Drawing pasted inside the lid. For a *Berks County Chest* with Adam and Eve Broadside in the lid, see figures 287 and 288.

[79] Once owned by Gus Pennypacker, Telford, Pa.

Most bizarre of all was the custom among certain sects of placing the certificates *in the coffin at burial,* with the idea that they should serve as passports to the world beyond. This seems to have been practiced by the Schwenkfelders, [80] one of the most highly cultured of the Pennsylvania groups, who also did not follow the custom of infant baptism — hence the Fraktur would more likely have been an illuminated Schwenkfelder hymn, perhaps, than a record of birth and baptism. In some cases, fortunately, these were removed just before burial, otherwise they would not have been preserved for us today. Rather similar is the instance of the *undertaker* who was also a *tombstone-cutter,* and who gathered from the various families in the community over a long period of time a whole chest full of certificates. From them he had been able to secure the correct information necessary for cutting names and dates on tombstones!

Fraktur pieces have been preserved in these five ways not only within Pennsylvania itself, but also in the neighboring states. From the mid-19th century down to today, they have been carried in strange and unusual ways into the remote corners of the United States, as well as abroad. While in the Rhineland in 1938, the author learned that an Ephrata manuscript had found its way into the British Museum. Though unable to examine it in person, a letter of inquiry to the Keeper of Manuscripts brought the prompt reply that there was indeed a copy of the *Paradisisches Wunderspiel, Ephratas, 1754* in the manuscript collection. How it came to be there, would no doubt make a story as unusual as the following one.

In January, 1772, at London, Benjamin Franklin came into possession of an Ephrata manuscript which had been sent him by John Peter Miller, of the Cloister. According to an ink note inside the front cover, it was lent in April, 1775, by Franklin before he left for Pennsylvania to none other than the notorious radical, John Wilkes, then Lord Mayor of London. Offered at auction in New York City in March, 1927, as late the property of a "London Concern," it was purchased by a collector who, having heard of the desire of the Music Division of the Library of Congress to possess it, turned it over to the national library. This was none other than the famous original manuscript hymnal, the *Turtel-Taube,* which was prepared partly by the Brethren of the Cloister and

---

[80] According to Rev. Lester K. Kriebel, of the Central Schwenkfelder Church, Pennsburg, Pa.

partly by the Sisters, out of esteem for Conrad Beissel, the Superintendent, and which the *Chronicon Ephratense* describes so carefully. And so, after nearly 200 years of exile in England, this choice Ephrata Fraktur hymnal came to rest in the Library of Congress.

The trail of Fraktur may thus lead us far from Pennsylvania where it was practiced, far from Bucks County where, in 1897, Dr. Mercer first discovered the German schoolmaster's paint box which led him to publish his pioneer pamphlet on *The Survival of the Medieval Art of Illuminative Writing Among the Pennsylvania Germans.*

## STUDIES OF PENNSYLVANIA GERMAN FRAKTUR

The bibliography of works on Fraktur, as will be seen in Bibliography D, is both brief and remarkably repetitious. Other than the original pamphlet by Dr. Mercer in 1897 and the most recent monograph on his own collection published by Henry S. Borneman in 1937, [81] the bibliography consists chiefly of hastily-written articles for various periodicals or for popular handbooks on early American arts and crafts. Practically no attempt has been made in these articles to introduce any new ideas or to expand those of Dr. Mercer, the temptation being rather to rewrite or slightly modify the material he had already presented and employ some new illustrations. Following his example, these studies have been devoted chiefly to a discussion of the existence of the Fraktur technique or to a description of the various Fraktur types. Few works have been attributed to those artists who actually *signed* their pieces, [82] and no attempt whatsoever has been made to group or attribute the many *unsigned* examples. Likewise, no serious attempt has been made to describe the chronological development of the Pennsylvania German Style of Illumination during its 100 years of existence.

Lest this be construed as criticism of Dr. Mercer's pamphlet, it should be acknowledged at once that his pioneer effort is so surprisingly accurate that it has never really become out-of-date. In fact, it was his very careful and accurate research which has led so many subsequent writers to lean so heavily upon his work. His description of the simple

[81] Borneman, Henry S., *Pennsylvania German Illuminated Manuscripts.* The Pennsylvania German Society *Proceedings*, XLVI (1937).

[82] *Ibid.*, and Lichten, Frances, *Folk Art of Rural Pennsylvania.* New York, N.Y.: Charles Scribner's Sons, 1946. Even in works as ambitious as these, few illuminators are actually identified with their works.

paint box used by a German schoolmaster about 1820, with its compartments and little glass bottles, its goose-quill pens and brushes, has often been repeated [83]  But his account of the art of Fraktur and its types constitutes a remarkable "staking out" of the field as a whole, and is as true today as it was 63 years ago  He emphasized the following facts:

> "First, that the art of Fractur was not confined to Bucks County or to the Mennonites, who had presented us with the first specimens seen, but that it had flourished throughout Pennsylvania Germany, among the Dunkers, the Schwenkfelders, and probably the Amish and Moravians.
>
> Second, that it had been chiefly perpetuated by deliberate instruction in German schools by German schoolmasters, and that it received its death blow at the disestablishment of the latter in Bucks County in 1854.
>
> Third, that the art, always religious, had not been used for the decoration of secular themes, such as songs, ballads or rhymes, but had expressed itself in
>
>> A.   Illuminated Song Books,
>> B.   The Title-pages to Small, Plain Manuscript Mennonite Song Books,
>> C.   Rewards of Merit on Loose Leaflets,
>> D.   Book Marks,
>> E.   Taufscheine or Baptismal Certificates with Marriage and Death Registers in Bibles . . ."

In addition, Dr. Mercer went on to list and describe examples of each of these types, many of which have since been presented to the Bucks County Historical Society. [84]   He also attributed two of them tentatively to *Jacob Overholt,* a teacher in the log schoolhouse near Deep Run, Bucks County, and to *Isaac Gross* of Bedminster. [85]   One could hardly ask for more from a pioneer work in a field which until then, according to Dr. Mercer himself, had been "little more than casually alluded to by any writer." No earlier notices have as yet come to the attention of the present writer, nor any mention of Fraktur illuminations seen by early travelers through the southeastern Pennsylvania counties, prior to this date, 1897.

---

[83] Mercer, *op. cit.,* p. 424.  See herein figure 72; also for a somewhat later Fraktur box with original Vorschriften signed and dated: "A. K. Kinsey. Box/ 1864" see figure 73.
[84] *Ibid.,* 425-431.
[85] See Appendix A, under Oberholtzer and Gross.

After Dr. Mercer had called attention to the existence of this "survival of the medieval art of illuminative writing among Pennsylvania Germans," had listed the more common types, and had employed the word "Fraktur" in describing it, subsequent writers down to 1925 contributed little new information. In their brief accounts, they usually stressed the high quality of the musical manuscripts which were produced within the Ephrata Cloister itself as opposed to the "crude," "puerile," "grotesquely drawn and garrishly colored" Birth and Baptismal Certificates and they emphasized the quaint and whimsical character of Pennsylvania German Folk Art as a whole.

The second substantial treatment of Fraktur as a subject in itself was contributed by T. Kenneth Wood. [86] Mr. Wood not only reviewed what had been recorded to date, but discussed the manner of their preservation (framed, Bible, chests), and the contents of the different texts. His chief contribution, however, was the arrangement of his article and the chronological sequence of his illustrations. He was also the first person to reproduce the later lithographed Baptism and Confirmation Certificates.

From 1925 on, scarcely a year went by in which something was not published relating to Fraktur writing. Excellent brief accounts were contained in the two handbooks of the Pennsylvania Museum of Art (1929) and the Metropolitan Museum of Art (1934); the Schuyler Jackson Auction (1933) of an entire collection of Fraktur constituted the first major dispersal. Since then, the Lorimer Auctions (April and October, 1944), the Hostetter Auctions (October and November, 1946), the private sale of the Nadelman Collection (1948-49), and the Arthur Sussel Auctions (October, 1958 and January, 1959), have been the only large scale dispersals of Fraktur collections

An important event in the Folk Art field as a whole was the first great exhibition of American primitives at the Newark Museum in 1930-31, [87] which in turn led to the definitive exhibition at the Museum of Modern Art in 1932, [88] when seven Frakturs were shown for the first

---

[86] Wood, T. Kenneth, 'Medieval Art Among the Pennsylvania Germans', *Antiques*, VII (May, 1925), 263-266.

[87] Newark Museum exhibition catalogue, *American Primitives*, edited by Holger Cahill and Elinor Robinson. November 4, 1930 to February 1, 1931.

[88] Museum of Modern Art, exhibition catalogue, *American Folk Art: The Art of the Common Man in America, 1750-1900*. New York, N.Y.: Museum of Modern Art, 1932. Items 72-78.

time in a public exhibition.  These included birth and baptismal certificates, decorative designs, Spencerian penmanship samples, and so on.

The years 1935 to 1937 saw a new burst of activity in the Fraktur field, with magazine articles, gallery exhibitions, the founding of the Pennsylvania German Folklore Society, and the publication of both Stoudt's *Consider the Lilies* [89] and Borneman's *Pennsylvania German Illuminated Manuscripts.* [90]  In the former of these, Stoudt went far towards dispelling the emphasis previously placed upon Pennsylvania German superstitions, pow-wow, etc.  No doubt these did and do exist, but the part they played in the consciousness of the individual folk artist must have been slight indeed.  Stoudt, while emphasizing unduly the Pietist background of Pennsylvania German Folk Art, achieved the point that the motifs had a *religious* rather than a *pagan* background, and that the *love of decoration for itself* must likewise be taken into account.

By far the most important contribution made to the Fraktur field since Mercer's pioneer pamphlet is Borneman's monograph (1937) on his own collection. [91]  It contains the most detailed description of the various Fraktur types to date and accurate color reproductions of some 39 outstanding specimens from his collection.  Towards the end of the volume is a list of some 100 artists whom Borneman believed executed various works in his collection. [92]  This collection is one of the most distinguished which has ever been gathered, and it is only too bad that the selection of material for reproduction was not more representative of the different phases of the art.  The book's chief shortcomings are that it is (1) limited to one collection, (2) not chronologically arranged, (3) limited to hand-drawn examples, avoiding any discussion of interesting printed works, (4) emphasizes unusual rather than typical examples, and (5) brings in much extraneous material.  Many details need more careful examination, such as the list of artists, the dating and listing of inscriptions, etc.  Although a great landmark, the book gives little real sense of chronology, or of the development and dissolution of the Fraktur technique.  The Fraktur work of the Ephrata Cloister has not been adequately treated, nor that of the Schwenkfelder group — two of the cent-

---

[89] Stoudt, John Joseph, *Consider the Lilies How They Grow: An Interpretation of the Symbolism of Pennsylvania German Art.*  Pennsylvania German Folklore Society *Publications*, II (1937).

[90] Borneman, *op. cit.*

[91] *Ibid.*

[92] *Ibid.*, pp. 49-50.

ers of the highest development of the art. Likewise, the attributions to
Christopher Dock are tentative and unconvincing, since they are not supported by sufficient evidence to show that the pieces were executed prior
to the date of the famous schoolmaster's death in the year 1771.

Reverend Kriebel in 1941 [93] presented a concise account of the field
as a whole, pointing up the three most important developments: Ephrata,
Christopher Dock, and the Schwenkfelder School (especially Susanna
Hübner). In addition, he summed up admirably the various interpretations of the motifs, a problem which has engaged the attention of many
writers on the subject.

Books like Drepperd's *American Pioneer Arts and Artists* (1942)
and his *Primer of American Antiques* (1944), Robacker's *Pennsylvania
Dutch Stuff* (1944) and Kauffman's *Pennsylvania Dutch American Folk
Art* (1946), all contain small sections on Fraktur, based chiefly on Mercer's early pamphlet. Frances Lichten (1946) [94] and John J. Stoudt (2nd
ed., 1948) [95] both devote larger portions of their books to Fraktur and
cite the identifiable works by a few more artists.

Of this group, it is Drepperd whose statements we need to examine
more closely. He would like to call them "script hangings" rather than
Fraktur, and traces them back to texts which he says existed in New
Amsterdam and New Sweden, but he gives no real evidence. He also
remarks upon their resemblance to William Penn's deeds, but this is
superficial since they in turn resemble letters of apprenticeship, deeds,
and other official or legal documents written throughout Europe during
the 17th and 18th centuries. And as far as dating is concerned, the
models after which the Pennsylvania German Fraktur-Schriften are fash-
ioned go back even further than the date of 1650 which Drepperd quotes.
If any Swedish Frakturs exist which are (1) *written* in Swedish, (2)
*signed* by Swedish artists, or (3) *decorated* with purely Swedish motifs,
they do not seem to have turned up as yet. As a matter of fact, an

---

[93] Kriebel, Lester K., 'A Brief History and Interpretation of Pennsylvania
German Illuminated Writings (Fractur-Schriften).' Historical Society of Montgomery County *Bulletin*, III, 1 (October, 1941), 20-31.

[94] Lichten, Frances, *op. cit.*, pp. 191-223.

[95] Stoudt, *op. cit.*, pp. 185-238.

analysis of the use of motifs, color, and general composition would seem to deny any such Swedish influence or connection. [96]

One might also attribute this work all over the United States to various immigrant groups, since examples turn up in New England with English background, in New York and New Jersey with more Dutch flavor, and undoubtedly in many other states as well. As has already been pointed out by the author in two articles, the pen-and-ink technique reenforced with color has been generally found along the whole eastern seaboard, particularly in connection with birth and family records. [97]

The results published in these brief accounts have been confirmed by another publication in Minnesota,[98] where many Pennsylvania German certificates were no doubt carried by immigrants who moved westward. As has been indicated, however, it was never practiced in precisely the same way elsewhere or with the same motifs, and nowhere was it so completely *homogeneous* as in the southeastern counties of Pennsylvania.

We can therefore sum up what has been written to date about Fraktur in this way: that its existence has been noted and its general development suggested, but that the greatest emphasis to date has been upon the more important *types and their contents*. The deficiencies of the literature available thus far on Fraktur can be summarized as follows:

(1) That these studies, and the illustrations on which they are based, have come chiefly from material available in *public museums* (excepting Mr. Borneman's volume). Since this is numerically small in comparison to the large body of Fraktur work in *private* collections, the conclusions are not always above question.

(2) That no detailed study has been made of the *immediate* Euro-

---

[96] Compare Drepperd, Carl W., 'Origins of Pennsylvania Folk Art', *Antiques*, XXXVII, 2 (February, 1940), 64-68, with Whitmore, Eleanore M., 'Origins of Pennsylvania Folk Art', *Antiques*, XXXVIII, 3 (September, 1940), 106-110, and also with Reichmann, Felix, 'On American Folk Art', *American-German Review*, X, 6 (August, 1943), 34-36, the latter being a review of Drepperd's *American Pioneer Arts and Artists*.

[97] Shelley, Donald A., 'Regional Examples of American Folk Art', The New-York Historical Society *Quarterly*, XXIX, 2 (April, 1945), 92-105. Also in 'American Primitive Painting: Illuminated Manuscripts', *Art in America*, XL II, 2 (May, 1954), 139-146, 165; 12 ill.

[98] Heilbron, Bertha L., 'Pennsylvania German Baptismal Certificates in Minnesota', *Minnesota History*, XXVII, 1 (March, 1946), 29-32.

pean background of the Pennsylvania German Fraktur style, the only references given being to the Medieval manuscript style.

(3) That no detailed study has been made for dating, or for the chronological and stylistic development of Fraktur. Nor have differences between the work done in various local groups, sects, or different counties and townships been analyzed.

(4) That no study has been made of the printed certificates and other broadsides decorated with Fraktur work, or of their relation to German printing in Pennsylvania as a whole, i.e. the printing of early German books, newspapers, and almanacs.

(5) That little attention has been devoted to the work of individual artists, and to the isolation of additional groups of Fraktur pieces which obviously are the work of one illuminator. That even the work of the Ephrata Cloister and Christopher Dock still await definitive treatment.

While some of these problems are beyond the immediate sphere of this monograph, in that they involve minute and extensive research not possible at this time, they will nevertheless be discussed sufficiently to indicate their status as of today. Since the illuminators were folk artists or possibly itinerant craftsmen as well, there are no institutional records or exhibition catalogues [99] to consult, and the problem of securing accurate biographical material on each artist thus becomes very difficult. Long hours of research and genealogical investigation will be necessary before many of those individuals will be identified. Nevertheless, wherever possible here, an attempt will be made to specify the field of activity of the various artists, as well as their particular type of production and characteristic features.

---

[99] Such as those of the National Academy of Design, New York City, from the year of its establishment in 1826.

# V. PENNSYLVANIA GERMAN FRAKTUR ILLUMINATION

LTHOUGH Fraktur work took many forms and varied widely in its contents, it was motivated by three chief aims. These aims, listed according to the frequency with which they appear, were: (1) to preserve a record of birth and baptism, (2) to emphasize a religious truth, and (3) to present an attractive and colorful design. It is sometimes difficult to isolate these various purposes one from the other since a single Fraktur may incorporate two, or even all three, of them.[100] While this situation complicates the problem of dividing the material into clear-cut categories — such as when a Bookplate suddenly is transformed to serve also as a Birth Certificate [101] — it is nevertheless possible to identify at least *eight* distinct types of Pennsylvania German Illuminated Manuscripts.

To demonstrate each of these types, a simple yet characteristic example will be chosen and its contents analyzed. Wherever possible, such variations as appear within each type at different periods or in the work of individual artists, will be pointed out. It is, in fact, such textual variations which ofttimes supply the necessary clues to solve problems of dating as well as of attribution. In this respect they are just as important as the designs, the handwriting, and the color of a Fraktur specimen.

Nor does this mean that these artists limited themselves to one type of work to the exclusion of all others. On the contrary, it can easily be demonstrated that many of them produced a wide variety of types embracing almost every form listed in the present chapter. Within any type, however, the illuminations written by one artist seldom vary in their text. Motifs, composition, and even the punctuation employed are apt

---

[100] See figures 142, 206, 232.
[101] See figure 142.

to remain the same. These constant factors help in grouping similar examples, in establishing the place of origin and approximate date of execution, and occasionally lead to a positive identification of the artist.

Fraktur specimens in any one of the following eight groups, it should be emphasized, may be printed as well as hand-drawn, may be in English as well as in German, and may be octavo or folio in size. This classification is based upon their *use,* while the sequence of the groups themselves is according to the *number* of examples found.

## PENNSYLVANIA GERMAN FRAKTUR TYPES

### *Birth and Baptismal Certificates*

The most common form of Fraktur, and one that also offers greater variety than any other, is the Birth and Baptismal Certificate. It is more accurate to use this inclusive term since, in most cases, one certificate was employed for both purposes. [102] If the baptismal portion is missing, it is usually a small-size certificate where space is at a minimum; in such cases the record is often carried into the margins of the piece in order to make the certificate complete. Occasionally a reference to confirmation is also made in the same certificate, but this seems to be the exception rather than the rule.

In the literature on Fraktur illumination, constant references have been made to Marriage and Death Certificates. Although the impression given is that they are not at all unusual, very few of them have been recorded in past publications, and the present writer has seen only a half dozen during 20 years of research. In other words, they are quite rare. It is far more common to find notations made *in writing* of marriage or death either at the bottom of the usual Birth and Baptismal Certificate, or on the reverse.

The situation in Pennsylvania thus differs greatly in this respect from that in Europe, where such Death Certificates or Memorial pieces were evidently fairly common. While following somewhat closely the continental prototypes in design and in general appearance, the Penn-

---

[102] Borneman, *op. cit.,* continuing previous writers, emphasizes *Baptismal Certificates* and gives equal status to Birth, Baptismal, and Wedding and Family Records (p. 14). Numerically, the Birth and Baptismal Certificates far outnumber all the others put together.

sylvania German artists adapted them to their own purposes. One rarely finds in this country a Fraktur which begins "Andenken an" or "Ein Geschenck für."

The European "Tauff-wunsch" or "Geburts-brief," on the other hand, was the chief form to be taken over in this country by the local artist. In his hands it became a definite form with virtually uniform text. [103] Once the text had been crystallized, the artist turned his attention to the decorative borders and he lavished such imagination and such creative effort upon them that the Birth and Baptismal Certificate became a separate field of art work apart from other Fraktur illuminations The owners being refugees, frequently reaching this land of plenty only after enduring horrible conditions aboard ship for several weeks, it is natural that they placed considerable value upon the written record of their births and early lives. In this period, for example, certificates frequently mention the European duchy, province, or city, in which the child was born. They had never owned land, or been free before, and they passed through such great hardships to get here, that they naturally went out of their way to preserve some record of their origin and background.

From a historical point of view, these Birth Certificates have far greater value than other Fraktur work because of their rich genealogical content. Because of their detail and accuracy, they supply invaluable records not only of the child whose birth they record, but also its parents, relatives, and the sponsors at the baptism. While they lack the force of a legal affidavit, since they are rarely signed by any witnesses, their great honesty of detail and religious origin go far beyond any such document used today. Nor do we know of any other section of the country where records such as these were so carefully kept at such an early date. In contrast to the New England family registers which list for each member of the family only his name and dates of birth and death in three columns, the precise and complete information of the Pennsylvania German certificates is remarkable.

As we shall see, the evolution and development of the text seems to go through definite progressions, attaining a more standard form by 1800 even in the hand-written types where the individuality of the artist

---

[103] Occasionally a Pennsylvania "Familien-tafel" or "Register" appears, but these are rare exceptions. See figure 236.

was more likely to play a part. The German becomes more correct, the spelling virtually unified, and the information contained in each certificate is presented in an established sequence. This naturally resulted from the great prevalence of the printed forms which, by 1800, were being run off in large quantities on every important German press in eastern Pennsylvania. [104]

The large majority of these certificates follow in their text two specific patterns, depending upon the approximate date of the Fraktur and the background of the artist. The earlier of these (Type 1) starts with the name of the child in large script and then continues with the account of the birth. [105] The later (Type 2) is the more usual Pennsylvania form, starting first with the story of the parents: "Diesen beiden Ehegatten" etc., and then continuing with the account of the child. While innumerable variations of these two occur, they divide the whole body of certificates pretty definitely into hand-drawn and printed ones, and both of them exist side by side. The first of these forms, however, is more apt to be 18th century and the second 19th century.

The later, common form (Type 2) begins with the full name of the father, then the mother, the mother's maiden name. the designation of sex, the name of the son or daughter for whom the certificate was made, the year, day, and month, the hour and even the minute of birth, whether the time is morning or evening, frequently also the sign of the zodiac under which the child was born, and concludes with the name of the State, County, and Township or City. [106] No fact is left to the frailty of human memory here! After the story of the birth comes the record of the child's baptism, with day, month, and year, the name of the minister and his denomination, followed by the names of the sponsors or godparents. The account continues, in a few instances, with betrothal or marriage, [107] and often concludes with a pencilled notation elsewhere on the certificate telling the date of the subject's death. [108]

---

[104] See Appendix B and C.

[105] See figures 76, 184-186, 205, 208, 214, 220-222, 232, 234. It should be noted that the German feminine endings "in" and "en" are carefully followed: Magdalena Nas*zin* (186) Anna Maria Sus*zerin* (205). and Anna Margareta Biedermani*n* (232).

[106] See figures 33, 83-86, 90-95; also Color Plates IV and V.

[107] See figure 89.

[108] See figures 84, 90, 91, 259.

## *Vorschriften or Writing Specimens*

Pennsylvania German Illuminated Vorschriften, by their very nature, far surpass the illuminated Birth and Baptismal Certificates in calligraphic beauty. While not relying solely upon decorative capital letters for their effect, the floral border designs of the Vorschriften never achieve the predominance they do in other fields of Fraktur, and are naturally kept subordinate in color and design to the religious text.

These writing specimens, a large proportion of which originate in Mennonite areas, are built around texts lifted from the Bible which have a moral or religious application in everyday life. [109] The only notable exception is the elaborate Vorschrift writing practiced by the Schwenkfelder group, especially the Hübner family, where the text is actually taken from the Schwenkfelder hymns. Instead of concluding with the usual alphabets of capitals and lower-case letters, and with numerals, the Schwenkfelder Vorschriften specimens continue with the various verses of the hymn chosen for illumination. [110] Because certain texts or hymns seem to be more popular than others, we find them used over and over again. This applies again especially to the Schwenkfelder work, where we find the same text and its accompanying motifs repeated verbatim again and again over a period of as much as 50 years. [111] The only change visible is the slight alteration in the color scheme due to the use of later pigments.

In contrast to the Birth and Baptismal Certificates where dates have little reference to the year of actual writing of the manuscript, [112] the dates given on Vorschriften can be accepted as final. This fact is of tremendous significance in determining the dates of the illuminated style of writing as a whole, and in giving us a key to its relatively late development — contrary to the assertions usually made regarding its early origin. Few indeed are the Vorschriften which bear dates in the 1760's and 1770's. It is with the 1780's that the period of greatest activity gets under way, and in the period 1790-1810 that it reaches its highest level of artistic perfection. It continues to flourish through the 1820's and the 1830's, but by the 1840's has begun to lose its virility. Its apogee is

---

[109] See figures 35-36, 136-141, 152-153, 157; also Color Plate II.
[110] See figure 166.
[111] See figures 170-173.
[112] See figures 83 and 85; also Color Plate IV.

represented by the Mennonite work of the 1790's, [113] and the Schwenk-felder work of 1800-1815. [114]

As with dating, we are also on surer ground in dealing with the names found on the Vorschriften than we were on Birth and Baptismal Certificates. Usually the distinction between the artist and the person *for whom* the piece was illuminated is carefully stated, if we read the inscription closely. Borneman's list of artists is filled with many names of owners rather than artists, if we check the original texts. [115] The present author accepts as artists' names only those where it is stated: "Geschrieben von mir Henrich Otto." He does not accept those pieces which are inscribed simply: "Diese Vorschrift gehört mir . . ." for this implies ownership, not creation. In the case of the Landis family pieces, the English equivalent "the property of Henry Landis" appears on the same Vorschrift along with the German text, thereby supplying irrefutable evidence of the contemporary meaning of this phrase. Further proof of this interpretation may be found in the fact that groups of Vorschriften, written and decorated in the same hand, bear the same inscription "Diese Vorschrift gehört . . . ," but conclude with *different names*. These are no doubt the writing specimens executed by *one* teacher, rather than the personal work of several different pupils.

In reality, the author knows of no proof that Fraktur writing as such was actually taught in the schools, as has often been stated. That the rudiments of *writing* were taught is quite evident, but if any pupils were taught Fraktur at all, it is very likely that only those found by the teacher to be especially gifted in this respect were given actual instruction. Birth and Baptismal Certificates seem to be signed less frequently than the Vorschriften or religious texts, which were used as writing copies and consequently involved more pride on the part of the artist.

Although the Vorschrift, like the Birth and Baptismal Certificate appears in both full and half-size, it is much more commonly seen in the smaller of these sizes. About four out of every five Vorschriften are in this half-size. Vorschriften in the quarter-page size are not uncommon, frequently being built around a single large capital letter. [116]

---

[113] See page 107 and figures 135-138; and 152-153; also Color Plate II.
[114] See page 112 and figures 160-171; also Color Plate III.
[115] Borneman, *op. cit.,* pp. 49-50.
[116] See figures 74-75, 159, 172, 174-175.

The Vorschriften are usually made of several component parts, each of which is enclosed in a separate section of its own. [117] Occasionally the title line itself is separated from the body of the text by a decorative border; sometimes a second, smaller Vorschrift is enclosed in a box at the lower left or right; sometimes these smaller sections are even turned on their sides; [118] and occasionally small birds or flowers are enclosed in a special section apart from the main body of the Vorschrift  Usually the whole Vorschrift is enclosed in its own decorative border — sometimes a very ornate one including small birds, stars, tulips, or candy stripes — and with solid color blocks at the corners.  Many times the border stripe is a different color on each side of the Vorschrift, with the corner-blocks where these stripes cross in a contrasting color.

The variety of these Vorschriften is apparent in the following description of a typical example:

TITLE—Large capitals and strapped lower-case letters,
    sometimes with ornaments intertwined.

BODY—Upper and lower-case single color (if two lines,
    caps in red and black; or red and black alternating
    words; or else black words with red swirls).
    —Small German Script religious quotation.
    —Small German Script alphabet, capital German Script
    alphabet, and German Script numerals 1-10 or 100-1000.

BOTTOM RUNNER
    —Occasional "Honor and Dominion . . ."
    —Frequently "diese Vorschrift gehört . . . Geschrieben den 10
    Febry A D 178. . ."
    —Or name and date in heart or box at corner of Vorschrift
    —Or date hidden occasionally in foliage at top.
    —Or very occasionally, musical bars with notes inserted at
    beginning or end of text body.

### Religious Broadsides

The various Fraktur types characterized here as Religious Broadsides, although at first glance they may seem rather unrelated, are so grouped because basically they have quite a few things in common: (1) their content is wholly religious and moralizing, (2) they are apt to be *either* hand-written or printed, (3) they are usually early in date, fre-

---

[117] See figures 36, 133-141.
[118] See figure 139.

quently 18th century, (4) they depend chiefly upon an unusual arrangement of text for their pictorial character, and (5) they are rarely seen today.

In contrast to the far more common Birth and Baptismal Certificates, and to the Vorschriften with their large size inscriptions in Fraktur letters, these broadsides take a labyrinthian or puzzle form. Easy to detect because of their unusual character, they are not always easy to decipher. In most cases they are large in format, the 1784 and 1785 *Irrgartens* being the largest of all Fraktur forms found.

### Das Goldene ABC Für Jederman

Although certainly not the most common, the Goldene ABC issued at Ephrata in 1772 (of which only two specimens have come to the author's attention) is one of the most unusual. [119] A Broadside issued on the Cloister Press, it has the added interest of having its borders filled in with a decoration in ink that ties up very closely with the earlier Fraktur work in illuminated Ephrata Choral manuscripts such as the *Turteltaube* [120] and the *Paradisische Wunderspiel.* [121] The typography likewise continues without change the individual character of the Ephrata imprints in the capital letters as well as in the borders. In this broadside the alphabet is used as a means of teaching a series of religious truths, each of which begins with a particular letter. At the bottom of the form, a series of tightly compressed boxes contains in each one an additional precept in rhyme.

Besides the rare Ephrata 1772 imprint, Goldene ABC's were run off at Reading and at Harrisburg in the early 19th century, probably from about 1810 to 1825. But even these forms, if they were at all common in their own day, certainly are not plentiful today. Those seen by the author, although they follow exactly the text of the Ephrata piece, rarely have any Fraktur decoration in the borders.

### Geistliche Irrgartens

Going back once more to medieval prototypes and ideas, the Geistlicher Irrgarten, the Seven Rules of Wisdom, and various Spirals and Circles, take on *labyrinthian* form. Chiefly 18th century, this form was later

---

[119] See figure 130.
[120] See figure 107; also Color Plate I.
[121] See figure 120.

taken over by 19th century Valentines and True Lovers' Knots. But in its original context, it seems to have been more generally associated with religious teachings and symbolism. [122]

Most frequently seen are the Geistliche Irrgartens which were printed by several of the early printing houses, beginning once more with the Miller (Philadelphia, 1762) and Ephrata presses, [123] and going on to Allentown, Bath, Harrisburg, and others in the early 19th century. In none of the 19th century ones, however, does the form change much from the Ephrata 1784, 1785, and 1788 specimens. [124] As in the case of the Goldene ABC's, only the 18th century examples seem to have merited the addition of Fraktur borders. The text gives an account of the Fall of Man with appropriate commentaries.

### Seven Rules of Wisdom

This form of labyrinth or puzzle is even rarer than the Irrgarten, only three examples having come to the author's attention, none of which were printed. All of these were Schwenkfelder. [125] More attention is given here to the colored Fraktur capitals reminiscent of Vorschriften. The text of Figure 39 read in its proper sequence would be as follows:

"Thue nicht alles was du kanst den es ist ein Hoffart.
Frage nicht alles was du nicht weist den es ist ein Furwitz.
Glaube nicht alles was du horest den es ist ein Leichtsinnigkeit.
Gib nicht alles was du hast den es ist ein Verschwendung.
Sage nicht alles was du weist den es ist ein Thorheit.
Urtheile nicht alles was du siehest den es ist ein Frechheit.
Begehre nicht alles was du magst den es ist ein Unve[rstand]."

A translation of the complete text would read as follows:

"Do not everything that you can for that is Pride.
Ask not everything that you don't know for that is Curiosity.
Believe not everything that you hear for that is Credulity.
Give not everything that you have for that is Prodigality.
Tell not everything that you know for that is Folly.
Judge not everything that you see for that is Impudence.
Desire not everything that you like for that is Stupidity."

---

[122] See figures 38 and 189.

[123] For hand-written examples see figures 27, 125, and 167.

[124] See figure 131.

[125] See figures 39, 169, and another example in the Juniata College Library Huntingdon, Pa., which is illustrated in the *American-German Review*, XI, 2 (December, 1944), pp. 15-16.

## Spirals and Circles

The use of Spirals and Circles is fairly common, and occasionally appears in conjunction with Birth Certificates and Vorschriften as well. Typical specimens are shown in Figures 40, 144, and 223. Usually some central motif or idea is surrounded by wheels or circles, each of which contains some religious prayer or admonition. In this respect, there are close analogies to the House Blessings and Spiritual Wonder-clocks which constitute the next group of religious broadsides we shall consider. The texts of these spirals and circles start at the center and read outwards.

## Haus-Segens

Carrying over the old European fondness for inscriptions, the Fraktur illuminators and printers turned out a whole series of House Blessings. As with the previous forms — the Goldene ABC and the Irrgartens — the lead was taken by the Ephrata press. In contrast to them, however, the House Blessing enjoyed more popularity and is not so great a rarity today. Printed as well as hand-drawn examples survive from both the 18th and 19th centuries, and quite a few of the better-known Fraktur illuminators seem to have at one time or another produced some House Blessings.

The texts of these vary slightly, but the general pattern is pretty much the same in all of them  A few typical specimens are sufficient for the purposes of this study. [126]

## Geistlicher Uhrwerk and Stundenweiser

These follow very closely the text and format of the House Blessings, but omit the blessing portion. In one example an entire grandfathers clock appears, [127] but usually the motif of the clock dial is the chief element of the composition, with each hour corresponding to a prayer.

### Illuminated Books and Bookplates

The earliest Fraktur writing in this country, as we have noted in the section dealing with Vorschriften, was practiced at the Ephrata Cloister from about 1745 onwards. This included not only the Wall-Texts in the Saal, but also books and bookplates such as the *Goldene*

---

[126] See figures 41, 190, 194.
[127] See figure 42.

*ABC*, the *Turteltaube*, various illuminated choral books, and the bookplates frequently found in the *Martyrbooks*. These books, as a matter
of fact, probably antedate the Wall-Texts since they would naturally
have served as the models for the larger pieces. If such be the case, we
can then say that the use of Fraktur illumination in connection with
books, namely that produced by the Sisters at the Ephrata Cloister, was
the earliest in this country.

While book illumination competed in no way with the much larger
production of Birth and Baptismal Certificates or Vorschriften, in variety
and ofttimes in beauty, it far surpassed both of them. It is indeed very
closely connected with both these fields, for it follows the same stylistic
patterns and was practiced by many of the same artists who produced
the larger and more ambitious pieces. It is only natural that the same
craftsmen who illuminated Birth and Baptismal Certificates or Vorschriften should also occasionally decorate a Book or a Bookplate. [128]
Yet being a more precise art and in smaller size, these books seem to
stem from a more limited number of artists, or local country schools. In
the case of the Bookplate, in the manuscript music notebooks, and the
printed songbooks especially, the name of the school and the county are
frequently identified.

Because of these limitations of size and purpose, plus the fact that
almost invariably books are dated carefully — both imprint and date of
illumination — the books form a much more reliable basis for dating
than almost any other form of Fraktur work. In most cases they were
produced for young children, as gifts or tokens of religious development
rather than to record dates of birth. [129] These dates, therefore, can be
accepted as the year of production, unless otherwise noted. This is in
marked contrast to the problem encountered with Fraktur Birth and
Baptismal Certificates, where dates frequently have little reference to
the year of production, as we have seen. [130]

The reasons why only a limited number of these little Fraktur gems

---

[128] Fine Bookplates were produced by many outstanding Fraktur illuminators:
Henrich Otto, Jacob Oberholtzer, Christian Strenge, Karl Munch, and Wilhelmus
A Faber, to mention just a few.

[129] See Borneman Bookplate illustrated in the *American-German Review*, IX,
4 (April, 1943), as a Cover design, inscribed as follows: "This beautiful song
book belongs to Anna Stauffer and was purchased for her by her father to the
honor of God and her own instruction, March 24, 1793."

[130] See figures 83 and 85.

have survived are obvious. In the first place, they were never produced in really large quantity, and furthermore they seem to have received pretty hard wear through handling. Bindings are frequently broken at the hinges, and pages are ripped and torn. [131]  As a result, many of the decorated Title-Pages have come loose and have been framed in order to preserve them. In other cases, these charming little illuminations were wantonly removed from the books in order to be sold as separate illuminations, although the written text on most of them betrays their source.

The main body of this type of Fraktur writing was done during the century from 1765 to 1865 — as in the case of Fraktur illumination as a whole — but the earlier Ephrata books would move the starting date up to 1745. Excepting these Ephrata books, the heyday of fine quality book illumination would correspond to that of Fraktur writing as a whole, or from about 1785 to 1835. This would be from the Schumacher-Otto period up to the breakdown of the Schwenkfelder style. Good quality illuminated books or bookplates are much more apt to date after 1800 than before it. The dates given on the Title-Pages of these books, as has been pointed out, are usually the actual dates of production

Illuminated Books and Bookplates are here combined as one subject since the same artists seem to have produced both, and since illuminated books frequently have bookplates at the front. In order to avoid duplication and repetition, it seemed best to include them in one classification. Among the many types of illuminated books which appeared, the most numerous were the Manuscript Music Books and the Printed Mennonite Song Books. [132]  The latter naturally predominate because they were printed in such large quantities, although many of them never were decorated with a bookplate. The following 10 classifications would adequately cover the field, although all but the first three would admittedly come under the heading of "rare":

1.  Early Ephrata Books [133]
2.  Mennonite Manuscript Music Books (horizontal) [134]

---

[131] Ofttimes these bookplates are only pasted in.
[132] Usually these bookplates appear as single-page designs immediately inside the front cover, and only occasionally as double-page designs (see figures 45 and 46). In several instances Fraktur designs appear inside *both* the front and back covers, and in one a portrait is painted on the inner side of the back cover of a volume from Salomon Henkel's library (Borneman collection). Less often, further embellishments occur throughout the book itself.
[133] See figures 43, 48, and 105-128; also Color Plate I.
[134] See figures 44, 143, 149 and 151.

3. Printed Songbooks, Testaments, and Bibles (vertical) [135]
4. Manuscript Copybooks [136]
5. Manuscript ABC Books [137]
6. Manuscript Schoolbooks [138]
7. Manuscript Business Ledgers [139]
8. Manuscript Weaving Pattern Books
9. Manuscript Surveying Books
10. Books of designs for "Kentucky" Rifles [140]

*Bookmarks, Rewards for Merit, and Small Designs*

Closely allied to the Bookplates and other illuminations found in books, are the small Fraktur pieces of all shapes and sizes which we call "Bookmarks." [141] They seem to have received this name chiefly because they are found at random through the pages of old books of all sorts, as if marking the place where someone stopped reading. There is little uniformity of size or shape, and they present a very miscellaneous group indeed. Occasionally they are inscribed as Rewards for Merit in the first or second class, in singing or in writing. [142] More often, they seem to be simply small, offhand designs, sometimes bearing a name or date, or a childish or religious saying: "this bird would rather be in the house" or "Das Herze mein, soll Dir allein."

At first glance, the simplicity of these might lead one to the assumption that they had been done by children in school, but further examination reveals that these Bookmarks and other small Fraktur designs are more often the work of those same artists who did the larger pieces. In many cases it is possible by comparison with the larger pieces to identify the makers of the small ones, through similarities of design, drawing, color, or motif. [143] Ofttimes the small pieces are found to be actual portions out of a larger Vorschrift or Birth Certificate by the

---

[135] See figures 45-46.
[136] See figures 47 and 144-147.
[137] See figure 48.
[138] See figure 50.
[139] See figure 49.
[140] E. Ricksecker's book of designs for gunstocks and barrels, mentioned by Cornelius Weygandt in *The Dutch Country* (p. 202) is dated 1836-37, but has not been seen by the author.
[141] See figure 51.
[142] See figure 52.
[143] Compare figure 54 with Stoudt, *op. cit.*, Color-plate II.

same artist. Those examples done by the children are more apt to be mid-19th century work, poor in drawing and garish in color, and quite obviously not the work of an adult.[144] These are most frequently animal subjects which have been lifted by the child artist from primers or other children's books.

In size, these Bookmarks range from 2 inches square up to 2 x 8 inches and are frequently irregular in shape — circular, trapezoidal, and so on. The large majority seem to be bookplate-size and smaller, and usually a vertical rectangle. In the case of Anna Altdorffer,[145] we have a set of four Rewards for Merit, all of which were presented at different times to a single child for special excellence (1787, 1787, 1790, and no date).

### Love-Letters, True-Lovers' Knots, Valentines, Ample Grove

One of the more interesting, but less common, forms of Fraktur illumination appeared in the continuation of the old European "Liebesbrief" or Love-Letter. If variety of techniques employed is any key to their popularity, they must have been of considerable interest, for they include in various forms Fraktur, Cutout, Fold-up, Pin-prick, and Drawn-ribbon work. In this respect at least, they clearly reflect their more popular European prototypes.

Inasmuch as the word "valentine" is of English derivation and is limited to the date February 14th, the European and Pennsylvania "Liebesbrief" is a much broader term.

### Liebesbriefe

These early German Liebesbriefe seem to have been given to a young girl at any time of the year a young man might so desire, and frequently the inscription gives only the year of presentation, not the day or month. On the other hand, many of them bear no date whatsoever, and hence might be given at any time by young and old alike.

The large percentage of these Liebesbriefe which have turned up in Pennsylvania date from 1770 to about 1810. They usually are of circular pattern, having been folded and then cut out. Afterwards, they were decorated by Fraktur writers and thus ofttimes can be attributed to

---

[144] See figure 53.
[145] See figure 52.

illuminators whose other works are well known to us.  Both the handwriting and the colors provide the necessary clues. [146]  They usually
consist of 8 or 16 hearts around a central motif, each of the hearts containing an amorous quotation.  The cut-out Liebesbrief is then mounted
upon a colored paper or cloth background to bring out the intricate designs of the cutwork.

The mistake of identifying all cut-work pieces as "valentines" has
frequently been made, in spite of the obvious character of the accompanying texts.  This cut-work technique is not limited to Liebesbriefe
alone, but appears almost equally often as the decorative borders of an
illuminated Birth and Baptismal Certificate.  These certificates, however,
are usually rectangular in form rather than circular, or circular within
a square as the Liebesbriefe themselves invariably are.

About 1800-1810, two new forms of Liebesbriefe in English rather
than in German appear.  These take two somewhat different forms, both
continuing the *labyrinth* idea, but employing it in a slightly changed
manner and without the decorative cut-work so characteristic of the
Liebesbrief: (1) the True-Lovers' Knot, and (2) the Fold-up Valentine

### True-Lovers' Knots

Turning from the circular form of the Liebesbrief, a labyrinth
based on a square plan was worked out to intrigue the fancy of the receiver.  The artist now addressed the subject wholly in English and employed a vast complex of squares, circles, hearts, and winding forms. [147]
Between the different members he inserted the usual hearts, flowers, and
stars, through which he entwined the inscription in labyrinth form, occasionally reducing portions of it to abbreviations or cryptograms.  Occasionally the usual Pennsylvania German distelfink or some other bird
appears at the top of the design, and in one case, profile portraits of
the donor and the receiver.

### Fold-up Valentines

Far more common than the True-Lovers' Knots are the Fold-up
Valentines which are also in English and are even more complicated and
elaborate in their form   Many times these are marvels of intricate design
sign and embody pictorial motifs rarely found in either the Liebesbrief

---

[146] See figure 55.
[147] See figure 56.

or the True-Lovers' Knot.  In one case which is quite unusual, four Clipper Ships appear along with the usual hearts, flowers, and birds.

The Fold-up Valentine begins just before 1800 and continues well down towards the middle of the 19th century  In its labyrinth style, it continues the Irrgarten, the Liebesbrief, and the True-Lovers' Knot.  But in reality, it is the culmination of these predecessors as regards intricacy of plan, artistry of execution, and amount of decoration — for it is completely decorated on *both* sides of the paper!

When delivered, it was folded into a small square made of interlocking triangles, much like a pin-wheel. [148]  "Each section as it is unfolded reveals some new sentiment and leads ultimately to the inside of the valentine, where the name of the enamored suitor is finally made known.  As each successive fold is unloosed, a new declaration of love and a fresh burst of color greet the eye.  This type of valentine frequently employs in the interior a labyrinth or maze, as in the present example, [149] indicating once more the lingering of a Medieval form.  While the verses employed are stock rhymes from sample books printed for this purpose, their arrangement is entirely original with the designer of each valentine, who sometimes adds new variations of his own." [150]

On the basis of their repetition of standard verses in English, their use of non-Pennsylvania German motifs, and because they frequently turn up in Bucks and Chester Counties, the author believes they are very probably of *Quaker* origin.

### The Ample Grove

This last strange type has only appeared in two examples, and apparently dates around 1820-30.  The mathematical problem it poses is too intriguing to pass by, so it will be pardoned if it is included at this point.

Carrying one step further the labyrinthian form of the True-Lovers' Knot and the Fold-up Valentine, the text of this unusual form represents the epitome of puzzle forms and is worth repeating here ·

---

[148] See figure 57.

[149] See figure 58.

[150] Shelley, Donald A., 'An Unusual Valentine', The New-York Historical Society *Quarterly Bulletin*, XXVII, 3 (July, 1943), 62-67; 2 ill.

"I am disposed to plant a grove,
    To Satisfy this girl I love,
This simple grove I must compose,
    Of nineteen trees in nine straight rows.
Five in each row I here must place,
    Or never expect to see her face,
Ye sons of Ad [am] grant me your aid,
    To satisfy this curious maid." [151]

### Miscellaneous Fraktur

In addition to the more common types of Fraktur illumination already discussed, there are many more which for one reason or another do not fit into these classifications. They differ in size and shape as well as in content from the more common forms, and are usually "one of a kind" pieces. Since they were produced for some very special occasion and by an individual, it is frequently difficult to relate them to the work of known Fraktur illuminators. Their chief interest lies in the extra variety they give to the field of Fraktur by virtue of their unusual character. Some of them, such as the New Year's Wishes and the Gift Tokens, constitute further late survivals in Pennsylvania of forms which were far more common in Europe.

New Year's Wishes are the best example of this transfer of a German and Swiss prototype to Pennsylvania. Although fairly common abroad, only five examples have come to the author's attention during the past 20 years. Those, and one or two Christmas Cards, [152] are the only instances of Fraktur pieces connected with a holiday still celebrated today, there being no Thanksgiving, Fourth of July, or Valentine's Day greetings, as we have noted. Of the five New Year's Wishes seen, all were 18th century and four could be connected with illuminators of other Fraktur pieces: Daniel Schumacher (2), [153] Hans Jacob Brubacher, the C.F. Artist, [154] and the C.M. Artist.

Other miscellaneous Fraktur specimens include an occasional Gift Token inscribed "Ein Geschenck fur.." in English or German, a Witch

---

[151] See figure 59.
[152] Borneman, *op. cit.,* p. 38, says "Christmas cards or greetings do not turn up in these manuscripts," but several small illuminated cards bearing Christmas sentiments have recently come to the author's attention. The word Christmas does appear, and references to the Christ Child leave little doubt as to their intent. See figure 60.
[153] See *The Historical Review of Berks County,* XVII, 3 (April-June, 1952), 71.
[154] See figure 61.

Charm and an Indian Hymn, the last two both from the Schuyler Jackson collection. The text "Wild Du bald ein Doktor werden" has appeared on several occasions. Isolated examples of unusual subject-matter called "hex" or "pow-wow" pictures are frequently found either to be fragments of larger compositions, or simply free-hand designs with no particular aim.

## Pictorial Fraktur Designs and Drawings

A large group of miscellaneous pictorial Fraktur pieces will not fit into the above classifications since they are not strictly speaking Birth Certificates, Vorschriften, or Religious Broadsides. In them, moreover, the Fraktur or inscription element is apt to be subordinated largely, if not entirely, to a pictorial approach. They seem to be simply designs executed by the illuminator for the sheer pleasure of making an unusual pattern or representation. In this respect they correspond closely to the off-hand pieces of glass blown at the end of the day by the glassblower from the scraps remaining from the day's work. It is this fact which no doubt explains why some of the most dramatic pieces of Fraktur take this form. The illuminator was free from any limitations of form or written text and could really "let himself go."

The term "balanced" designs is used because they usually are perfectly arranged geometrical designs which consist of some central motif with balanced members on either side. Occasionally one finds "all-over" designs, geometric interlaces, and the like; at other times they border on the pictorial, but still retain the balance feature, and are totally lacking in perspective or space-representation. Rarely do names, dates, or inscriptions appear.

They appear in all sizes from full Certificate size down to the quarter-size. [155] They are both vertical and horizontal. Perhaps as a result of their very irregularity of size and shape, one finds them in their original handmade frames much more frequently than other forms of Fraktur work, and the frames are usually well-suited to the individual design.

While it is this classification which the *layman* today has in mind when he speaks of "Fraktur drawings," rather than the Vorschriften or

---

[155] See figures 62-69.

PLATE II. Huber Artist, Mennonite Vorschrift, 1790

*Author's collection*

Certificates, in a sense this category is farther removed from the original idea of Fraktur than any of the above types of Pennsylvania German illuminated manuscripts. It is because of this lack of Fraktur inscriptions as well as the ever-nearer approach to a purely pictorial representation that this classification is taken up last. The kinds of subject-matter which appear in the various groups listed below are obvious and therefore need no explanation here:

(1) ABSTRACT
(2) RELIGIOUS

| Adam & Eve | Adoration of the Shepherds |
| Prodigal Son | Baptism of Christ |
| Pelican | Ascension of Christ |
| Crucifixion | Last Supper |

(3) TRADITIONAL OR FOLK SUBJECTS

| Seven Swabians | The Four Trades |
| Swarm of Bees | Tragic Ballads |

(4) HISTORICAL

| Penn | Hessian Soldier |
| Franklin | The Great Comet |
| Washington | The Great Whale |
| Taylor | Various Horsemen |

(5) ARCHITECTURAL OR LANDSCAPE

| Pennsylvania Houses | Castles |
| Farm Buildings | Churches and Schools |

(6) ANIMALS
(7) STILL LIFE
(8) PORTRAITS

Under the last heading will be considered only those representations which presumably were taken from life. Fraktur drawings of Washington, Jackson, Taylor, etc., which had only political or symbolical significance will be counted out. The portraits taken up here are the production of itinerant workers, who traveled through the Pennsylvania countryside during the 1820's and later, when Fraktur was still being produced on a large scale. Many of them bear identifications or birth records written in Fraktur letters.

This production of portraits was actually a rather limited one, due to the attitude of the Pennsylvania Germans as a whole toward self-glorification. Portraiture, or representation of one's self, to them seemed "worldly" and when found at all, is apt to turn up on the periphery of the German section rather than within it. Even as regards oil paintings in general, when we have passed beyond the early Moravian portraitist

Johann Valentin Haidt, the Quaker primitive Edward Hicks, the Lancaster County painter Jacob Eichholtz, the Lancaster County primitive John Landis, and the York County chronicler Lewis Miller, we are left with a small group of unknown portrait painters in watercolor, and a miscellany of several unknown overmantel painters and portrait painters in oil. Landscape paintings of Pennsylvania German farm life or interior genre scenes are rare indeed. [156]

These small and repetitious portrait watercolors can be divided into two or three groups which are fairly homogeneous: (1) the so-called Stettinius type, and (2) the Jacob Meinsel type. The former deals chiefly with standing portraits in rudimentary landscape backgrounds, [157] and the latter seems to follow more of an interior, genre style employing man and wife, and occasionally whole family groups seated in a stenciled or painted room. Two unusually fine examples owned in Reading, Pa., show the interiors of a Hatter's Shop and a local Merchant at his Counting Desk.

Never really common, these portrait watercolors are highly prized by Pennsylvania German descendants today and rarely can be seen except in the owner's "front parlor." In gathering material for this monograph, the author made it a point to photograph also these occasional specimens of primitive art, but 20 years of searching has produced only about 75 examples. They pose one of the most intriguing identification problems in this field, since they follow such clear-cut, stereotyped forms.

## PENNSYLVANIA GERMAN FRAKTUR TECHNIQUES

One of the facets of Fraktur work which has never received the careful attention it deserves is the wide variety of techniques employed by the illuminators. Concentrating upon the classification of the many Fraktur types we have just discussed, the tendency has been to speak of the hand-written, part-printed, and printed types, and to pass rather quickly over the many interesting technique developments and combinations which appear. It is these variations which show the true *ingenuity* and *individuality* of the folk artists. Many of these unusual techniques

---

[156] See Bibliography C under "Painting" for Preston and Eleanor Barba's detailed articles on Lewis Miller's travel books, containing many portraits, genre scenes, landscapes, etc.

[157] See figure 69.

used on the hand-written as well as on the printed Frakturs will be described here, some of them for the first time.

The reasons for this neglect are easily explained  First, since most of the early accounts of Fraktur were in magazine form and space was limited, it made a much simpler story to keep to the three main types mentioned above in order to give some idea of their chronological sequence. It seemed natural that the hand-drawn examples should be much earlier in date, for the early date of the first printed specimens had not yet been discovered.

Second, the tendency has always been to look down upon the Printed Certificates and Broadsides as being *artistically inferior*. Borneman, for example, speaks of them as "the printed and inartistically decorated certificates," although he is perhaps the first to allude to their early date. [158]  Kenneth Wood was the first to mention the lithographed examples, differentiating them from the block-printed pieces, but Borneman although he mentions Currier & Ives in his list of printers, states only that the certificates later "were printed in color" without distinguishing between the various printing media. [159]  Util the author's 1945 article in the *Quarterly Bulletin* of The New-York Historical Society, no mention had been made of the stipple-engraved examples. Also, very little notice had been given anywhere to cutwork and pin-prick.

As was the case with our classification of Fraktur types, almost all the Pennsylvania techniques have their counterparts in Europe, but with typical local adaptations. [160]  With one or two notable exceptions such as the Printed Certificate and Pin-prick work, the proportion of examples in each technique approximates that found in Europe. While the Printed Certificate never received the tremendous development abroad that it did here, Pin-prick, which was very popular abroad, never really got started here due to the preference for the Cut-out technique.

Although the sequence of techniques discussed is roughly chronological from hand-written Fraktur to printed and lithographed ones, it must constantly be kept in mind that the two — printed and hand-drawn — *flourished side by side*. The problem of their relative dating will be taken up in the next chapter. For example, the question of which came

---

[158] Borneman, *op. cit.*, p. 16.
[159] *Ibid.*, p. 15.
[160] See figures 11-32.

first, the printed center with hand-drawn borders, or the handwritten center with crude stamped borders, is not entirely clear. And printed broadsides such as the 1762 Miller *Irrgarten* (Philadelphia and the 1772 Ephrata *Goldene ABC,* antedate most of the hand-drawn Frakturs. [161]

Five individual techniques are worthy of study here. While it is not possible in every one of these media to show the method or procedure followed by the craftsmen, the author has been fortunate in most cases to locate half-completed or discarded examples which shed considerable light on this subject. Most of these are the work of prolific, and hence identifiable, illuminators whose other products are also illustrated in the accompanying Plates. Characteristic examples of each of the five categories listed below are illustrated:

(1) HAND-DRAWN
   (a) Pen and wash
   (b) Cross-hatching, stippling, etching
   (c) Penmanship specimens
   (d) Watercolor portraits
(2) BLOCK-PRINTED
   (a) Part-printed
   (b) Crude stamps
   (c) Applied designs
   (d) Colored backgrounds
   (e) All-printed
   (f) Printed and color-blocked
(3) CUTWORK AND PIN-PRICK
(4) STIPPLE-ENGRAVED
(5) LITHOGRAPHED
   (a) Black and White
   (b) In color

### Hand-Drawn Fraktur

### Pen and Wash

It is the Pen and Wash technique which in every respect embodies the true meaning of Fraktur. While it is second in quantity, naturally, to the mass-produced printed forms, the amount of such handwork done far exceeded the author's original ideas, as already pointed out in the Preface. It is possible that it may exist today in even larger quantities

---

[161] See figure 130.

in private collections as yet unknown, although in view of the extensive coverage of material by the author over the past 20 years, this is very doubtful

A perfect demonstration of the Pen and Wash technique has come down to us in the form of four pages of hand-drawn Fraktur work by Christian Peters. [162] Although no longer bound together, they must originally have belonged to a manuscript Copybook or ABC Book which he followed in preparing his illuminations. A fifth page shows the last 10 letters of a Fraktur alphabet and a complete Roman one, suggesting the existence of additional pages as yet undiscovered.

In the first page a capital letter "J" is outlined in pen and ink, leaving vacant portions of the letter which Peters intended to fill in with color. [163] The sections of the capital letter involving interlace he has already completed in black-letter work, thereby suggesting his closeness to the European originals. The second page goes a step further in showing not only how he executed his capital letter, but also how he laid out the first line of his Vorschrift and employed faint guide lines to follow in spacing out the remainder of his text. [164] In the third page he has begun to fill in various colors throughout the first line (Verse 484), but oddly enough he follows no regular sequence of colors such as one usually finds. [165] The fourth page shows a completed Vorschrift, which, although it is certainly from his hand also, nevertheless has a noticeable European flavor as regards the floriated capital letter and downhill slant of the written text. [166] The previous pages show the more careful layout one finds in the Pennsylvania German specimens as well as the less ornate treatment of capital letters. Christian Peters' signed and dated masterpiece, which is one of the most ornate examples of Fraktur that has come to our attention, is in the Brooklyn Museum [167] and came from the same source as the five smaller pages.

One might imagine that a fair number of such technique demonstration sheets, or incomplete Fraktur specimens, would have survived the years, but in reality they are not often seen. In contrast to the Peters

---

[162] See figure 74.
[163] See figure 74a.
[164] See figure 74b.
[165] See figure 74c.
[166] See figures 74d and 75.
[167] See figure 229.

examples which can be dated from his masterpiece of 1777, the only two other ones which have been seen by the author are both 19th century, one of them having been drawn by Enos Godshalk in the year 1820.

### Cross-Hatching, Stippling, and Etching

Sometimes in order to gain contrast and richness in their lettering or designs, illuminators resorted to unusual texture effects achieved outside the realm of color. The use of cross-hatching, [168] stippling, [169] and "etching" are those most often seen. Even in the earliest Fraktur work done at the Ephrata Cloister, we find examples of all of these. The filling in of backgrounds with etching or stippling, or with tonal treatments, [170] produces an effect not unlike stippled dower chests.

The practice continued right down into the 19th century when, as we shall find, it gained new life and greater richness in the hands of the highly gifted *Schwenkfelder* decorators. Their great contribution was the use of brilliantly-colored strapwork, diaper patterns, checkerboard, and spiral patterns. [171]

### Penmanship Specimens

The calligraphic element of Fraktur work was destined to receive special attention all the way along the line, from the Ephrata Cloister work through to the itinerant professional penman's exhibition sheets of the mid-1850's and 1860's. [172] The extra attention given to *schnörkel* (or elaborate penmanship flourishes) and the inclusion in Fraktur borders of birds and animals executed in pure calligraphic style, appears in the Ephrata, Mennonite, Schwenkfelder, and general 19th century schools.

### Watercolor Portraits

These early 19th century likenesses are executed chiefly in watercolor, but frequently include a Fraktur inscription or identification at the bottom, [173] or else are outlined in pen and ink. While they may have

---

[168] See figure 76.

[169] See figure 77.

[170] See figures 107, 113, and 114; also Color Plate I.

[171] While the Mennonite Vorschrift illuminators employed stippling and diapering to a limited extent, it was the Schwenkfelder group with their bold designing and brilliant coloring who really capitalized on this idea.

[172] It is a short step from Ephrata into the work of Jacob Oberholtzer and other Mennonites who used interlace, and thence into the work of professional penmen. See figures 79-80.

[173] See figures 69 and 81.

only a minimum of Fraktur work on them, they are included here because they occasionally served as Birth Certificates [174] and therefore present another form of hand-drawn Fraktur.

Even Lewis Miller, the itinerant watercolorist of York, Pa., produced a Family Register form in Fraktur. [175]

### Printed Fraktur

The story of the rise and development of the printed forms provides one of the most interesting chapters in the history of Fraktur. Although this involved Goldene ABC's, Irrgartens, Haus-Segens, and many other types as we have noted, it reached its highest development in the printed Birth and Baptismal Certificate.

The demand for these in the southeastern counties of Pennsylvania had reached such proportions that every printer felt called upon to supply forms for the use of the local citizenry. First Ephrata, then Reading, Harrisburg, and Allentown became the chief centers for mass production of these certificate forms. Wood, Nolan, McMurtrie, Borneman, Stoudt, and Shoemaker have all touched upon them, but the details of the story have been bypassed in their enthusiasm for hand-written Fraktur specimens.

### Part-Printed Forms

To fill the demands of the Pennsylvania Germans for Birth and Baptismal Certificate forms which the local minister or school teacher could fill in, the printers supplied a page with the text arranged in a rectangular block at the center. [176] The space for the names and dates were left blank and the borders provided ample opportunity for decoration, if the owner so desired. [177]

The first text arrangements varied considerably. Corresponding to the earlier hand-written forms which began with the name of the child, some early printed forms began "Gezeuget von..." [178] At least as early as 1784, however, a standard form beginning "Diesen beiden Ehegatten..." appeared. By 1790, the Reading presses had already improved upon the plain rectangular text-block form by introducing the heart-form, in which the main text was enclosed within a large heart

---

[174] See figures 69 and 81.
[175] Contained in a manuscript owned by The New-York Historical Society.
[176] See figures 82-84.
[177] See figures 82, 84, and 240-241.
[178] See figure 82.

at the center of the Certificate and two stanzas of baptismal hymns appear within smaller hearts at the lower left and right corners.[179]  Although this achieved a more decorative design, it created irregular areas for the decorator to fill, a problem which soon led to new and original developments.

### Crude Wood-Block Stamps

One of the first auxiliaries to the printed forms, both the rectangular and the heart-shaped types, was the use of somewhat crude but extremely decorative woodcut blocks.  Sometimes these appear in orderly formation, such as on the Ephrata-Otto certificates,[180] and sometimes in random arrangement in vacant areas along the borders.[181]  The former blocks usually contain multiple designs, whereas the latter random type consist of single motifs that are irregularly and unevenly stamped here and there according to the fancy of the decorator

Among the former, a long horizontal textile-like block and two vertical blocks each containing three birds and miscellaneous flowers predominate; these are the trademarks of Henrich Otto and the Ephrata press.  The small block stamps with single motifs used by the Reading printers are usually barn-signs or stars, tulips or other flowers, parrots or smaller birds, mermaids,[182] and occasionally human figures.  Some of these bird and mermaid stamps may be very early, since they also appear on some handwritten certificates dated in the 1760's and 1770's.

The use of stamped borders continued down well into the 19th century, as late as 1860, and even after the lithographed forms (which must have been considered more modern and more attractive pictorially), had been in use for some time.[183]

### Applied Designs

The next step in the decoration of certificate borders is one which has passed unnoticed by previous writers.  In contrast to the somewhat plain and primitive character of the Reading stamped pieces, a deficiency which was improved in the Otto pieces by the addition of hand-drawn

---

[179] See figure 85.
[180] See figures 83, 86, and 242; also Color Plate IV.
[181] See figures 82 and 85.
[182] See figures 85 and 197.
[183] See figure 87.

connecting garlands of leaves and flowers as well as by spectacular lettering, the Reading decorators developed a technique of applied cut-outs
which achieved equal and perhaps greater richness.

These applied cut-out designs are combined, usually, with hand-
drawn borders by Friedrich Krebs.    Their use appears to be confined
entirely to the Reading imprints of Schneider & Co., and to certificates decorated by Krebs.    In fact, the appearance of a few of these applied cutouts upon hand-drawn specimens suggests very strongly that the idea
may have been a Krebs invention!

If so, where did Krebs secure these applied designs and what forms
do they take?    At first glance, one might not even notice these small
embossed and gilded designs with colored backgrounds in yellow, lavender, and orange which are pasted to the certificates, so soft in tone are
they.    The frequent appearance of various Saints, [184] duly labeled and
in rectangular blocks, at first suggested the possibility of religious tokens
of some sort.    But the subsequent discovery of hunting scenes, ladies
and gentlemen playing cards at a table or playing musical instruments,
was against this theory.    The finding of one such certificate with nothing
but various kinds of birds upon it and another consisting entirely of
animals, further complicated the problem.    And then, amidst all of
these were tulip, urn, and heart shapes. [185]    It was these latter shapes
which ultimately gave the clue to the origin of these applied cut-outs.

At various times they had been identified by antique dealers as the
labels off packages of tea.    Another suggestion was that they had been
used as labels on the bolts of fabrics sold in the country stores throughout the Pennsylvania German community.    Examination of a group of
such labels, however, revealed little similarity of form and design, and
in each case the size and price of the material per yard were clearly
marked.    That these applied designs had been produced just for this
purpose, for use on Frakturs, seemed unlikely in view of their irregularity and offhand quality.    Still no satisfactory explanation of their source
was forthcoming.

One could only conclude that Krebs, or whoever the decorator may
have been, was adapting something intended for a totally different use
to his own special purpose.    This, in fact, has since proved to be the

---

[184] See figures 91 and 249.
[185] See figures 91 and 249.

case. Careful examination revealed that the tulip, urn, and heart designs not only did not have any definite outline around them — such as the Saints did, for example — but that they also had an allover floral *repeat* pattern that had *no relation to their shape.* [186] This fact suggested the possibility that sheets of paper, embossed with floral designs, were being cut up into various shapes. A checkup of the figural groups of hunters, musicians, etc., likewise revealed irregular shapes, as if the decorator were cutting around his chosen motif in such a way as not to interfere with an adjoining one. What were these sheets of paper, embossed with religious, secular, animal, bird, and floral motifs intended to be used for?

The first clue to this problem came in the George Horace Lorimer Sale (1944), when a Child's Schoolbook was sold which had as its cover this same embossed paper. The second clue appeared in the Claude W. Unger Collection, where the author not only found a certificate form torn in two ,parts both of which were covered with animals of every size and variety from a tiny squirrel to a huge elephant, [187] but also an uncut gilded sheet embossed with Adam and Eve in the center surrounded by a multitude of birds, [188] some of which actually appeared on certificates photographed by the author.

Additional sample sheets, containing similar subject-matter, were found in Plimpton Library at Columbia University, as well as several books describing and recording the various forms, printers, and place and date of printing. Apparently these embossed sheets of designs were quite popular in Europe where they were used for *bookbindings* and for *endpapers!*

Perhaps the most ornate example of these cut-out designs applied to a Birth and Baptismal Certificate is in the Reformed Church Library at Lancaster, Pa. [189] The only instance which has come to the author's attention in which these embossed designs have been used in other Fraktur work, was an example in the Nadelman Collection [190]

---

[186] See figure 91
[187] See figure 90.
[188] See figure 88.
[189] See figure 89.
[190] A cutout bird applied to a hand-drawn vine.

## Colored Backgrounds

In some cases, Krebs went even further to achieve richness of decoration. Instead of simply applying these embossed designs in the borders of his Birth and Baptismal Certificates and filling out the remaining space with his flowing Fraktur designs, he toned in the entire surface of the paper (excepting the large central heart and the two smaller ones) with a pastel shade of buff, pink, lavender, or yellow. [191]

That this coloring of the background was done *after* the embossed designs had been applied to the certificate is proved by the fact that in several cases the applied designs have come loose and have exposed the white, untinted paper beneath. It was on top of this colored ground, then, that Krebs proceeded to fill in empty spaces with the winding vines, tulips, crowns, and sun and moons, which are virtually his signature.

## All-Printed Forms

It was not long until the technique of mass production had eliminated even these hand-drawn motifs used to connect, or fill the spaces between, the printed designs. [192] This made any special penmanship unnecessary except that of writing the name, dates, etc., of the subject. Now the artist had only to fill in the colors of the angels and birds in the borders by hand. Everything else was machine-made. It is at this time, about 1800, that the printed Birth and Baptismal Certificate takes on its mechanical, monotonous look, [193] which is relieved only by the riotous color splashed on top of the printed designs by "intensity loving" Pennsylvania Germans. When not satisfied with the designs before him, the craftsman simply ignored them and painted brilliant patterns of his own right over the top of the printed outlines.

## Printed and Color-Blocked Forms

But even this last remnant of handwork, as far as the printed certificates are concerned at least, was short-lived for by 1825 the printers had perfected a means of stenciling in the border colors also by means

---

191 See figures 90-91.

192 See figures 92-93.

193 The deciding factor here is *exact repetition*, as opposed to the earlier stamped borders where each grouping is different. Here, also, the blocks are finer cut and are more *balanced* in their arrangement.

of color-blocks. Although they had printed border designs *in outline* in color before this, [194] they had not attempted solid color printing. [195]

Chief center for the production of these color-blocked certificates was G. S. Peters at Harrisburg after 1828; Allentown, although its printers took over Peters' Angel Design almost verbatim, seems never to have printed with color-blocks. Perhaps this is not unusual, since G. S. Peters himself did not invariably use color-blocks, as is apparent from examples which still turn up that are hand-colored in traditional gaudy style. His use of color-blocks was carried on later by Theo. F. Scheffer, also at Harrisburg. [196]

Oddly enough, this technique never seems to have taken hold in Reading where people apparently preferred the variety of handwork and the brilliance of color which stencil-blocks could not provide. This production at Harrisburg is one of the early predecessors of modern color-printing today, for Peters soon found he could use several color-blocks together. He then expanded into publishing religious broadsides [197] and books in color, especially juveniles. [198] His later certificate forms, broadsides, books, and pictures were printed in four colors: red, yellow, green, and blue.

### *Cutwork and Pinprick* [199]

Both these techniques were popular in Europe during the late 18th and 19th centuries, but in Pennsylvania only the former received much attention. Examples of Pinprick which have come to the author's attention would not exceed 12, and most of the Cutwork that has survived is the work of only a very few artists, among them Christian Strenge [200] and Wilhelmus A. Faber. [201] While some of the Pennsylvania examples date in the 1780's and 1790's, most of them were executed after the turn of the century, probably between 1810 and 1820.

Since so little has been written about Cutwork thus far, we are doubly fortunate not only in having a fine group of finished specimens

---

[194] See figure 86.
[195] See figures 94-95.
[196] See figure 262.
[197] Way to Eternal Life, Life of Christ series, The Ages of Man, etc.
[198] Joseph and His Brethren, The House that Jack Built, etc.
[199] Borneman, *op. cit.*, p. 38, "punch work and cut work."
[200] See figure 55.
[201] See figures 96-98.

to choose from, but also some partially completed examples of Faber's own work which reveal just how he worked. In the first sheet we have the uncolored piece of white paper, which has been folded in half and then cut through with a sharp knife to preserve a solid oval panel at the center surrounded by a border of hearts and winding vines in silhouette. [202] It should be noted at once that most Cutouts seem to have been folded only once for cutting, thus accounting no doubt for their crispness. In the second sheet, the cutting has been completed and the center panel with its hearts and vines outlined in the red and yellow watercolor lines so characteristic of Faber's work. [203] Remarkably enough, when the uncolored form is laid over the colored one, opening for opening they match in every detail. Their accuracy is amazing, thereby suggesting the possible use of patterns.

In a third example, a typical completed Faber Cutout of unusual and much more elaborate design may be seen. [204] In the case of the Weidner family of Berks County, he made Cutout certificates for five members of the same family: Father and Mother, and three children (two of them born on the same day evidently were twins!). The apogee of Faber's cutwork technique was reached no doubt in the intricate example in the Brooklyn Museum collection, fully signed and dated 1818. [205] The latinizing of Faber's name, his designs, and the names of the families for whom he worked, all suggest Swiss origin.

The few examples of Pinprick work which have appeared are Love Letters [206] or Valentines, two of them of quite late date (1835), with red satin ribbon drawn through their edges, an unusual technique among the Pennsylvania Germans. [207]

### Stipple-Engraved Certificates

The city of Reading, which carried the printed certificate to such high development, also produced the Stipple-Engraved technique practiced so successfully by Carl Friederich Egelmann and Gabriel Miesse. Of these two gifted artists, little has been published to date, although both are well worth much more careful investigation. The former is

[202] See figure 96.
[203] See figure 97.
[204] See figure 234.
[205] See figure 98.
[206] See figure 99.
[207] See figure 100.

the author of the only Pennsylvania German engraved Fraktur Copybook as well as several outstanding certificate forms, [208] and the latter (perhaps his pupil) ably carried on the Stipple-Engraved tradition. Egelmann also illustrated several books as well as numerous Almanacs printed at Reading during the 2nd quarter of the 19th century. Although Stauffer lists Egelmann, [209] he apparently was not familiar with the man or his engravings, which seems strange indeed in view of his own origins in Lancaster County, Pa.; Miesse is not even listed.

Illustrations from Egelmann's *Copybook for the Instruction of Youth* and some of the copperplates engraved by Gabriel Miesse, including his own Bookplate, are to be seen in Figures 267-279. Most unusual is the latter's certificate form showing the *Baptism of Christ*, which has all the earmarks of an Italian primitive!

### Lithographed Certificates

Lithography in black-and-white. as well as in color, soon lent itself as a medium for the production of Birth and Baptismal Certificates, as well as for Marriage Certificates  And whether they originated in adjacent Philadelphia or distant New York City, they were as apt to be in German as in English. [210]  Even N. Currier and Currier & Ives engaged in producing these *in both languages* following. remarkably enough, the standard text form established in the Ephrata-Otto examples of 1784.  Their alternate "Family Register" form, however, must not have enjoyed much popularity in the Pennsylvania German area, since only one example has come to the author's attention.  The rather surprising activity of N. Currier and Currier & Ives in this unusual field received comparatively little attention even from such an authority as Harry T. Peters, in his various books on their vast activities.

In the list of "Fraktur Printers" given in Appendix C, those producing Lithographed Certificates are so designated.

---

[208] Shelley, Donald A., "Illuminated Birth Certificates, Regional Examples of an Early American Folk Art", The New-York Historical Society *Quarterly*, XXIX, 2 (April, 1945), 101, illustrated on page 105. Herein see figures 101, 270, and 271.
[209] Stauffer, D. McN., *American Engravers upon Copper and Steel*, I (1907), p. 80.
[210] See figure 102.

## PENNSYLVANIA GERMAN FRAKTUR MATERIALS

The actual materials and media used in any craft provide interesting facts for speculation, and those used by the Fraktur illuminator are no exception. While in most cases we may assume that the merest essentials were available, the character, history, and use of these few items make the many differences we note in various Fraktur pieces. As might be expected, there were books published on the proper manufacture and use of these materials necessary for Fraktur writing. The earliest of these probably dates back as early as Theophilus of Paderborn (Germany), in the 12th century, who described recipes for making tempera which coincide with those used six centuries later in Pennsylvania by local craftsmen.

In the 16th century, when the use of Fraktur as a typeface, as well as Fraktur illuminating were being practiced on a large scale, quite a few books were issued regarding methods of illumination. It is interesting to observe that most of these were published in the Rhineland area where Fraktur as a typeface and written letter was being most actively developed. Borneman reproduces the Titlepage of one of these showing the various tools of the illuminator, and we may discern there the various brushes, pens, etc., which he was supposed to employ. [211] It must be remembered in this connection, however, that the implements of the local Pennsylvania craftsmen were no doubt limited, and apt to be somewhat fewer and more primitive than those shown here. This little volume is one of three mentioned by Borneman as foreign sources of information dating from 1560 to 1566. [212] No doubt there were many others between that time and the first Pennsylvania ones.

Those which he cites as being printed in America, date chiefly around 1815-20. [213] There are no doubt earlier ones also.

---

211 Borneman, *op. cit.*, pl. I.
212 *Ibid.*, pp. 41-42 :   1560 *Kunstbüchlein*, Frankfort
                1566 *Kunstbuchlein*, Frankfort
                1566 Boltzen's *Illuminirbuch*, Rufach (Elsass)
                     (first issued at Basel in 1548).
213 *Ibid.*, pp. 39-46:   *Das Grosse ABC Buch*
                Ambrosius Henkel
                New Market, Shenandoah County
                Virginia, 1817-1820.
      page 44:   *Die Land-und Haus-Apotheke*
                Johann George Hohman
                Reading, 1818.
      pp. 42-44·   *Oeconomisches Haus-und Kunst-Buch*
                Johann Krauss
                Allentown, 1819.

Inasmuch as Fraktur writing was actually practiced chiefly by professionals and not done by every farmer and his housewife, we naturally would not expect to find a great many of these color books — at least not many in comparison to the dyeing books, which after all every housewife would have needed for everyday purposes. Copies of these three American books of instruction on dyeing and the home arts in general are not exceedingly rare, copies of some of them having appeared in sales in recent years.

## Paper

Although early deeds and indentures, notably some of those printed at the Ephrata Cloister about 1765, were executed upon parchment, [214] no Fraktur illumination has come to the author's attention which was *not* done upon paper.

This early paper is excellent in quality and will far outlast any of our papers today, as well as those of the later 19th century. With its high rag content and its fine surface, it provided an excellent vehicle for the use of the penman. It consequently is responsible not only for the high quality of the lines the craftsman was able to achieve upon its surface, but also for the fact that so many of these early documents are preserved today. Had they been executed upon inferior paper, they would long since have disappeared as a result of disintegration. Whether framed or not, therefore, the durability of the paper upon which the Birth and Baptismal Certificates and other Fraktur pieces were executed has kept them fresh and strong

Occasionally one finds the paper has suffered a little, usually from the following reasons: (1) excessive dampness sometimes stains and mildews the edges, (2) constant folding frequently has broken the paper into two pieces, and (3) in the earlier period at least, one frequently finds that the ink has eaten through the paper completely. This latter feature is especially characteristic of the Ephrata music books, where sometimes the end bars of an entire music book have been eaten through from the first page to the last. For further explanation of this "rusting" reaction of the early ink upon paper, see foot-note 228.

One of the interesting bits of research yet to be carried out with these certificates would be a study of the watermarks which occur on

---

[214] See specimen in the Pennsylvania Historical Society, Philadelphia, illustrated here as figure 129.

the paper. Because so many of them are framed and cannot be removed easily, it is virtually impossible to say at this time what the source of most of this early paper may have been. We know that large quantities of paper were manufactured at the Ephrata Cloister [215] as well as in the early Rittenhouse mills, and the watermarks found thus far substantiate this. What other mills might also have provided paper for this purpose, it is difficult to say at this point.

Since the Certificates and other Fraktur illuminations in Pennsylvania usually take certain specific shapes and sizes, it is interesting to observe what these are, and to realize at the same time how the original size of the sheets of paper was responsible in large degree for the final size of the Fraktur piece. They naturally do not all conform by the quarter-inch to certain specific sizes, but with minor variations our Birth Certificates, Vorschriften, Designs, etc., do fit into three chief sizes as follows:

(1) Large, or folio, size        13 x 16 inches
(2) Medium, or half, size.       13 x  8 inches
(3) Small, or quarter, size      6½ x  8 inches

Even most of the small illuminated Music Books follow this same format with page sizes ranging around 6½ x 4 inches, or half the above smallest Certificate size. The chief variations fall in the period after 1820, when the 16-inch width frequently comes out 15 or 15½ inches, and the 13-inch height changes to 12½ or 12 inches. But within these limits, the above standard sizes continue through the entire history of Fraktur writing. They may vary from vertical to horizontal in usage, but the outside size still remains the same.

Just as in early American portraiture, where the size of canvas used may provide a clue as to the painter (as in the case of Ezra Ames), so in Fraktur certain illuminators seem to have favorite sizes.

### Pens

Perhaps the tool which played the most important part in these illuminations was the pen, for it was the implement which was used to lay out the composition of the certificate as well as to fill in the infor-

---

[215] Hark, J. Max, *Chronicon Ephratense: A History of the Community of Seventh Day Baptists at Ephrata, Lancaster County, Penn'a.* Lancaster, Pa.: S. H. Zahm & Co., 1889. See pages 209-211, and 213.

mation regarding the individual for whom the certificate was being made. On the steadiness and flexibility of the pen, therefore, depended the artistic quality of the Fraktur design.

Some penmen were very careful about their materials, especially their pens, and the works which they produced are therefore of very high quality.[216] Other illuminators were not so careful, and their lines are therefore apt to be thin, weak, and nervous in their execution. [217] It is this factor of technical perfection which frequently differentiates the work of the novice from the work of an experienced Fraktur decorator. It may also mark the difference between a fine old work of the period and a modern attempt at imitation or forgery, as we shall see later. So characteristic is the penwork of certain artists, that it provides the major clue for isolating their works from those of other contemporary illuminators.

It was the quill pen, rather than the steel pen, which the Fraktur penman used. [218] Its flexibility and jagged character only served to enhance further the picturesque angularity of the Fraktur letters executed by the early artist. This flexibility, as we shall see, led the illuminator to shade his letters very decoratively and to add extra flourishes or "schnörkel." By the time the steel pen had been developed, the golden age of Fraktur was already past, although many of the older craftsmen undoubtedly must have continued using the quill pen even after this date. [219]

Quill pens, like the paper and the colors used by the Fraktur illuminator, were procured in a simple but definite way. Just as the paper was handmade and the colors were neutral earth colors, the quills were taken from the wing of a goose. [220] Not any wing would do; it had to be a specific one. These instructions were contained in the Henkel *ABC Buch* printed at New Market, Virginia, and quoted by Borneman [221] According to this book, the second, third, and fourth quills were preferred

216 See Jacob Oberholtzer, figures 40, 47, and 142-147.
217 See "Weak Artist", figure 209, and "Flat Parrot Artist", figure 210.
218 See Copybook *Title-pages* with quills, bottles of ink, etc., figures 47 and 144.
219 See figure 78.
220 Mercer, *op. cit.*, p. 424.
221 Borneman, *op. cit.*, p. 39.

## Pencils

As a general rule, any pencil work was limited to the guide lines for the lettered text of the Fraktur illumination[222] — and even these were usually executed with a stylus rather than a pencil.[223] From the author's observation, if any great amount of pencil drawing was done in connection with the layout of the designs, then it must have been erased, since few traces of it remain on the certificates. Since the pen-and-ink lines are normally quite clear and clean, furthermore, one doubts that any erasing could have been done because the ink would then tend to blot and the lines would spread on the paper.

Towards the middle of the 19th century, on the other hand, one begins to find more pencil. In children's drawings especially, it is quite prominent. Daniel Peterman, for example, used it quite freely and never made any attempt to erase it or draw in ink over it. As a matter of fact, he seems almost to have substituted it for pen and ink outlines.[224]

## Brushes

From Mercer's statement about the brushes supposed to have been found in the Fraktur box,[225] it is impossible to say whether or not the story about the cat-hair brushes was taken from the usual Benjamin West anecdote as told by John Galt or not.[226] Perhaps it was, but at least it is certain that whatever brushes were used were of a definitely primitive type. Inasmuch as the chief function the brush performed was simply fling in areas of color, it had little actual effect upon the appearance of the Fraktur penwork itself. Only in the later period do we begin to find forms drawn without benefit of pen-and-ink outlines, but from the execution of detail in these later pieces, it was possible to secure a fairly fine point with the brushes they used.

## Inks and Inkwells

The inks used in Fraktur writing deserve special study since they play such an important part in the initial conception of the work. Next

---

[222] See figures 74b, 74d, 201, 225, and 234.
[223] See figures 43, 203, and 206.
[224] See figure 217.
[225] Mercer, *op. cit*, p. 424. ". . . its longest compartment contained goose-quill pens and brushes made of the hair of the domestic cat"
[226] Galt, John, *The Life, Studies, and Works of West.* London: T. Cadell and W. Davies, 1820. See p. 19.

to the pen itself, they perhaps play the chief role in fixing the character of the piece. Inasmuch as the inks are so distinctly separated from the colors themselves, they are treated separately here. For, as we have seen, the Certificate was first laid out with quill pen and ink, the coloring of initials and designs being left until afterwards. [227] In some cases, the ink lines never were actually filled in with color because the penman decided that it was not necessary to complete the entire surface in color.

While various colored inks were occasionally used, black and red seem to have been the chief ones. Sometimes the consistency of these varied, due to their homemade origin, so that the effect of several colors is achieved either by thinning or thickening the ink. The black, when thinned out, becomes brown, even buff, in color; the red, likewise, becomes orange or rust-colored. This is especially true in the earlier period where more emphasis is placed upon the penwork and not so much upon the color, and where there is apt to be less color and a narrower assortment of color.

*Black ink,* as will be noted especially in the Ephrata manuscripts, has a tendency to eat through the paper. The manner in which it does this seems the same as in European manuscripts, and results apparently from the chemical composition of the ink itself. As abroad, gall-apples (or gall-nuts) are the chief ingredient, and after constant exposure to air, a chemical reaction sets in which may be compared to ordinary rust. [228] This rust eventually eats its way through the paper wherever there is sufficient ink to make it possible. As a result, the Ephrata manuscripts with their bars of music ending at approximately the same point on every page, frequently are eaten through from cover to cover. Ephrata Fraktur work, Daniel Schumacher, Master C.M., and other late 18th century artists frequently exhibit this same defect, and occasionally as late as the 1840's and 1850's one also finds it. It seems to be limited to black ink, moreover, for it never appears in any other colors.

*Red ink* played a very prominent part in the earlier Fraktur pieces, where it was used not only for portions of the decorative designs, [229] but also for lettering. In some of these, portions of the letters or por-

---

[227] See figures 74a-74d.
[228] The chemical reaction is as follows:

$$\text{Fe-Tannic Acid (of Gall Apples)} + \text{Water} = \text{Ferro-Oxide}$$
(iron salt of tannic acid - *black*)     (humidity)     (ferrotannic acid or *brown* rust)

[229] Schnörkel, hatching, feathering, etc.

tions of each word, are executed in red ink and the remainder in black. [230] Occasionally alternate lines appear in red and in black, [231] and sometimes extra colors appear, such as in an inscription following a red-green-black, red-green-black system. As a general rule, however, inks other than black and red were not much used until the mid-19th century.

*Inkwells* appear in the Mennonite Copybooks of the 1780's as well as in the 1821-31 Egelmann (Reading) Copybooks. No doubt they were early blown glass or pottery ones, as Borneman has suggested. [232]

## Colors

The decorative designs of the penwork in Fraktur writing were ably supported by vigorous colors, chiefly reds, yellows, greens, and blues. These were remarkable in their intensity, especially through the glossy surface achieved by the use of *cherry gum* or *gum arabic* to increase that intensity. Even certain painted pieces of furniture show this same use of glossy substance in certain colors. [233] Noted by Mercer in his book, [234] this is no new idea since, as Borneman pointed out, it goes back ultimately to Theophilus of Paderborn [235] It also accounts for the flaking off of color from Fraktur specimens due to dampness and sticking when they have been folded together.

Not all Frakturs employ this method, however. Especially after the turn of the century, one finds increasingly the dull and flat watercolors which have not been treated with this same vehicle, and which present a totally different effect. These certificates lack the sparkle and crispness of the earlier ones. [236] Some writers claim that this medium is limited to certain counties or to certain artists, but this is a dangerous generalization. Others say it appeared about the Civil War period, [237] but again one must accept this broad statement with caution, since some of the

---

[230] See figure 35.

[231] See figure 40.

[232] Borneman, *op. cit.*, p. 39.

[233] Dower chest decorations.

[234] Mercer, *op. cit.*, p. 424.

[235] Borneman, *op. cit.*, p. 41.

[236] See figure 210.

[237] Jackson Collection, Schuyler B., *Sale Catalogue* (1933), p. 28, "The use of cherry-tree gum as a medium apparently ended with the beginning of the Civil War."

very earliest artists employed these flat watercolors. *Ephrata work,* for example, can be identified readily because of the use of this flat water-color.

As in the case of inks, the choice of colors in the earlier period was limited, while later we find odd shades of all sorts which suited the taste of the period. The reds, yellows, blues, and greens of the earlier period are amplified by the addition of oranges, purples, and even *gold or silver.* While these latter colors are not common, they do exist. It is interesting to discover this last hand-me-down from the medieval art of manuscript writing. The examples on which they have appeared belong to no special period, but range in date all the way from 1776 down to 1856. [238] As has happened frequently with specimens of cherry-gum work, however, they have *flaked off* or discolored considerably.

### Straight-Edge

A straight-edge or ruler was virtually a necessity for the Fraktur penman. With so much emphasis upon borders and border designs, he could not very well be without one. Also, for laying out the lines of text for his Certificates or his Vorschriften, he needed some sort of guide to follow.

While one as ornate as that described by Borneman is certainly not an absolute necessity, [239] no doubt such types in triangular section did exist. A simple flat one, however, as shown in the 1566 Boltzen von Rufach *Illuminirbuch* Titlepage, [240] would have been much more likely. This type did exist in Pennsylvania, for several of them have come to the author's attention. Usually, if they contained any design at all, it was a simple heart opening to hang the straight-edge on a nail.

### Compass

While the compass was also a necessity at times, its use is not nearly so prevalent as the straight-edge. It occurs chiefly in laying out some of the circular Labyrinths or Valentines, where the greatest accuracy was necessary. In other more usual instances, such as the work of the Mount Pleasant Artist, [241] clock dials and the heads of people are

---

[238] The New-York Historical Society, *Cutout,* dated 1776.
[239] Borneman, *op. cit.,* p. 40.
[240] See figure 2.
[241] See figure 220.

first outlined in ink with a compass and then the hair and other facial details added on top. It served as a guide line, in other words, to achieve the shape of the human head.

One or two illuminators, who based their designs more upon geometric forms, also employed the compass. We find it especially often in the form of barn signs which are composed entirely of circles, hearts based upon circles, and other stylized flower designs. [242] As in the case of the straight-edge, the compass is used to lay out a rather complicated geometric design and then the details are added freehand by the illuminator.

### Stylus

In some instances, instead of using pencil to lay out the lines which guide the text of the Certificate, a stylus or sharp edge seems to have been employed [243] — much in the same way as we find upon the decorated Dower Chests. While this custom is not a common one, it does appear in quite a number of instances which have come to the author's attention. The stylus has likewise been used occasionally by the more geometric illuminators in laying out their forms, such as the Wetzel illuminator, [244] Strenge, and others.

### Knife

A small knife would be part of the required equipment of the Fraktur writer, since his quill-pen would need careful attention. Apparently this is born out by the New Market *ABC Buch* (Henkel), which offers instructions as to the proper manner of sharpening the blade. [245]

Occasionally, as we have already seen, this knife was no doubt put to other uses, such as cutting out portions of the paper to increase the effectiveness of the designs [246] This style of work, although it was practiced by a few decorators, never was taken up by the main body of Pennsylvania Fraktur writers, and is more than likely the effort of a

---

[242] Ehre Vater Artist, Susanna Hubner, John A. Landis, and others.
[243] For use of stylus and pricking see Jones, Leslie Webber, 'Pricking Manuscripts: The Instruments and Their Significance', *Speculum, A Journal of Mediaeval Studies*, XX1, 4 (October, 1946), 389-403.
[244] See figures 62 and 205.
[245] Borneman, *op. cit.*, p. 3C.
[246] Christian Strenge (figure 55) and Wilhelmus A. Faber (figures 96-98 and 234).

few European craftsmen who were expert in the tradition and who continued to practice it here after their arrival. Like European Pinprick, it never was really taken up by the local Pennsylvania decorators.

## Frames

An integral part of any picture is its frame, whether appropriate for it or not. And with Fraktur, this is even more definitely the case for quite a wide variety of types appear upon them — types which seem to have been developed especially for them and in which they frequently turn up even to the present day.

It is proper, in closing this chapter on materials and tools, to scrutinize these moldings which belong to several different periods and which occasionally help in fixing the date of a somewhat puzzling Fraktur specimen. Just as we speak of Currier & Ives frames, we can speak of Fraktur frames, for there are certain types of moldings which seem to be restricted to the Pennsylvania German area and to have been used most commonly on these illuminated pieces. The frames found on these Frakturs are cut from rather heavy moldings, boldly profiled, and frequently beaded at the outer or inner edges. Usually in black, the monotony is often relieved by edgings in yellow, red, or contrasting colors now softened by age and hard wear. From about 1800 onwards, blocks begin to appear at the corners of the frames, sometimes emphasized by a change of color, a bit of design, or a different kind of wood. But even in these, the flat or reeded moldings of the frames themselves continue to be quite heavy and deeply profiled.

While most Fraktur frames are of wood, a few examples exist where paper has been employed for the same purpose. In these, heavy paper or cardboard has been worked into the shape of a frame, and then painted either a flat color or else stippled with a darker color over a lighter one, just as we shall find in the case of the regular beveled wooden frames. [247] In a few instances these paper frames appear to have been covered or bound at the edges with pieces of fabric, but these are most unusual. [248] We mention these paper and cloth frames only in passing, for they are certainly far from being common.

---

[247] See figures 54 and 81.
[248] See figure 53.

The more common wooden frames are usually finished in one of two ways: they are either left in the natural wood, or are painted in plain or decorative fashion   Both these types exist in a wide variety of shapes and sizes such as one would scarcely think possible until actually making a study of them.   If it were not for the fact that they obviously have never been separated from the certificate which they contain, one would certainly think that they were much later, and somewhat unrelated, additions.

## PENNSYLVANIA GERMAN FRAKTUR DESIGNS AND MOTIFS

In the first section of this chapter, devoted to Types of Fraktur, Pennsylvania German illuminated manuscripts were identified by the purpose for which they were used, as indicated by their text, with only occasional references to their layout, designs, or motifs.   Here we shall examine the individual designs themselves and the manner of their use.

Even more impressive than the written inscriptions in Pennsylvania German art, perhaps, is the profusion of decorative motifs and designs. To the casual observer, their dive.sity and charm are the real sum and substance of Pennsylvania German Folk Art.   In fact, it was their "quaintness" and naiveté which first attracted the interest of collectors and antiquarians to this field; the knowledge and appreciation of the form and local construction of their furniture, for example, came later with specialization.

It is in the field of decoration that the Pennsylvania German craftsmen made their most significant contribution.   It is their bold, clearcut designs which stamp objects as Pennsylvania German — so much so that anything with decoration is automatically called Pennsylvania German whether it really is or not.   Decoration, in other words, has become synonymous with this locale.   Even New York and New England decorated pieces are thus occasionally misattributed to Pennsylvania.   And the problem of European importations is even more complicated.

But just as the European *forms* were altered in adapting them to Pennsylvania, so the *designs* underwent sufficient changes that make it possible to distinguish the difference.   And with Fraktur itself, just as the various European types were taken over in Pennsylvania, so the motifs were adapted with minor changes.   Thus, when color and form are not adequate to distinguish European importations, slight alterations in the use or interpretation of the designs themselves ofttimes supply the necessary clue.

Wherever one looks in Pennsylvania German Folk Art, regardless of medium, one finds a richly decorative style based upon flower, bird, and animal forms. As has been stated by Downs, "indeed nothing was so trivial as to be scorned by woodcarver, painter, iron caster, or potter." [249] Questions have always been raised as to the explanation of this development, its meaning, and the degree to which it may or may not be original in this country.

In seeking an explanation or reason for this highly decorative style, one automatically turns to the background of the people themselves. In the Rhineland, in fact in most of Central Europe, a tradition of painted furniture, glass, illuminations, and decorative pottery was already well established by the middle of the 18th century. In those regions which were strongly *Catholic,* there was already a profusion of votive pictures, wardrobes with religious scenes painted on the door panels, and printed broadsides incorporating the favored subjects of the Catholic Church. In those regions where Catholicism was not so strong, taste ran more towards use of everyday subject-matter which the decorator found all around him: architectural designs, birds, flowers, and other familiar motifs.

Now it must be recalled that the background of the many groups which came to Pennsylvania, no matter what their place of origin, was *Protestant* rather than Catholic and that anything reminiscent of the hierarchy of the Catholic Church was anathema to them. Religious subjects such as the Baptism of Christ, the Ascension of Christ, the Crucifixion, the Last Supper — in fact virtually all of those themes which make up medieval iconography — are rarely found in Pennsylvania German Folk Art, whether it be Fraktur or a related medium. A half dozen or so instances among Fraktur drawings are the only exceptions to this rule. [250]

In place of the religious motifs of the European pieces, the Pennsylvania German Folk Artist substituted a new iconography of

---

[249] Downs, Joseph, *A Handbook of the Pennsylvania German Galleries in the American Wing.* New York: The Metropolitan Museum of Art, 1934, p. 5.

[250] These are usually Crucifixions, Adam and Eves, Baptisms, etc. See figures 63, 200, and 233.

floral, geometric, animal, and bird motifs which he made up for himself from the subject-matter he found around him in everyday life. Not that these were unknown in his European fatherland: on the contrary they were quite common there, but their use and development was less advanced. In Pennsylvania, on the other hand, beginning with very simple ideas, the artist treated these designs based upon everyday flowers in a completely original manner and went far beyond the patterns used by his European predecessor. Flowers and birds were, after all, constant reminders of the beauty which the Folk Artist found all around him. [251]

The degree to which these decorators were conscious of the implications and meanings of the motifs which they employed, has always posed a difficult problem. Some early writers have alluded to a few simple concepts which no doubt were known to the Pennsylvania German Folk Artists, but have not credited them with an extensive iconographical knowledge. More recently, especially since the 1930's, the tendency has been rather to read all sorts of complicated meanings into the artist's use of certain motifs on a chest or Fraktur illumination. [252] That the entire background is a religious one there can be no doubt, but that each Folk Artist or craftsman possessed an intimate knowledge of iconography and deliberately chose his designs to convey a special meaning, could hardly be proved. [253] A third school of thought has singled out their *decorative character* as the sole raison d'être for the colorful Folk Art motifs. [254] This group of writers would rule out any influence of custom or folk beliefs.

---

[251] Wood, Ralph, editor, *The Pennsylvania Germans*. Princeton, N.J.: Princeton University Press, 1942, p. 39. "The Pennsylvania German Farmer," by Walter M. Kollmorgen (Chapter II): "The wealth of flowers tended on Pennsylvania German farms obviously has a cultural lineage tracing back to Europe, and is closely related to a love of color on buildings, walls, bureaus, cupboards, chests, dishes, birth certificates, and mementoes. Their passion for flowers has long been one of their notable traits.

Nearly three-quarters of a century ago a German historian pointed out that nowhere in the Rhineland did the "Blumenschmuck" equal that in the "Pfalz," from which many of the Pennsylvania Germans came. It is not uncommon to find several dozen potted flowers in a house receiving almost daily attention. On some farms potted plants are kept even in the windows of the cow or steer stable . . ."

[252] Especially in such volumes as Stoudt's *Consider the Lilies*, his 'The Meaning of Pennsylvania German Art' in *The Historical Review of Berks County*, III, I (October, 1937), 3-8, and in his more recent *Pennsylvania Folk-Art: An Interpretation* (1948).

[253] Borneman, *op. cit.*, p. 52.

[254] Gilbert, Russell W., *A Picture of the Pennsylvania Germans*. Pennsylvania History Studies, #1, published by The Pennsylvania Historical Association, Gettysburg, 1947.

The author believes rather that it was *a combination of all these factors* which is responsible for the rich development of decorative designs. He is inclined to agree with the suggestion of Downs that "Sentiment, love of nature, and symbolism provide the key to the exuberant decoration lavished upon dower chest and bandbox, pie plate and birth certificate, fireback and sampler."[255]  The author believes that the vast preponderance of floral decoration can be attributed to the fact that their hymnology was predominantly a floral one and that, as several writers have suggested recently, their decoration can be traced to this inspiration rather than to folk beliefs regarding the precise meaning of each flower (tulip or pomegranate), each bird (parrot or peacock), or each animal (lion or unicorn).

At various times writers have alluded to the "fantastic" and unrealistic character of the designs. Borneman finds the birds, for example, quite removed from reality and impossible to associate with actual species.[256]  Freely treated they most certainly are, but no doubt is left as to their true nature. The classic example is the Parrot, or more properly the Paroquet, which so many authorities have stated was never found in Pennsylvania; hence, they say, it must go back either to some European bird they had known before they came here, or else it must be based upon a purely imaginative concept. Such is not the case, for it can be demonstrated that at the period when these Fraktur illuminations were being made, the Carolina Paroquet (*parque carolinensis*) was common as far north as Pennsylvania and New Jersey, and was constantly ravaging the apple orchards and destroying fruit.[257] The existence of several drawings by J. J. Audubon, covering the period 1810-30, can hardly be overlooked.

The same writer who found the designs so fantastic above, also finds them to be "mythological and religious symbols of great antiquity — Zoroastrian, Pythagorean, Gnostic, Rosicrucian, and even legendary Atlantean symbols — as befits the traditions of the often heretical sects that settled in Pennsylvania."[258]  This statement surely covers a wide field of knowledge for such a simple people!

---

255 Downs, *op. cit*, p. 5.
256 The characteristic forms of doves, distelfinks, etc., are easily recognized.
257 See Lichten, *Folk Art of Rural Pennsylvania*, p. 272 and Shelley, *op. cit.*, 126.
258 Jackson Collection, Schuyler B., *Sale Catalogue* (1933), Introduction.

Ot'ler writers have gone out of their way to show how all these motifs go back to early Nordic symbols of various types. [259] This is largely the result of a tremendous flood of pro-Nazi propaganda writings which burst forth in Germany prior to, and during, the last war. Great emphasis was put upon what one writer has aptly termed the "Urvätererbe" with special attention given to the Spinnenrad, Sechsstern, spirals, etc., which are much less common in Pennsylvania German Folk Art than in European German. [260] The labyrinth idea would be an exception.

These involved historical explanations of European authorities are really not required in order to account for the Pennsylvania German's love for what was all around him. Still predominantly a farmer at heart, he ha l a keen a| preci.tion and love for nature. And he had never been free before or had owned land of his own. With the possible exception of the unicorn, Sophia, and the horseman, the motifs can all be associated with everyday nature.

There is no question that many of the motifs of Christian Art were taken over from pagan sources, that many of the motifs of Folk Art — while having simi'ar | agan background — are actually used in a religious (or Christian) rather t'ian mystical (or Pagan) sense in European Folk Art. But many of these are not transferred to Pennsylvania at all, or if they are, t ey have usua'ly lost contact with the original meaning, and are interpreted and drawn in new and different ways.

The connection of the whole Folk Art movement with the arts and designs of the Near East has always been a provocative subject. The similarity of approach, motifs, and even the techniques themselves, [261] has frequently been pointed out. No doubt trade routes and the Turkish invasions into Central Europe provide the simple explanation. The two chief routes would have been through Italy northward, and from the Balkan countries up through the valley of the Danube. The richness of the fo k arts of Roumania, Hungary, Austria, and the Central European countries seems to favor the latter explanation, especially when one considers the tremendous barrier presented by the Alps. In the opinion

---

[259] Mahr, August C, 'Origin and Significance of Pennsylvania Dutch Barn Symbols', *The Ohio State Archaeological and Historical Quarterly*, LIV, 1 (January-March, 1945), 1 32

[260] Zaborsky, Oskar v., *Urvater-Erbe in deutscher Volkskunst.* Leipzig: Koehler & Amelang, 1936.

[261] Sgraffito, pierced decoration, etc.

of the author, the possible third (and round-about) route through North Africa into Spain and Southern France would have contributed little to this development.

That the general movement was to the westward seems clear also from the fact that the whole decorative style as it spread out becomes thinner and less luxuriant, as we move to the West. Even within Germany and the Rhineland itself, the farther one goes from the well-springs of Central European Folk Art, the less flamboyant and rococo the decoration becomes. As we go northward down the Rhine, the use of color becomes more restricted and the designs are more judiciously fitted to the forms, are less rococo. It was from the *middle Rhine* areas, we must keep in mind, that most of the Pennsylvania Germans came.

The repertoire of designs which the Pennsylvania artists developed was an unusually rich one. While drawing upon the lore of the Old World, it also made full use of the New. In contrast to the turmoil of the Rhineland and the profusion of designs running over the European forms, the peaceful countryside of Pennsylvania as well as the limited means at the artist's disposal in the New World encouraged decorations that were somewhat less brilliant in color and more studied in their presentation. The Pennsylvania designs have a sense of *repose* and *reflection* in them, along with the exuberance of newly-born national and personal independence. A sense of *balance* and *orderliness* is everywhere apparent.

Some idea of the wide variety of motifs employed in the Pennsylvania Fraktur may be gained from the following list. One becomes so accustomed to the hearts and tulips, that some of the more unusual and delightful designs should be pointed out. For the sake of brevity, the motifs are here arranged in groups according to their frequency: (1) Flower and Fruit, (2) Bird and Animal, (3) Geometric and Abstract, (4) Religious, (5) Secular, and (6) Architectural.

In dealing with each of the above classifications, only a few of the more popular designs can be discussed here. Wherever possible, their European prototypes will be named and the various meanings that are ascribed to them cited. Considerable research has been done in this field, especially in Germany, directed towards compiling a dictionary of

Folk Art terms and tracing the ancestry of the more common forms. [262]
It is interesting to compare the German or European interpretations with
some of the ideas advanced by various writers in the field of Pennsylvania German Arts and Crafts.

### Fruit and Flower Designs

The *Tulip* was the most favored of all flower motifs, whether on
pottery, glass, china, painted tin, butter molds, furniture, or on Fraktur.
So prominent was it on their pottery that Edwin A. Barber called his
pioneer book "The Tulip Ware of the Pennsylvania German Potters."
The tulip led all the Pennsylvania German motifs in receiving special
attention from the Folk Artist.    Sometimes on one object alone may
be seen a dozen or more treatments of this one motif, in varying stages
of development from the simplest 3-petal form to examples containing
within themselves other flower motifs, or even houses. [263]

Brought from the East into the West, the tulip was first seen at
Vienna about 1559.    According to Downs, it was brought into Germany
from the Near East by a Swiss botanist. [204]    It soon became a favored
flower, so much so that a regular "tulip madness" developed in Holland,
leading to speculation in tulip bulbs much as in our stock market today.
It is not surprising, therefore, to find the tulip in Rhineland decoration,
but it never was used there to the extent it was here in Pennsylvania.
In Europe it held second place to other flowers such as the pink and the
carnation, [205] but in Lancaster and Berks Counties it yielded to none.

The meaning of the tulip, symbolical or otherwise, has been the
cause of much speculation.    Used in *three's*, it has been thought to represent the Trinity, [260] but such an arrangement could just as easily be the
result of a desire for central balance as well as of a religious interpretation.    The fact that one does not frequently find the tulip used in this
way, certainly suggests that knowledge of such an iconographical motif
was not widespread.    Eberlein believes that the tulip symbolizes life,

---

[262] Erich und Beitl, *Wörterbuch der deutschen Volkskunde*.    Leipzig: Alfred
Kröner Verlag, 1936.
[203] See figure 170.
[204] Downs, *op. cit.*, p. 5.
[205] See European figures 15, 18, 20, 23.
[266] Downs, *op. cit.*, p. 6.

love, and immortality [267]   Stoudt more recently has attempted to identify the tulip with the *lily*, [268] and other authors have even confused
it with the *lotus!* [269]

*Fuchsia or Pomegranate, Carnation, and Rose* often share honors
with the tulip because of their gaiety and exotic form.   Edwin A. Barber
quotes Reverend Hilderic Friend as stating in his *Flowers and Flower
Lore* that "the fuchsia in Germany has long been regarded as sacred,
since it is one of the first signs of the returning life of spring." [270]

Barber also mentions the *Forget-Me-Not* and the *Lily-of-the-
Valley*.[271]   To these we should certainly have to add the Pink or Aster,
the Bell Flower, the Violet, and the occasional use of entire Baskets of
flowers.

*Vines, Leaves, and Trees* also play a part in Pennsylvania German
decoration.   Although trees are occasional y found in later pieces during the
19th century, vines and leaves were used to fill in empty spaces in
Fraktur designs from earliest times   Winding vines or garlands of small
leaves were employed even more successfully to tie together the various
elements of floral designs such as Henrich Otto's. [272]   *Palmettes* appear
especially prominently in the Schwenkfelder work.

*Grapes, Apples and Strawberries.* in fact most of the fruit motifs,
begin to appear in the early 19th century.   *Cornucopias, Ears of Corn,*
and various common fruits and vegetables become more popular as the
vogue for printed Birth Certificates spreads.

### Birds and Animals

Second only to Hearts and Flowers is the multitude of Birds and
Animals that abound in the borders of Fraktur drawings and certificates.
Whereas the former frequently have some relation to actual wildlife, the

---

[267] Eberlein, H. D., and Hubbard, C v.d. 'Illuminated Monastic Manuscripts
Were Origin of Fractur-Painting', *American Collector.* V, 8 (September, 1936),
4-5.
[268] Stoudt, *Consider the Lilies*, 1937, and *Pennsylvania Folk-Art,* 1948
[269] Erich und Beitl, *op cit.*
[270] Barber, Edwin A., *Tulip Ware of the Pennsylvania-German Potters.* Philadelphia, Pa : The Pennsylvania Museum and School of Industrial Art, 1903
Cf. p 82
[271] *Ibid.*, pp 83-84.
[272] See figures 186-190; also Color Plate IV

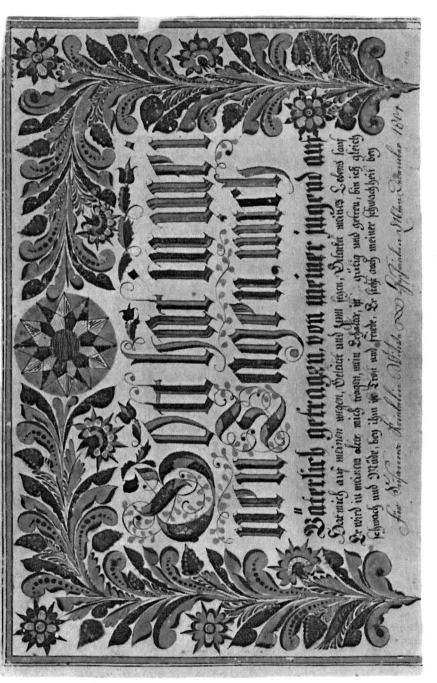

PLATE III. Schwenkfelder Vorschrift, 1804
*The Schwenkfelder Historical Library, Pennsburg, Pa.*

grotesque beasts we see are more likely either to be lifted from Coats-of-Arms or to be pure figments of the imagination of the Folk artist.

*The Parrot,* or Paroquet, is the most common local bird motif. [273] As already pointed out, while it is not known in the state of Pennsylvania to-day or in any of the adjoining Middle Atlantic States, at one time this bird was one of the worst scourges of the fruitgrower. Late in the summer when apples were ripe, a flock of them could ruin a year's crop in a short space of time simply by tearing the fruit apart to get at the seeds. Readily identifiable because of their curved beaks and brilliant color, the folk artists used this already decorative subject-matter to excellent advantage. Henrich Otto was the first illuminator to visualize the great possibilities of this motif, which continued to be one of the trademarks of Pennsylvania Fraktur right down to the very end.

*The Distelfink* (thistlebird) or Goldfinch, ran a close second to the Parrot. A common bird with colorful markings, it vied with the *Scarlet Tanager* for second place. The Distelfink was especially popular on the small Fraktur drawings or bookmarks of the 19th century.

*The Dove,* so well loved by everyone despite its mournful song, also appears prominently. It sometimes symbolized the human spirit, but more often simply conveyed the sentiments of the heart, signifying love and conjugal felicity. Its somewhat heavy, curvilinear form was beautifully presented by Folk artists, particularly by Francis Portzline. [274]

*The Peacock, Pelican and Eagle* are all three motifs which have a great deal of medieval character behind them. Though a barnyard fowl and a respected weather prophet among the Pennsylvania Germans according to Joseph Downs, [275] the *Peacock* stood in ages past for the Resurrection of the Dead. While far from common, the peacock does appear in Fraktur and other Folk Arts from the time of Henrich Otto and Georg Hübner (the potter), down to the mid-19th century in the works of Francis Portzline. In manufacturing Spatterware for the Pennsylvania German trade, even the English Staffordshire potters made the peacock, or peafowl, one of their chief patterns, and went so far as to create several variations of the pattern. Usually, the tail of the peacock is not spread.

---

[273] See Lichten, *op. cit.,* p. 272; also herein p. 84.
[274] See figure 218.
[275] Downs, *op cit.,* p. 6.

*The Pelican,* Barber states, "is often figured in old German manu-scripts as a symbol of maternal devotion." [276]   It seems much more likely, however, to be the transplantation of the Medieval Catholic motif of the Mother Church.   Another far from common design, in the hands of the Pennsylvania German Folk artists it became the excuse for a lovely, rhythmical pattern of feather motifs in red, yellow, and black, with the young Pelicans reduced to a mere element of the design.

*The Eagle,* and its many varied treatments, provide a fertile field for study.   Both single and double-headed, it appears in every medium of Pennsylvania German Folk Art and on both hand-drawn and printed Fraktur.   Although the single-headed variety (sometimes with shield and stars) is beyond question the "Bird of Freedom" and has been lifted from the Great Seal of the United States, the double-headed eagle is just as surely lifted from the old Hapsburg emblem and occasionally even has the crested heads. [277]   The double-headed eagle has sometimes been called a dove, but this is open to question since the talons are still ex-tended although the arrows and olive branch are missing.   Final proof that these Hübner birds joined together as a heart are intended to be eagles and not doves, is supplied by a large sgraffito plate in the Brook-lyn Museum, [278] which has an inscription just above the head which reads: "Hier ist Abgebilt ein dobelder Adler."   After 1800 the single-headed eagle becomes more common, usually with the shield, and in the printed forms of the 1840's and 1850's has a ribbon in its mouth bearing various inscriptions.

About 1800, a group of new bird subjects appears including pairs of *Robins,* or Lovebirds, the *Swan or Duck,* and more rarely *Owls, Storks,* and *Hummingbirds.*   Although *Butterflies* appear occasionally in hand-drawn Fraktur certificates, they are much more common in the later printed forms.

Animal forms in the earlier period again indicate preference for those having medieval European background, especially the *Deer, Rooster, Lion,* and *Bear.*   The *Unicorn,* from medieval days the fabulous guardian of maidenhood, enjoyed particular popularity in the late 18th century on decorated dower chests as well as on illuminated manu-

---

[276] Barber *op. cit.,* p. 36.

[277] See figure 234.

[278] Lorimer Collection loan; for illustration see Stoudt (1948), p. 319.

scripts. [279] They usually are shown rampant in balanced pairs, occasionally singly opposite a lion or horse, and frequently with chains around their necks. [280] Wherever they appear, regardless of medium, the Unicorn is one of the most picturesque motifs found in Pennsylvania Folk Art.

*Horses and Dogs* indicate the debt of the early pioneer to his daily indispensable companions. Even *Cats and Snakes* appear occasionally in 19th century Fraktur, whereas *Lambs, Crocodiles,* and *Whales,* are less often encountered.

### Geometric and Abstract Designs

The Pennsylvania German Folk artist was every bit as adept in handling geometric and abstract designs as he was his hearts, tulips, peacocks, and unicorns. Many of his most striking achievements are products of the ruler and compass, and of his feeling for bold pattern and outline. Ofttimes the success of his composition depends heavily upon these basic formal patterns of squares, rectangles, triangles, and hexagons; or upon circles, spirals or interlaces (in the same way as his barn signs and labyrinth forms); or upon the endless picturesque borders he developed using combinations of triangles, diamonds, striping, winding lines, etc. Even cross-stitch patterns, such as one finds upon the samplers of the early 19th century, occasionally appear in Fraktur.

He frequently employed compass and ruler to execute pictorial motifs such as the *Sun, Moon,* and *Stars,* as well as occasional witchball designs. [281] Subjects like the *Mariner's Compass* or *Clock Dials,* which became increasingly popular in the 19th century, were certain to be produced mechanically rather than free-hand. And on occasion, as we have noted, even the outlines of human heads were first drawn with the aid of a compass. [282]

### Architectural Designs

While not so common as previous design forms, *Architectural motifs* turn up here and there throughout the entire history of Fraktur illumination. From the early Ephrata Chart and the first Frakturs suggesting

---

[279] See figures 287 and 289.
[280] By contrast, lions never seem to have chains; see figures 61, 67, and 187.
[281] See figure 222.
[282] See figure 220.

castle designs down to the mid-19th century, the folk artist seems to have been conscious of their pictorial possibilities. And when he did not actually represent a building, he often employed columns or columns-and-arches in his designs. [283]

Chief among the architectural motifs, of course, is the local *Pennsylvania House*   Although at first resembling more the Rhineland crenellated castle [284] or the typical peasant dwelling, representations of local Lancaster, Berks, and Montgomery County architecture finally began to appear. [285]   After 1800, we find the center-hall house, paneled doors, and quoined corners so characteristic of Pennsylvania   And usually the illuminator does not limit himself to showing us only the house, but includes the front yard or garden, with the picket fence that surrounds it.

An occasional *Barn*, or even a *Mill*, also finds its way into Fraktur, but it is with the local *Schoolhouse* or *Church* that the artist really lets himself go. The structural detail of every window and door, and particularly the tower, receive careful attention. Though many of these may be the work of children, they show great care and mastery in their **execution**.

In the later printed Certificates and House Blessings, a great many architectural woodcuts turn up, including both houses and public buildings. *Pavilions* with fountains and statuary are also seen   *City Views* are rarely found except in a few early hand-drawn certificates and later in the "Way to Heaven and Hell" broadsides and G. S. Peters religious colorprints.

### Religious Motifs

Many of the motifs already discussed have a bit of religious meaning in them, but others are still to be considered. The ever-present *Heart* for example, although it may have either religious or domestic meaning, is more apt to have the former. On early tombstones, stoveplates, and pottery, it is frequently accompanied by a religious inscription. On Frakturs, if inscribed, it usually contains the ubiquitous "Das Herze mein, soll Dir allein."

---

[283] See figures 66, 142, 179, 205, 233.
[284] See figure 201.
[285] See figures 66, 179.

The Pennsylvania *Heart*, let it be noted, also has an unusual form; being made up of two circles, it is most frequently quite round and heavy looking. Ofttimes the two circles are shown complete within the heart and occasionally even have a star or barn sign motif contained within these two circles. In priority of use on Frakturs, the Heart might even precede the Tulip, so popular is it. When it does not appear as a border motif, it is likely to be used to enclose the text panel or otherwise make up the overall composition. [286]

The *Crown, Cross,* and *Fish* are apt to embody similar religious connotations. Whereas the *Crown* [287] is a frequently-appearing motif in both hand-drawn and printed specimens down to the early 19th century, the Cross and Fish are less commonly seen. To the Pennsylvania German artist, no doubt, the *Cross* [288] again smacked of Catholicism, and the Christian meaning of the *Fish* had become less clear in the transfer from the Rhineland to Pennsylvania. Although the Fish appears occasionally on pottery plates, both slip and sgraffito, it is rarely seen on Fraktur specimens.

The religious symbolism of the *Pelican* has already been noted in connection with other bird and animal motifs. [289]

The *Angel* is by far the most common of all the motifs involving the full-length figure. At first it appears only as an *Angel's head* with wings, particularly on early hand-drawn Frakturs and on the first Ephrata-Otto printed forms. [290] Corresponding very closely to the motifs found on early tombstones, this was identified by Stoudt in *Consider the Lilies* as the Virgin Sophia. Shortly afterwards the full-length *standing or flying Angels* appear, blowing a trumpet or bearing a palm, usually in pairs with one coming from each side of the composition. [291] About 1814, a standard *pair of Angels* appears, one of which bears a wreath and the other holds a Dove of Peace. [292]

No explanation is required for the usual themes of the Nativity, Baptism of Christ, Preaching the Gospel, the Last Supper, and the Cru-

---

[286] See figures 76 and 77.
[287] See figures 193 and 198.
[288] See Stoudt (1948), pp. 159, 172, and 174.
[289] See pages 89-90.
[290] See figures 188 and 190; also Color Plate IV.
[291] See figures 192, 207, 240, and 245.
[292] See figure 254.

cifixion, or for such subjects as Adam and Eve, the Prodigal Son, the Way to Eternal Life and Damnation. As has been noted, figures of Saints as well as some of the themes just listed, appear on the gilded and embossed Applied Designs. For the most part, however, religious iconographical subjects are rarely seen in Pennsylvania German Folk Art.

### Secular or Folk Themes

Though we may call these secular, even these themes border on religious subject-matter, and include such subjects as the Baptism of a Child, [293] a Bride and Groom, [294] a Kneeling Child, or a Singing Class. They are probably the rarest of all the figure pieces. Semi-portrait subjects such as Busts of a Man and Woman, Heads of Children, or a profile of the Princess of Brunswick, [295] are more often seen than full-length figures. Sometimes human figures appear singly, as in the work of Francis Portzline, but more often they occur in pairs such as the Man and Wife by John Zinck, [296] or similar pairs by other artists. Friederich Speyer, on the other hand, preferred to use *pairs of Women,* in place of the more common balancing Angels. In one or two rare cases, George and Martha Washington are placed opposite one another.

*Historical and Folklore Subjects* constitute a field that is as yet unexplored. Besides portraits of Washington, Franklin, Taylor, and Jackson (based on known likenesses), representations of the United States Seal and occasional Clipper Ships appear. Folk themes such as the *springing Horseman* with trumpet, [297] pistol, or sword, the *Hunter* on foot, the *Great Whale,* the *Five Maidens under a Tree,* and the *Seven Swabians,* have only lately begun to receive careful attention. Folk ballads and Folklore no doubt will provide the explanation for these and other similar themes in due course.

In contrast to New England illuminations, *Coffins* scarcely ever appear in Pennsylvania German Fraktur work. Nor is the *Swastika,* or whirling cross, as common as had once been thought.

---

[293] See figure 233.
[294] See figures 226 and 227.
[295] See figure 201.
[296] See figure 237.
[297] See figure 199.

# VI. DEVELOPMENT OF THE PENNSYLVANIA GERMAN STYLE OF ILLUMINATION

O reconstruct the history and development of the illuminated style in Pennsylvania is not an easy problem. So little has been done beyond mere classification of the types, main techniques, and schools, that any serious stylistic investigation must start virtually from scratch. Beyond establishing the existence of the Ephrata and Schwenkfelder schools, and mentioning a few outstanding calligraphers such as Christopher Dock, Henrich Otto, and Susanna Hubner, little effort has been made to analyze the characteristics and dates of their work or to fit them together to build up a picture of the illuminated style as a whole. Even the identification of individual artists has proceeded remarkably slowly, and information regarding some key figures is surprisingly misleading.

In the opinion of the author, however, most of these apparently divergent styles can readily be connected once they are placed in their proper historical sequence. The realization that each of the religious sects involved represents the transfer to Pennsylvania of a different European background, educationally as well as artistically, is most important in understanding this problem. It is not just a problem of techniques or designs, but one of time. Time, or *dating,* is a key factor in this development. The date of arrival of each of the groups, their particular educational level, their religious ideas, and their relationship with neighboring sects, all have a bearing upon the character and development of the Fraktur work they produced. No doubt many of the smaller groups lost their identity artistically, but major movements are easily discernible.

To get a more accurate picture of the chronological development of the illuminated style, *dates* other than those on the Frakturs themselves must be taken into account. One index to the progress of the communities where such work was being done is the dates of formation of the eastern Pennsylvania counties themselves. The amount of activity within these is clearly reflected in the rapid breaking up of some of them to form new counties with new county seats. The pattern of this development is repeated about 25 years later in the establishment of German printing presses in these same centers in more or less the same sequence.

The *German Imprints* issued from these local presses are the second factor which has been underestimated in the study of Fraktur thus far. Not only were the text and decoration of the printed forms taken over from the hand-drawn ones, but frequently the same decorator worked in both fields. Another facet of this relationship which has been completely overlooked thus far is the use of motifs borrowed from dated, printed certificates in hand-drawn Frakturs [298] This is far more prevalent than has been realized, from the Otto forms of the 1780's right down to mid-19th century imprints

Inasmuch as many of the outstanding artists who drew their own Frakturs also decorated these printed forms, and since a large percentage of these forms actually bear imprint dates, their importance in building up a chronology of Pennsylvania German illuminated manuscripts cannot be denied. While bibliographers only recently have begun to take into account this phase of the activities of the early German presses in Pennsylvania, [299] an excellent picture of the development of printing can be secured in this way. Since the printed forms were so popular that they had to be re-issued year after year, changes in firm names are clearly recorded. The list given in Appendix C, containing 35 locations, over 100 printers, and more than 250 separate imprints, is the most complete ever made, and is drawn from the 65 public and private collections examined by the author over the past 20 years. In the same way, newspapers also are important for dating. Some certificates actually bear the imprints of newspaper offices, or can be dated by the imprints of newspapers produced by the same printers. Almanacs and their imprints must likewise be observed.

---

[298] For *Otto* (figure 188) parrot influence see figures 191, 198, 202, 203, 210, 215, 240, 241, 248, and 263; for *Krebs* (figure 198) direct influence see figure 263; for *J. Bauman* (figures 250 and 251) deer and bird influence see figures 214, 223, and 264; for hand-drawn copies of later printed certificates compare *Angel I* (figure 254) with figure 265, and *Angel IV* (figure 257) with figure 266.

[299] Such as Alfred Shoemaker's checklists of imprints of the German presses in Northampton and Lehigh Counties, as well as more recent biographical sketches of the printers of various other Counties published in *The Pennsylvania Dutchman*. See Bibliography D, under "Printed Fraktur."

A chronology of Fraktur illumination, therefore, must take into account the widespread use of printed forms regardless of the Fraktur type. And since they continued to be produced so regularly right down to the late 19th century, they ofttimes provide a yardstick against which to measure difficult dating problems. Whereas in the past they have been frowned upon as "mass production" and therefore aesthetically inferior, in reality they have a great deal to commend them, as will be apparent to anyone who studies them carefully. Much ingenuity and creative effort went into developing printed *Taufschein* forms sufficiently attractive to compete with the hand-drawn certificates, as well as into discovering new modes of decoration. When properly designed and colored, they are readily the equal of most of the hand-drawn work. Those who look down upon the artistic merits of the printed forms have forgotten for the moment that there are many handwritten Frakturs which are equally as unattractive as a poorly printed one!

## *Methods of Analysis*

To aid in isolating the work of the various schools and artists, and in showing how they all go together to form a homogeneous style, every possible means of analysis and dating Fraktur has been used. These can be classified under three main headings:

(1) observation of types, techniques, materials, and designs,

(2) comparison with printed Fraktur forms of the same period,

(3) application of specialized selective techniques of identification developed by the author for testing difficult attributions.

The first two methods of analysis have already been discussed in some detail, but the third method deserves careful consideration at this point.

In seeking means to aid in the identification of difficult Fraktur pieces, several possibilities present themselves. While all of these may be classified as *direct evidence* inasmuch as they are contained within the Fraktur itself, they fall into three types:

(1) information contained in the text,

(2) errors and corrections, and

(3) the physical form of the Fraktur itself.

When used to *supplement* other more obvious identifications such as similarity of design and color, these clues are highly reliable.

As textual information, for example, *closeness of dates* among a group of pieces is quite important since the period of activity of an artist is apt to be somewhat limited. If we keep in mind the fact that Birth and Baptismal Certificate dates are not necessarily those of the making of the piece itself, the works of any one artist usually bear very close dates. The *names of Counties* in which the Frakturs were written also play an important role. While we know that most illuminators did travel about a great deal, the major portion of their work should originate from a few adjoining counties. The *family names* contained in the text are often important for identification, since the same decorator frequently would produce work for several branches of the same family. For this reason, it is advisable to check the various names which occur especially on Birth and Baptismal Certificates, including not only the principals but also the Sponsors or Witnesses and, where mentioned, the *Minister* who officiated. In cases such as Daniel Schumacher, we know that the minister and Fraktur writer were one and the same person. The *use of German or English* and combinations of the two, sometimes help verify attributions, such as Friedrich Krebs, Wilhelmus Antonius Faber, the Mount Pleasant Artist, and Francis Portzline.

*Errors,* or corrections of errors, frequently supply an amusing kind of negative evidence that can be used to support attributions. Constantly inscribing the *wrong name* in the space provided for it, crossing it out, and substituting the correct one for it, is a weakness of the Martin Brechall and Francis Portzline pieces. *Consistent misspelling* of some word in the works of a single artist occasionally will assist the grouping of his pieces. *Misinterpretation of motifs* regularly in one person's work helps in much the same way.

The physical form of the Fraktur also tells a great deal. The *handwriting* is one of the most important factors in identifying the artist, even if the certificate form has been filled in by another person. A comparison among several examples soon reveals similarities or differences in script, capital, and lower case letters, and particularly in the numerals employed for dates or Scripture chapter numbers.

In printed certificates the *typography,* like the calligraphy in handwritten ones, provides an invaluable clue in dating and identification problems.  Peculiarities of type fonts such as the design of capital letters, shape and sizes of letters, and odd decorative motifs, distinguish the earlier printed forms from the later ones.  The large heavy typeface of the first Ephrata and Reading certificate forms stands out in marked contrast to the later 19th century smaller ones.

*Borders,* and improvised motifs used as borders, serve to identify the work of a single artist because being impromptu, and relatively unimportant in the design as a whole, they reveal differences in personality much in the same way that handwriting does.  In printed forms, also, the reappearance of certain designs or woodblocks in borders enables one to identify the press from which the certificate was issued.  As will be found in the chapter on printed forms, it is sometimes just the very arrangement or sequence of the blocks that identifies the printer.

The *materials* employed by the illuminator also supply clues, such as the use of odd sizes or shapes of paper, the presence of unusual colors of ink and the combination or repetition of these colors, the consistent use of cherry-gum gouache or watercolor, and the proportion of pen and brush work.  Occasionally, other minor personal idiosyncracies appear, such as the tendency of Francis Portzline to cut small triangular sections from the corners of his certificates, or Kreb's habit of edging his pieces with a colored border, and an unidentified Decorator who wrote in the lower right-hand corner of his pieces the price of each one.

## Theories to Date

Before beginning our chronology, it might be well to review the various schools of Fraktur work mentioned in publications thus far. Although Mercer in his early pamphlet mentioned the *Ephrata* illuminations, for some reason which is not clear, he failed to discuss or describe them. [300]  All subsequent writeups of Fraktur have devoted considerable space to the Ephrata work, calling it "religious" and the remainder "secular" — a distinction that has not held up since virtually all Fraktur has a religious background.  Borneman, although he had a fine group of Ephrata manuscripts and books, devoted only a page and a half to this subject while Stoudt, first in his 1937 and then in his 1948 edition, has given the most detailed and fully-illustrated account to date. [301]

---

[300] Mercer, *op. cit*, p. 425.
[301] Stoudt, Pennsylvania Folk-Art: An Interpretation (1948), pp. 131-183; 67 ill.

The work and teachings of *Christopher Dock,* schoolmaster of Skip-pack, have been the focal point for the existence of a second school of Fraktur among the Mennonites and the Schwenkfelders. Brumbaugh,[302] as well as Borneman,[303] have attempted to isolate manuscripts which would show his style of decoration and his handwriting. These efforts have not been entirely successful, in the opinion of the present writer, since most of the examples reproduced are either *undated,* or can with certainty be dated in the 1780's and 1790's, in other words *after* Dock's death in 1771.

The third, or *Schwenkfelder School,* of which the chief examples have been preserved in the Schwenkfelder Historical Library at Penns-burg, Pa., was first publicized by Borneman[304] and subsequently by Reverend Kriebel,[305] one of the leaders of the Schwenkfelder Congrega-tion today. In both cases, the brief discussion revolved around the chief figure in this school, Susanna Hübner, with no mention of the broader development of which she represents the peak.

To date there has been no attempt to classify Fraktur beyond these three specialized schools which were responsible for a great many of the best Pennsylvania German manuscripts produced. Borneman's account, which is the only detailed one thus far attempted on Fraktur, continues with a brief discussion of Folk Art, an extensive list of individual "pen-men and colorists," and concludes with the story of an itinerant penman of 1875.[306] Since his list includes many Mennonite and Schwenkfelder artists, it duplicates and somewhat confuses his previous discussion of the illuminations produced by these individual schools. While it is not always possible to draw distinct lines between these groups of manu-scripts, the various illuminators of the Hübner, Krauss, and Kriebel families might more properly have been listed with the Schwenkfelder School to avoid overlapping. Furthermore, in this author's opinion, some of the names included as those of the artists are actually the names of the *owners* of the Frakturs instead — as an examination of the

---

[302] Brumbaugh, Martin G., *The Life and Works of Christopher Dock.* Phila-delphia, Pa.: J. B. Lippincott & Co., 1908. Pp. 272; several illustrations.
[303] Borneman, *op. cit.,* p. 48.
[304] *Ibid,.* p. 48.
[305] Kriebel, Lester K, 'A Brief History and Interpretation of Pennsylvania German Illuminated Writings (Fractur-Schriften)', Historical Society of Mont-gomery County *Bulletin,* III, 1 (October, 1941), see p. 30.
[306] Borneman, *op. cit.,* pp. 48-50.

Schwenkfelder Historical Library specimens and the Borneman collection itself will reveal.

In the following account of the chronological development of the Pennsylvania German Style of Illumination, the Ephrata, the Dock (Mennonite), and Schwenkfelder Schools will be re-appraised and more fully treated.    They will likewise be supplemented by active movements among the "church people" in Lancaster and Berks Counties, and particularly by the vogue for the printed Taufschein which received its greatest impetus in the city of Reading, whence it spread all over eastern Pennsylvania and into Maryland, Virginia, Ohio, Indiana, and even New York City.

Since so much of this activity centered in and around county seats, it is frequently possible to cite designs or motifs as being more common in one county than another, or being used in somewhat different form. While these *county types,* as we shall call them, are not as distinct as in the painted dower chests which Esther Stevens Fraser so adequately identified and classified many years ago, [307] there is a considerable degree of stylistic similarity.    Wherever possible, such analogies with County types in other media will be referred to, whether they be painted furniture, pottery, china, or decorated tin.    The earlier picturesque iron stove-plates, Stiegel glass, and local country pewter produced between 1740 and 1760, antedate for the most part the Fraktur period and thus have only a limited influence in Pennsylvania German decorative arts.    Fraktur illumination, on the other hand, extended from this first 18th century florescence of Pennsylvania German artistry down through most of the 19th century, constantly strengthening and rejuvenating this Folk expression and preserving the motifs which distinguish it from other American Folk Art.

## THE EPHRATA SCHOOL (1745-1755)

Fraktur illumination not only appeared in America first at the Ephrata Cloister in Ephrata, Pa., but also reached its greatest perfection there. [308]    Oddly enough, in spite of this fact and in spite of the

307 Fraser, Esther Stevens, 'Pennsylvania German Dower Chests', *Antiques,*
     Part 1.   XI, 2 (February, 1927), 119-123.
     Part 2.   XI, 4 (April, 1927), cover and 28-283.
     Part 3.   XI, 6 (June, 1927), frontispiece and 453, 474-476.
   308 An account of a Borneman Collection exhibition at the Carl Schurz Memorial Foundation printed in the *American-German Review,* IX, 4 (April, 1943), 34, states "They [decorated choral books] came into full bloom at Bethlehem." The editor surely meant Ephrata.

record of the Cloister's activities kept by Brothers Lamech and Agrippa, the *Chronicon Ephratense,* [309] we still know surprisingly little about the individual artists who did this extraordinarily beautiful work, the sources of their inspiration, or the scope of their activity.  Ephrata illuminated manuscripts today are so widely scattered and so rarely heard of, that considerable field work will have to be done before these questions can adequately be answered.  Several of them have crossed the Atlantic or have otherwise traveled around in a way that is little short of fantastic. While it is perfectly true that they do still turn up, [310] they are such collectors' items that they never reach the light of day.  During the past 20 years the author encountered very few such examples.

The Ephrata Cloister, perhaps the nearest approach to medieval life to be found anywhere in America, was established by Conrad Beissel on the banks of the Cocalico Creek in Lancaster County in 1728.  A detailed account of the history of the Cloister during its earlier years need not be presented here, since it is readily available elsewhere,[311] and because it is only in the 1740's that the Cloisters enter into the story of Fraktur.  Of the three main buildings erected in the 1740's when the Cloister took on a new lease on life under Beissel's leadership, only two remain today, the *Saal* and *Saron.* [312]   The Saal, or meeting room, was built in 1740, according to Brumbaugh [313] who has recently restored it under the custodianship of the State Historical Commission; Saron, or the Sisters' House, was erected in 1742.  Unfortunately the large *Bethania,* or Brothers' House, built about 1743 was destroyed by fire in 1917. The two large remaining structures with numerous smaller buildings such as Beissel's cabin, the bakehouses, etc., provide one of the most interesting groups of buildings of the period extant today.  They are built of clapboard and plaster with very little iron, even the hinges being of wood.

The period of particular importance in the history of Fraktur begins just after the erection of these large buildings, or late in 1745.  It was at this time that the Ephrata printing press was set up, the paper mill established, and the Music and Writing Schools organized.  The 5, 6,

[309] Hark, J. Max, *Chronicon Ephratense. . .* Lancaster, Pa., 1889.
[310] *Antiques,* LII, 4 (October, 1947), 260-262.
[311] See Bibliography B. under Hark. *op. cit.,* Sachse, Stoudt, Oswald, etc.
[312] See figures 103 and 104
[313] Brumbaugh, G. Edwin, 'Continental Influences on Early American Architecture', *American-German Review,* IX, 3 (February, 1943), 8.

7, and 8-part music sung here was unlike any elsewhere in the world and drew enthusiastic praise from travelers who came great distances to hear it. [314] While Beissel must have drawn somewhat upon his previous experience in Germany as a violinist, the Ephrata musical notation (which is quite different from anything else we have seen), must have developed chiefly out of a specific need. The Superintendent, as Beissel was called, even created special menus for the Brothers and Sisters in order that they might develop certain kinds of voices for this choral work. [315]

For those who had no particular talent or interest in music, Beissel established a Writing School, the products of which are unique in the history of manuscript illumination. [316] Since they are in book form, involve choral music, and are usually decorated throughout, they are in many ways more strictly "illuminated manuscripts" than other Pennsylvania German Fraktur work which consists usually of single pages. The period during which these unusual Ephrata Choral Books were produced covered roughly one decade, from 1745 to 1755. It is these rare volumes and various related Fraktur specimens, which are of special interest to us here, and which, in their peculiar calligraphic character, differentiate the Ephrata illuminations from all other such work executed in Pennsylvania.

A brief description of these illuminations is given in the *Chronicon Ephratense,* although unfortunately more attention is devoted to the musical aspects and to their contents than to their artistic features. The following passage is of particular significance here:

"Before we conclude this chapter, let us mention the writing-school, where the writing in ornamental Gothic text was done, and which was chiefly instituted for the benefit of those who had no musical talents. The outlines of the letters he (Beissel) himself designed, but the shading of them was left to the scholar, in order to exercise himself in it. But none was permitted to borrow a design anywhere, for he said: we dare not borrow from each other, because the power to produce rests within everybody. Many Solitary [inmates] spent days and years in these

---

[314] Sachse, Julius F., *The Music of the Ephrata Cloister, also Conrad Beissel's Treatise on Music as Set Forth in a Preface to the 'Turtel Taube' of 1747.* Pennsylvania German Society *Proceedings,* XII, 9 (1903), 11.

[315] *Ibid.,* pp. 67-68.

[316] See figures 105-131; also Color Plate I.

schools, which also served them as a means of sanctification to crucify their flesh. The writings were hung up in the chapel as ornaments, or distributed to admirers." [317]

During the decade, 1745-1755, quite a group of choral books, religious manuscripts, and Fraktur charts were produced. Several of these were completely handwritten for special presentation copies, as we shall see, but a large precentage of them, especially those books containing the words to the hymns, were printed on the Ephrata press. Even the "Registers" or Indexes of the hand-written musical manuscripts were printed. Hand-illuminated bookplates were added to quite a few copies of the *Martyrbook* printed at Ephrata in two parts (1748 and 1749), the largest book published in the Colonies prior to the Revolution. [318]

These bookplates specified the Cloister name of the Brother to whom the copy belonged, such as "Ludwig Stein,"[319] "Michael Mayer,"[320] and so on. Other copies of the *Martyrbook*, such as Borneman's, also have occasional Fraktur pages inserted as illustrations. [321] The variety of the Ephrata Cloister productions will be apparent from the following list of recorded works:

| | |
|---|---|
| 1745, May 13, | Ms. *Roses of Sharon* Book |
| 1746 | Mss. *Turteltaube* |
| 1747 | Printed *Turteltaube* |
| 1748-49 | Printed *Martyrbook* |
| 1750 | Ms. *Christian ABC Book* |
| 1751 | Mss. *Paradisisches Wunderspiel* |
| 1754 | Printed *Paradisisches Wunderspiel* |
| c.1755 | Mss. *Saal Charts* |

In 1759 Conrad Beissel died, leaving control of the Cloister to Peter Miller. Without the creative force of Beissel behind them, the Music and Manuscript Schools seem to have died out — or at least the great urge for colored illumination seems to have spent itself. Occasional printed religious broadsides were issued in the 1770's and 1780's

---

[317] Hark, *op. cit.*, pp. 168-169.
[318] See figures 108 and 109.
[319] See figure 43.
[320] Borneman collection.
[321] A full-page *Crucifixion* scene in typical Ephrata manuscript style.

bearing the Ephrata imprint, particularly from 1784 to 1788, but little evidence of Fraktur is seen otherwise. [322]  In 1786, the *Chronicon Ephratense* was published and by 1789, Peter Miller had also died.  By the end of another decade, 1799, the Cloister Press had passed into the hands of Johannes Bauman, whose Birth and Baptismal Certificates we shall consider later. [323]  Thus ended more than a half-century of activity at this unusual Cloister in Pennsylvania, survivor of the cloister of medieval times in Europe and progenitor for the illuminated manuscript style on these shores.

With regard to color and motifs, the Ephrata work is unmistakable. As to its origins and the penmen who executed it, there is little evidence available.  The only reference to the problem of its origin is contained in the *Chronicon Ephratense,* where it states: [324]

> "It is reported that the angels singing antiphonally appeared in a vision to St. Ignatius, and thus their methods found their way into the church.  It is possible that in former ages they were more in use in the convents; now but little is known of them.
>
> Yet one of these tune-books came over the ocean, and we are informed that, being engraved on copper, it was printed at Augsburg, but we cannot answer for it . . ."

In spite of the author's special trip to Germany in 1938 to find sources of Fraktur illumination in general and these Ephrata books in particular, no such tune-book could be located.  In his search he visited many Folk Art museums and libraries, especially music and manuscript divisions containing early printed music books and pattern books, not just in the Rhineland itself, but in adjoining areas from which the Pennsylvania Germans came.  No prototype combining Fraktur lettering and floral illumination with multi-part choral music as in the Ephrata books could be found. [325]

No doubt Sisters Anastasia, Rahel, and Iphigenia were especially expert at Fraktur writing, [326] but obviously more hands were involved in producing all of this Ephrata manuscript work.  Who actually pro-

---

[322] See figures 129-131, Haus-Blessings, Labyrinths, etc.
[323] See figures 86 and 250-251.
[324] Hark, *op. cit.,* p. 167.
[325] Also the Rothschild Music Library at Frankfort, the Lutherische Kirchenmusik Institut at Heidelberg, and many others.
[326] Stoudt, *op. cit.* (1948), p. 135.

duced the many illuminated copies of the *Turteltaube* and the *Paradisisches Wunderspiel,* may very well indeed never become known.

The distinctive colors in all of these manuscripts are one of the trademarks of the Ephrata work. The pen outlines executed originally in black ink now turned brown with age, are filled in with flat washes of watercolor or stippled with the point of the pen. No cherry gum is used here to brighten the color. It is the softness of the colors that gives these manuscripts their unusual character, soft blues and greens with occasional touches of rust. The areas of color are tastefully placed at the headings of the pages, between hymns, or along the edges of the bars at the outer margins of the pages. [327] The most ambitious and successful of these appear on pages where they have been employed to fill out space left blank by the hymn, usually at the lower right of the page. Occasionally, they extend the full height of the page. [328]

Tulips, pomegranates, carnations, and a multitude of small flowers abound here. Also hearts, vases, or urns with plants growing from them, and even an occasional cross may be seen. [329] Doves, with flowers issuing from their mouths, are the only bird motif that appears. [330] Occasional figures of Brothers or Sisters in their simple cloaks are found, outlined with utmost simplicity. [331] Almost more important than these motifs, however, is the varied assortment of checkerboard, diamond, diaper, stipple, and other patterns employed to fill out these outlines. Executed with the pen and not in color, these *overall repeat patterns* are as characteristic of the Ephrata work as the peculiar assortment of designs and colors. [332] A definite textile or lace background seems apparent in these minute patterns filling carefully-drawn outlines, [333] which might be explained from the fact that the Ephrata group came originally from the town of Krefeld, a great textile center in northwestern Germany close to the Dutch border.

Attempts to trace influences of the Ephrata Cloister in Fraktur work done elsewhere in eastern Pennsylvania, have thus far yielded very little. On the one hand, there was very little illumination being done out-

---

[327] See figures 120 and 121.
[328] See figures 107 and 128; also Color Plate I.
[329] Stoudt, *op. cit.,* pp. 172 and 174.
[330] See figure 107.
[331] See figures 121, 123, and 127.
[332] See figures 107, 113, 114, 119, 127, and 128
[333] See figures 107, 113, 114, and 122; also Color Plate I.

side the Cloister at that early date (1740's and 1750's) and on the other, one could hardly expect noticeable influence even at a later date, especially since we know that these Ephrata musical manuscripts were so closely held.    Certainly the artists who did these would never have ventured outside of the Cloister area, and it is very unlikely that outsiders would have entered the grounds often enough to receive any such influence.

The only possible exception to this would be the *Snowhill Cloister* which was established in Franklin County, near Waynesboro, as a mission church.    Manuscripts executed at Ephrata were lent to Snowhill for copying and, in the opinion of the author, some of the examples now identified as the work of the Cloister were actually produced at Snowhill. Noticeable changes in the quality of the penmanship take place: the color becomes much brighter through use of brilliant reds, greens, and yellows, and the drawing of the motifs becomes less competent. [334]    The ink of the outlines becomes much blacker and the whole effect is much sharper, and more scratchy, than in the Ephrata work.    But it is in the Fraktur titles particularly that the loss in quality is evident.    The flowing, rhythmic letters of Ephrata are replaced by nervous, uncertain characters.    A close study of the Snowhill work has been impossible due to its being closed during the long-extended negotiations for state ownership.    If and when this takes place, a story almost as fantastic as that of the Ephrata Cloister itself should be forthcoming.

## THE MENNONITE SCHOOL (1760-1856)

Perhaps the most widely appreciated of the Fraktur schools, because it has constantly been used to illustrate Pennsylvania German illumination as a whole, is the Mennonite work produced chiefly in Bucks County. Mercer, in his early pamphlet, [335] suggested that up to his time (1897), it was the *only* type known and revealed as the result of his extensive research "First, That the art of Fractur [sic] was not confined to Bucks County or to the Mennonites, who had presented us with the first specimens seen, but that it had flourished throughout Pennsylvania Germany, among the Dunkers, the Schwenkfelders and probably the Amish and Moravians . . ."    Certainly, within the field of Fraktur as a whole, it extends over quite a period of years and maintains a homogeneous char-

---

[334] See figure 128.
[335] Mercer, *op. cit.*, p. 425.

acter. Its greatest period, moreover, coincides with the highest period of Fraktur development, so that in a very real sense it may be said to be the backbone of Pennsylvania German illumination.

Keystone of this whole Mennonite movement was the *Mennonite School,* a fact which is repeatedly impressed upon us by inscriptions ending with the word, "schulmeister." [336] Mercer likewise recognized this background and reported "Second, That it had been chiefly perpetuated by deliberate instruction in German schools by German schoolmasters, and that it had received its death-blow at the disestablishment of the latter in Bucks County in 1854 " [337]  By this date, of course, the itinerant Fraktur writer had long since replaced the schoolmaster but, as is quite evident, the quality of the Fraktur work had suffered and the production was quite uneven

While the names of only a few of these schoolmasters have come down to us, the schools in which they taught have been clearly designated in some Fraktur pieces, and will ultimately no doubt lead to the discovery of the teacher's names.  Earliest, and most outstanding among them, of course, is *Christopher Dock.*  The importance of his contributions to early pedagogy is beyond question, but the identification of his Fraktur work leaves much to be desired. [338]

Dock's work as a schoolmaster of Germantown, then Skippack and Salford, has been acknowledged as a major force in the development of Fraktur technique.  But the examples which have been identified as his work thus far derive from a later period, if we can judge from a comparison with similar dated specimens by other illuminators. [339]  On the other hand, it must be admitted that many of the specimens attributed to Dock (with text partly in English and partly in German) have much in common, and thereby suggest a common source.  It is entirely possible that this common source is Dock's *real* work, and that to him therefore should go the credit for advancing it.  If this were the solution, then where are the original Dock Vorschriften that served as the models for these, and why should bona fide examples of his work be so scarce?  If

---

[336] Christian Strenge, C. M. Artist, etc.          .          ..
[337] Mercer, *op. cit.,* p. 425.
[338] See figures 132-134.
[339] See Brumbaugh, M. G., *The Life and Works of Christopher Dock* (1908), and Borneman, *op. cit.,* pl. 20.

he worked as assiduously as most writers believe he did, how is it that no Fraktur specimens signed by him have turned up to date?

Shortly after Dock's death, there began to appear a whole series of beautifully illuminated Mennonite song-books. [340] These provide a valuable key to the identification of works of this Fraktur school, since in most cases the location of the Mennonite school is clearly identified. If one takes into account slight stylistic modifications, these demonstrate the development of the Mennonite style from about 1780 through to 1835. They are directly related to the larger *Vorschriften,* which present still another phase of the activity that centered in the Mennonite singing and writing schools. In the cases of Christian Strenge. Christian Bachman, and Henry Hill, they signed their full names and dated their larger Fraktur pieces; on their bookplates, if any information occurs at all, it is usually the name of the township and county in which the school was located. Some of these illuminated title-pages also occur in printed songbooks, Testaments, or Bibles. [341]

The schools mentioned certainly give one an idea of the tremendous spread of this work. Northampton, Montgomery, Berks, Lancaster, and even Chester Counties had their Mennonite schools as well as Bucks. In fact, the appearance of similar specimens in all of these counties suggests that either one or two books must have served as models, or else the penman-schoolmaster must at various times have taught or traveled around to all these locations.

It is the Deep Run School (Tiefenbroner) in Bedminster Township, Bucks County, which seems to have been the focal point for most of this activity. There today, inscribed in chalk on the beams of the ceiling of the old school building which is still standing, are the bars of music taught to the children in that early day. [342] Not only are these still visible, but they likewise are related in style to these early illuminated songbooks.

Jacob Oberholtzer was the teacher in the old log schoolhouse near Deep Run, and it is to him that many of these illuminated Mennonite manuscript musicbooks have been attributed. It was Mercer who first mentioned Oberholtzer as the teacher "who probably produced the *Vorschriften Büchlein* of Margretha Wismerin, 'Vorgeschrieben den October

---

[340] See figures 143, 149.
[341] See figures 142, 150.
[342] See figure 148.

4th, 1781'." [343]    The existence of a large number of Mennonite musicbooks, as well as a half dozen or so fine *Copybooks* or *Vorschriften
Büchlein,* all of them from schools in this immediate area and decorated
by the same hand, [344] establishes beyond any question the presence of an
accomplished Fraktur writer.    The identity of Jacob Oberholtzer was
definitely established several years ago by a Fraktur Bible Title-page and
Taufschein handed down in the Rupp family, which he actually signed. [345]
All the characteristics of his decoration and penmanship style are apparent here.

That Oberholtzer must have continued at Deep Run as teacher for
at least a decade, is implied by the dates of the musicbooks and copybooks, which extend from 1781 to 1791.    While slight changes in design and in color take place, the style of composition and handwriting
change very little.

Meanwhile, similar books dating from 1784 to 1799 turn up from
Franconia, Hereford, and Plumstead Townships (in addition to Bedminster) in *Bucks County,* from Upper Salford Township in *Montgomery County,* from Pikeland and Vincent Townships in *Chester
County,* from Tulpehocken and Wismer Townships in *Berks County,*
and from Strassburg Township in *Lancaster County.*    So alike are the
colors, designs, and handwriting of all these that they must be the work
of one very gifted illuminator.    The 18th century examples are done
chiefly in red, yellow, blue, and black with occasional touches of pink or
green, whereas those dating after the turn of the century employ red,
yellow, and black.    About 1830, the favorite colors changed to red, yellow, and green.

The colors, designs, and general compositions of all of these are
reflected in the larger Fraktur *Vorschriften* so popular among the Mennonites.    Angels heads, flying angels with trumpets, five-petaled tulips,
and leaf borders all reappear in larger form in these Vorschriften. [346]
Other than angels, little use of the human figure was made.    Especially
characteristic are the neatly lined borders in several colors which many
times serve to separate units containing small Fraktur designs that are com-

---

343 Mercer, *op. cit.,* p. 426.
344 See figures 47, and 143-147.
345 See figure 142.
346 See figures 142-143.

plete in themselves.  Occasionally these small units are turned up on end without regard for the remainder of the *Vorschriften*; at other times, even the text within these borders is turned on end. [347]  Of chief note, however, is the *simplicity* of these blocked borders which frequently change color as they turn the corners. [348]  The vertical and horizontal ink outlines run to the edge of the paper, and the tiny squares which occur at the corners are usually filled in with a contrasting color that is different from the adjoining borders.  In some pieces, a faint sawtooth edge is introduced inside the main colored border and is composed of many faint pen lines drawn close together. [349]

These Mennonite *Vorschriften* are executed in both cherry-gum gouache and in flat watercolor, depending upon the artist and the area in which he worked.  The date of the Fraktur pieces has little to do with the choice of medium.  The colors of the Mennonite work, though brighter than Ephrata, are apt to be softer and less rich than the strong earthy colors of the Schwenkfelder work.  One has the feeling of great delicacy and sparkle, as opposed to the pungent and crisp colors of the Schwenkfelder work. [350]  The Mennonite illuminators liked to alternate red and black words one after the other, or to alternate red and black lines of text.  Ofttimes adjoining blocks of text are written in different colored inks.

In the Mennonite work, the love of good penmanship persisted into the 19th century.  Carefully drawn Fraktur capitals and meticulously written script text are evident throughout [351]  And very few, indeed, are the examples where occasional passages of interlacing do not appear within the letters or between the lines  Long after other decorators began to deteriorate, the Mennonite work holds its quality.  In its carefully laid out and carefully written aspects, it has much in common with the compositions of the Ephrata decorators.

Outstanding in the Mennonite School in addition to the above-mentioned Jacob Oberholtzer, are such artists as Christian Strenge, Christian Bachman, Hans Jacob Brubacher, Abraham Dirdorff, Rudolph

[347] See figure 139.
[348] See figures 36, 37, 152, and 154.
[349] See figures 44, 150, 151.
[350] See figures 153, 155-156; compare Color Plates II and III.
[351] See figures 152 and 155; also Color Plate II.

Landes, and many others. [352] Most of these were primarily *Vorschrift* writers and can be identified beyond any doubt because they signed many of their specimens. Few, if any, of them seem to have produced *Taufscheins* and thus in this respect very closely parallel the work of their neighbors, the Schwenkfelders. Just as the Bucks County and Lancaster County artists seem to have specialized in *Vorschriften* embodying Mennonite hymns, so the Schwenkfelder illuminators restricted their work to this one field. Many times, superficially, the Vorschriften of these two schools resemble one another. A careful stylistic analysis of a doubtful Fraktur specimen, however, will usually reveal its origin in one of these two schools. The colors, designs, and compositions of each differ noticeably from the other.

It is interesting to note that here again, as at Ephrata, the best work seems to come from closely-knit religious groups which, through a relative degree of isolation from other people, achieved an identity of their own.

## THE SCHWENKFELDER SCHOOL (1769/71-1854)

If the *earliest* and finest Fraktur was produced at Ephrata, and the *most consistent* in the Mennonite schools, certainly the *most decorative* and colorful illuminations were turned out by the Schwenkfelders. Centered in Montgomery County chiefly around Pennsburg, members of this sect are considered to be the most highly educated group that entered Pennsylvania If this be true, and certainly on the basis of the extensive literary evidence available at the Schwenkfelder Historical Library at Pennsburg today one cannot doubt it, there is no need to seek further explanation for the high quality of their illumination. So much of the Fraktur work of this one school has been preserved in this small area, however, that it is virtually unknown outside. Hence it has not received the attention it so richly deserves. It parallels the Mennonite work so closely, also, that it has no doubt often been confused with it.

The Schwenkfelders were followers of Casper Schwenkfeld and came from Silesia. This latter fact is of particular note because of their proximity to the Central European melting pot. Originating farther to the East than any of the other Pennsylvania German groups, they

---

[352] See figures 152-157.

were located on the trade routes leading directly into the Near East, and were therefore fully exposed to all the motifs, colors, and techniques constantly being brought into the West along this route down the Valley of the Danube.  It is the impact of these designs and influences which explains the Eastern flavor in Schwenkfelder Fraktur illumination, to which so many writers have called attention.  Nowhere in Fraktur are these *richer colors* and *more luxuriant designs* of Central and Eastern Europe more apparent than in this Schwenkfelder illumination. [353]

As has been noted in our study of the products of the Mennonite writing and singing schools, the illuminations of these two groups have much in common.  In the first place, both groups took the texts for their *Vorschriften* from their own hymnologies   Second, and even more important, they received similar instruction in the art of Fraktur.  Whether some of the early members of the Schwenkfelder families such as the Cassels, Hübners, and Kriebels attended Mennonite schools is not clear, but the similarity between their work in the 1770's and 1780's is quite remarkable.  Perhaps this close resemblance is due to dependence upon similar engraved copybooks, but it is not long-lived, for by 1800 a completely independent style had been developed that is unmistakable.

The Schwenkfelder style is embodied in its present form in the work of three or four chief Schwenkfelder families: the Hübners, Kriebels, Seipts, and Anders.  While Susanna Hubner is the only individual whose Fraktur hymns have been illustrated to date, [354] other illuminators are equally expert and equally representative of this school. Susanna Hübner, David Kriebel, [355] Abraham Hubner, [356] and others are but a few of the artists whose work is outstanding.

The period of greatest development is 1800 to 1835, but the high point would be in the period from 1800 to 1815.  The reason for this is that, unlike the other schools of illumination, the designs were handed down in these families and were copied, and re-copied, by new generations of children.  Thus, designs that are first seen around 1810 recur again and again down to 1830 and 1840   In the cases of some initials like the capital "S" in *Steh Auf* [357] or "H" in *Heilig,* [358] not only are

---

[353] See figures 160-164; also Color Plate III.
[354] See figures 165-169.
[355] See figure 160.
[356] See figures 158-159.
[357] See figures 170-171, and 173.
[358] See figure 174.

the complete compositions repeated, but the capital letters themselves are lifted out of the designs and used as practice exercises by the children. [359] In this respect, the attitude of the Schwenkfelders was different from that of Beissel who said, "We dare not borrow [designs] from each other, because the power to produce rests within everybody . . ."

So well copied are these Schwenkfelder forms, however, that many times it is only the brighter inks or the addition of some obviously later detail to the design which makes it possible to distinguish the earlier *Vorschriften* from the later. In the 1830's, a broad simple style depending more upon brushwork and less upon penmanship appeared. Occasional bookplates and balanced, conventional Fraktur designs clearly characterize this phase of Schwenkfelder Fraktur. [360] At the end of its development, 1840-50, a new kind of decorative design begins to appear and the first signs of weakening Schwenkfelder technique become evident. [361] This is accompanied by even more frequent use of flat watercolors as opposed to the earlier richly applied cherry-gum gouache.

The two distinguishing features of the Schwenkfelder work are its color and its designs. Intense vermilion red and deep yellow predominate, played against occasional areas of dark slate blue. Sometimes all three are combined in a single Fraktur letter, thereby giving it a richness and brilliance unsurpassed elsewhere. Green, although it appears occasionally in leaf designs, is usually dark and shaded with black outlines. For the most part, the outlines of the Fraktur inscriptions are faintly drawn in black or red ink, and then heavy quantities of cherry-gum gouache colors are filled in. Their brilliant color and decorative treatment of letters bring these Schwenkfelder illuminations very close to Medieval forms. [362]

Ingenious use of egg-and-dart motifs, strapwork, checkerboard, and diamond-shaped patterns reenforces their strong colors. Borders are either plain or, if they receive any attention at all, are doubled and tripled into complex decorative forms far beyond the requirements of the normal Fraktur piece. Diagonal bandings and scalloped hidden-eye motifs redouble and repeat one another until a composite border of five

---

[359] See figure 172.
[360] See figures 176-177.
[361] See figures 178-180.
[362] See figure 174.

or six individual decorative bands is developed.[363]  In much of the Schwenkfelder work, also, extra diagonal borders, sunbursts, circular motifs, or hearts from which spring floral designs, are used to fill the corners of the composition.  Susanna Hübner, in particular, favored diagonal members at the corners of her *Vorschriften*.[364]

Perhaps the most characteristic stylistic innovation of the Schwenkfelder illuminators, however, is the use of extra horizontal short lines around the Fraktur letters and the luxuriant development of leaf and flower forms.  The first of these serves especially well to distinguish this work very neatly from the Mennonite school.  Whereas both schools employ horizontal interlaces or bands running across inscriptions, and whereas both employ rudimentary leaf forms of concentric quill pen lines to fill vacant spaces within or around such inscriptions, it is only the Schwenkfelder artists who completely fill in spaces between the Fraktur letters and along the inside of the main borders with these repeating red and black horizontal or vertical lines.  The illuminations of the Kriebel family are especially rich in this feature.[365]  These horizontal and vertical lines are used in conjunction with the feather-like concentric lines which enrich the capital letters of their *Vorschriften*.[366]

Augmenting the already rich treatment of the capital letters in Schwenkfelder work, are leaf and flower forms of unusual luxuriance. Leaf upon leaf in alternating or repeating colors, proceeding from simple to complex, make these illuminations a never-ending source of pleasure.[367]  Even across these leaves, dotted, checkered, or other patterns appear with remarkable results.  At times echoing the stylized leaf forms of Ephrata, these are at once freer in execution and gayer in color.

Tulip, carnation, rose, and heart motifs appear everywhere, particularly the tulip or palmette plant emanating from a heart.  Susanna Hübner was particularly fond of this latter motif.[368]  Perhaps the height of decorative design was achieved in the varied treatment given that favorite Near Eastern theme of the *Tree of Life* or *Urn and Plant*.[369] While one finds the motif constantly used by the Hübners and Kriebels,

---

[363] See figures 160, and 183.
[364] See figures 165-166, and 167.
[365] See figures 161, 171.
[366] See figure 161.
[367] See figures 162-164; also Color Plate III.
[368] See figures 165-169.
[369] See figures 164 and 170.

no two are ever alike as regards either the urn itself or the plant. The greatest inventiveness appears here, with each composite form somewhat similar in its overall silhouette but vastly different in every one of its parts. The ancient *Urbogen* motif appears frequently in these Urn and Palmette compositions. [370]

Occasional flower motifs become so stylized that they resemble stars. The basic star form used by the Schwenkfelder artist, however, is unmistakable. For some reason, he preferred the six-pointed or "sechsstern" type and in every instance that has come to the author's attention, he elaborated upon this form. Frequently this appeared as a twelve-part form, but only because of his penchant for painting one side of a projecting point red and the other blue, or because of some similar decorative means to achieve extra sparkle and brilliance. [371]

In this connection, a few words should be said regarding the Schwenkfelders' use of the ruler and compass  In the hands of many artists, resort to such mechanical devices has been synonymous with an immediate loss both of character and of eye appeal. In this case, on the contrary, great gains were made in every respect. Judicious use of the ruler and compass to augment the picturesque free-hand designs which form the vocabulary of this distinctive school, has resulted in Fraktur of the highest decorative quality. [372]

## WRITTEN TAUFSCHEINS AND TAUFSCHEIN WRITERS

In the three schools of illumination which we have considered thus far — Ephrata, Mennonite, and Schwenkfelder — the absence of the Taufschein or the Birth-and-Baptismal Certificate is quite apparent. The religious nature and emphasis of these groups no doubt accounts for this. What references to birth do occur, such as in occasional Bookplates, or smaller Vorschriften, make a simple statement of fact and contain none of the detailed information of the full-fledged Geburts-und-Taufschein.

To pass by the Taufschein schools which flourished adjacent to, and contemporary with, these religious sects would be to overlook one of

---

[370] See figures 155 and 170.
[371] See figures 162-164, and 181; also Color Plate III.
[372] See figures 181-182.

the most fertile fields of Fraktur illumination. For among the "church people," Lutherans and Reformed, these Taufscheins far outstripped the *Vorschriften* both in quantity and in decorative subject-matter. In fact, aside from the mass-produced printed Fraktur forms which provide the largest single phase of this work, the hand-illuminated Taufschein is the chief development. These began prior to the time printed forms appeared and, as we have seen, derived directly from European proto-types. They continued right down through the 1860's, moreover, despite the development of the printed, stipple-engraved, and lithographed forms. In fact, the same artists who illuminated these hand-written Taufscheins often decorated printed forms also.

The field of written Taufscheins is a fertile field for investigation not only because of the large quantity produced, but because of the artists who created them and the wide variety of motifs employed. Since a religious precept no longer occupied the position of first importance in the composition of the *Taufschein,* the decorative borders became of prime interest. The artist allowed his imagination the greatest freedom, and simple floral designs were soon augmented by vigorous and dynamic representations of birds, insects, animals, and human figures of various kinds (flying angels, dancing couples, etc.). On occasion, even archi-tectural motifs were introduced. It is the presence, and the combination, of these motifs which enable one to gather together, and to isolate, the work and stylistic characteristics of artists as yet unnamed.

In the earlier period, no doubt many of these Fraktur writers were ministers (like Daniel Schumacher who signed himself as a Lutheran minister),[373] or school teachers (like Dock, Oberholtzer, Strenge, etc ).[374] It was not long, however, until these were supplanted by the professional penman or "Fraktur-schreiber" who traveled through the countryside of Pennsylvania much like the intinerant portrait painters of the 19th cen-tury. The manner in which they secured information about recent births and baptisms from the local ministers has already been described by many writers, and even some accounts by the itinerant artists themselves have come to light. [375]

---

[373] See figures 184-185.
[374] See figures 132-134, 142-147, and 152.
[375] Borneman, *op cit*, p. 50   Ferdinand Klenk's working notebook (1875), an itinerant penman in Jackson Township, Lebanon County. Also Lichten, *op cit.,* pp. 197-198   August Bauman, an itinerant Fraktur writer, active as recently as the beginning of the 20th century.

From the names of the ministers who performed the baptisms, the dates of the certificates, and the combinations of designs, it is possible to reconstruct fairly accurately the careers of the more productive Taufschein writers, even though specific details of their lives are not yet available. [376]   Much of this information may, indeed, never become known, since it is only occasionally that they signed their names. As folk artists, creating over and over again a limited artistic form they were capable of achieving, they were following a *folk tradition* in which the individual as such was not of primary importance. Hence, very few Fraktur illuminators ever signed their pieces, but those who did, did so fairly consistently.

In presenting the story of the development of hand-written Fraktur, limitations of space permit the identification of only a few of the artists listed in Appendix A. For purposes of clarity, most of those presented here are known to have signed at least one piece, although several unknown "Masters" will also be mentioned. From the many illuminated manuscripts studied, experience has shown that artists usually specialized either in Taufscheins, or else in Vorschriften and the related smaller religious text items.

Since the Certificate writers began in the earliest period and continued right down to the late 19th century, the hand-written Taufscheins present a very complete picture of the development and decline of the Pennsylvania German Style of Illumination. In that picture, the following artists played a prominent role: Rev. Daniel Schumacher, Henrich Otto, Friederich Speyer, Friedrich Krebs, H. Seiler, Karl Münch, Abraham Huth, Martin Brechall, Durs Rudy, Ludwig Crecelius, Daniel Peterman, Johannes Bard, John Zinck, Henry Lehn, John Landis, and Francis Portzline. Taufschein writers whose names are as yet unknown to us, but whose works deserve attention are: the Flying Angel Artist, C. M. Artist, the Cross-legged Angel Artist, the Mount Pleasant Printing Office Artist, and the A. W. Artist.

The history of attribution in the Fraktur field has been a very brief one since, as has already been pointed out, most of the articles

---

[376] Fragmentary notes on the lives of Valentin Schuller, Krebs, and Dulheuer by Shoemaker, and on Miesse by Dr. Oda, have recently been published in *The Pennsylvania Dutchman*. See Bibliography D, under *Fraktur: hand-written and printed*.

written in the earlier period featured the Ephrata "religious" manuscripts as opposed to the "secular" illuminated certificates by nameless folk artists. Prior to Borneman's book in 1937, [377] the only attributions made were those of Mercer (1897) [378] and of Cahill (1932). [379] Mercer tentatively attributed a Mennonite songbook to Jacob Overholt [sic], [380] a bookmark to Isaac Gross, [381] and mentioned "two aged masters of the craft still survive in the person of Jacob Gross of New Britain, and John H. Detweiler of Perkasie." [382] The work of none of these, however, was illustrated. Holger Cahill in his *American Folk Art* catalogue [383] both listed and identified the work of Francis Portzline by illustrating one of his characteristic works: the Birth Certificate he illuminated for his own daughter, Maria Portzline. [384]

In his 1937 volume, Borneman identified and illustrated the work of seven additional artists: Johannes Klinger, Johannes Renninger, C. M. Artist, Christopher Dock, Susanna Hübner (2), Jacob S. Bicksler, and Rudolph Landes. [385] He also reproduced in color an illuminated page from an Ephrata *Paradisisches-Wunderspiel* (1754) and in black-and-white an example of Leonhard Wagner (1507), the designer of Fraktur type. Of the seven identified Pennsylvania specimens, those of Johannes Klinger and Christopher Dock do not specifically state: "geschrieben von mir . . ." or some correspondingly definite fact and are, in the writer's opinion, open to question.

Stoudt, in his *Consider the Lilies* (1937), [386] illustrated several Susanna Hübner pieces, a baptismal certificate "printed for Heinrich [sic] Otto" and a detail of a "Geistlicher Ihrgarten [sic] printed at Ephrata in 1785 and illuminated in lily motif by Heinrich [sic] Otto," a pattern "Heinrich [sic] Otto is believed to have carried . . . with him as he itinerated to paint chests and illuminate Taufscheins," and a baptismal certificate "from Joseph [sic] Bauman's Ephrata Press."

---

[377] Borneman, *op. cit.*
[378] Mercer, *op. cit.*
[379] Cahill, Holger, *American Folk Art: The Art of the Common Man in America, 1750-1900.* New York: Museum of Modern Art, 1932.
[380] Mercer, *op. cit.*, #1, p. 426.
[381] *Ibid.*, #3, p. 429.
[382] *Ibid.*, p. 432.
[383] Cahill, *op. cit.*, #74, p. 38.
[384] *Ibid.*, #74.
[385] Borneman, *op. cit.*
[386] Stoudt, *op. cit.*

In his New-York Historical Society *Quarterly* article (1945), [387] the author added to Henrich Otto the identification of his important contemporaries, Reverend Daniel Schumacher and Friederich Speyer, as well as the early 19th century illuminator Martin Brechall, and the engraver, Carl Friederich Egelmann.

Frances Lichten (1946) [388] illustrated works by the as yet unknown Christian Peters, Reverend George Geistweite, the A. W. Artist, Maria Hübner, and Daniel Peterman   She illustrated as *printed by* Johann Valentin Schuller, a detail of one of the certificates *decorated by* him (the certificate itself says "Verfertigt").   Recent biographical material discovered by Dr. Shoemaker not only indicates his forms were printed for him at the *Adler* Press in Reading, but also gives some clues as to his activities. [389]

Stoudt, on the jacket of his *Pennsylvania Folk-Art* (1948), [390] reproduced a work of Christian Strange [sic], but failed to attribute Andreas Kaufman's 1795 *Vorschrift* (p 201) or his own Mennonite hymnal (p.213) to the same artist, although Strenge's characteristic yellow distelfink appears on each of them.   Among his many Fraktur illustrations, a majority of which are Ephrata work, he included works by Huppert Cassel, Jacob Oberholtzer, Reverend Daniel Schuhmacher [sic], and continued to identify an Ephrata certificate as printed by Joseph [sic] Bauman.   Although he also included signed Frakturs by the A.W. Artist, Georg Teibel, and H. Seiler, he failed to identify them.

The following lists give the names of those Fraktur illuminators whose work has previously been identified through actual illustration, as well as

---

[387] Shelley, *op. cit.*

[388] Lichten, *op. cit*

[389] Shoemaker, Alfred L., 'Johann Valentin Schuller — Fractur Artist and Author', *The Pennsylvania Dutchman*, III, 10 (October 15, 1951)

"We know of three Johann Valentin Schuller ballads  one on the murderer Johannes Schild, who killed his father and mother in Alsace Township, Berks County, on August 12, 1812; another is on the suicide of Andreas Emrich in 1811 in Northumberland County; and the third is a warning occasioned by sun spots in May and June 1816 .

There were two Johann Valentin Schullers, father and son. . . Senior died on this farm [in Northumberland County] in 1812  He was survived by his wife Magdalena, and four children — Johann Valentin, Jr, the oldest son; George; Anna Margaret, wife of Nicholas Eckel, and Christina, single.

I have been unable to establish whether it was father or son who was the fractur artist. The son was the author of the ballads  We also know that Junior handled *Taufscheins*. Several entries in the Adler (Reading) account books prove this. For instance, on February 16, 1813, he bought 150 certificates. . ."

[390] Stoudt, *op. cit.*

PLATE IV. Henrich Otto, Birth Certificate. Printed c.1784

*Titus C. Geesey collection, Wilmington, Del.*

those whose work will be illustrated here:

| PREVIOUSLY IDENTIFIED | IDENTIFIED HERE |
|---|---|
| Jacob S. Bicksler | Christian Bachman |
| Martin Brechall | Johannes Bard |
| Huppert Cassel | Andreas B. Bauer |
| Christopher Dock | Hans Jacob Brubacher |
| Carl Friederich Egelmann | Ludwig Crecelius |
| Rev. George Geistweite | Abraham Dirdorff |
| Maria Hübner | C.F. Artist |
| Susanna Hübner | Wilhelmus Antonius Faber |
| Rudolph Landes | Abraham Hübner |
| C.M. Artist | Abraham Huth |
| Gabriel Miesse | Friedrich Krebs |
| Jacob Oberholtzer | David Kriebel |
| Henrich Otto | John Landis |
| Daniel Peterman | John A Landis |
| Christian Peters | Henry Lehn |
| Francis Portzline | Karl C. Münch |
| Johannes Renninger | Durs Rudy |
| Johann Valentin Schuller | C. Scherich |
| Rev. Daniel Schumacher | H. Seiler |
| Friederich Speyer | Georg Teibel |
| Christian Strenge | I.T.W. Artist |
| A.W. Artist | John Zinck |

Some 35 nameless Folk artists, numerous examples of whose work have survived and can be grouped by designs or compositions, can likewise be added to the above list. Sooner or later signed specimens of these illuminators may appear which will reveal the identity of the artist. Examples of most of these have been included among the illustrations. [391] The majority of them belong to the first half of the 19th century and, if one can judge from the variety of Counties named on their certificates, must have been itinerant Fraktur writers who moved about very freely throughout the Pennsylvania German region.

The imprints of some 20 Pennsylvania German printers and 6 lithographers are also illustrated here, most of them for the first time.

With the exception of Otto, Speyer, Krebs, Schuller, Brechall, Egelmann, and Miesse, the artists listed seem to have produced hand-written

---

[391] See figures 201-237; also Color Plate V.

certificates exclusively.  Since the manuscript work of the first four of
these artists played such a key role in the Fraktur story, they are introduced here rather than in the succeeding chapter with Fraktur *printers*.
The outstanding work of the last two of these, C. F. Egelmann and G.
Miesse, will be taken up in the chapter devoted to stipple-engraved Taufscheins, since no hand-written Frakturs by them have come to the author's
attention.

### The Formative Period — Late 18th Century Artists

The existence of the Fraktur writing school at the Ephrata Cloister
in the mid-18th century and the extraordinary works produced there,
have led many writers into the error of believing that a great quantity
of illuminated Taufscheins and Vorschriften were also produced in
this same period.  They have supported this contention by pointing to
Taufscheins bearing early birth dates, evidence which we have seen cannot be relied upon. [392]  The existence of dated iron stove-plates, tombstones, "Stiegel" glass, and pewter prior to the Revolution, have also
been cited as proof of this contention.  In reality, however, the amount
of Fraktur illumination (aside from the Ephrata work), which can be
proved to have been executed prior to the Revolution, is very small
indeed.  And the few artists who signed examples dating in the 1760's
and early 1770's, can in most cases be found still working in the 1780's.
Exceptions to this rule would, of course, be artists like Christopher
Dock (who died in 1771) and the unknown Georg Teibel (whose works
all date in the 1760's).

The chief representatives of this *Formative Period* (1760-1800)
constitute the great quartette of early Pennsylvania German Fraktur
illuminators: Reverend Daniel Schumacher, Henrich Otto, Friederich
Speyer, and Friedrich Krebs.  Of these four, only two have received any
attention thus far: Rev. Daniel Schumacher and Henrich Otto, both
hand-illuminators.  Although Otto has been known for some years because of his decorations on early printed certificates, Schumacher was
first identified by the author in April, 1945, [393] and has since that time
been extensively illustrated in Stoudt's latest book. [394]  Since no stylistic
analysis of their work has been attempted elsewhere, brief outlines will

---

[392] See figures 82-85.
[393] Shelley, *op. cit.*, pp. 97-98, illustration on page 98.
[394] Stoudt, *op. cit.*, (1948).  Plates 230-237 are identified as by Schuhmacher
[*sic*], but he fails to recognize Plate 194 as also one of his works.

be given here with appropriate illustrations. Single works by several of the more active known and unknown artists of this same period will be included also in order to round out the picture.

REVEREND DANIEL SCHUMACHER is of particular interest here for several reasons. Not only does he typify the Minister-Fraktur writer of the 18th century, but he fully signed and dated virtually every example of his work that has come to the writer's attention. In these inscriptions, he variously described himself as an "Evangelical Lutheran" or as "Lutheran" minister and indicates very definitely that he issued the certificate at the time he baptized the child. These dates range from 1761 to 1781, thereby indicating a career extending over at least two decades. [395] As is typical of most Fraktur writers, his style changed very little during this period of activity and aside from slight improvements in the direction of greater refinement, wider variety of motifs, and less script writing, there is little difference between his earlier and his later works. Carefully balanced compositions, delicate penwork, occasional cross-hatching, and relatively pale colors characterize his illuminations.

Considerable European flavor still pervades his work and this flavor is heightened by the text-form he uses, which begins with the full name of the child in large letters and continues "hat das Licht dieser Weldt erblicket . . ." The studied repetition of his phrasing, the words employed, and his signature as a minister of the church, give all of these the import of an official document. Although Schumacher served as minister to several Lutheran churches in Berks and Lehigh Counties, [396] the late Claude W. Unger stated that he was ultimately removed as a minister, but continued in spite of this to operate on his own authority. A few of his pieces stem from Northampton County, also. The *Church Book* reproduced by Stoudt from the Albany Church, may be the one described to the author by Mr. Unger just before his death. Suffice it to say that the very correct language, the careful craftsmanship of Rev. Schumacher's illuminations, and the variety of their subject-matter, suggest a person of no mean ability and intelligence.

---

[395] See figures 184-185.
[396] Early, J. W., *Lutheran Ministers of Berks County*, Reading, 1902. See pages 21 and following.

JOHANN HENRICH OTTO, [397] despite the meager facts known about him, has for many years dominated the Fraktur picture. Just as the name "Stiegel" connotes the finest form and color in glass, so Henrich Otto (as he is generally known) connotes the finest in early Fraktur. Like Stiegel, he was active in Lancaster County and, like Stiegel, he used flower and bird forms to great advantage. On occasion, however, Otto went far beyond the realm of flowers and birds into unicorns, lions, pelicans, mermaids, and seahorses. All of these motifs he treated with rare imagination and great feeling for decorative pattern.

Perhaps the most artistic feature of Otto's Fraktur work, however, is his unusually fine lettering. Whether employing large ornate capital letters, block letters, or tiny script, he treated them with equal competence and taste. If there be any question about his work, a glance at the numerals and the penmanship flourishes he constantly employed between lines of text, will resolve that question. His obvious pride in lettering carries over into his printed certificates which, however, never quite achieve the grandeur of his hand-written Frakturs. It is his large and ornate capital letters that appear singly in these Frakturs which point consciously toward their immediate prototype, the European *Copybook*. Within the last decade, one such copybook printed at Halle turned up in an estate sale of one of the early families of Ephrata, Pa., [398] containing several alphabets, the largest of which duplicated in detail the large capitals of Henrich Otto.

Since we know that several of Otto's children were baptized in the church at Ephrata and his printed forms come straight from the Ephrata Press, such similarities are of decided importance. Whether he had any real connection with the Cloister itself is not clear, but he certainly employed its press and type. [399] Most of the certificates he issued are for Lancaster or Berks County families, and when drawings of his have been found inside the lids to dower chests, they have usually been Lancaster or Berks County chests. It is these freely executed drawings which by their decorative character and vigorous color have excited the admiration of antiquarians and, because of their balance and composition,

---

[397] Otto's full name is given on one or two early certificates, including the one he illuminated for his own daughter, Anna Barbara Otto, see figure 238.

[398] See herein page 25, and foot-note 64.

[399] Compare figures 131 and 189; also Color Plate IV.

have caused so much speculation on the possibility that Otto might also have decorated dower chests. [400]

In addition to the characteristics already noted, Otto had a distinct predilection for using colored inks, especially yellow and pinkish red. These lend softness and extra charm to his work. His constant use of large flowers seen frontally or in profile, and connected by winding vines or chains of leaves, leave very little doubt in problems of attribution. His borders, and the motifs they contain, are as neatly laid out as his Fraktur lettering, and evince a feeling of quiet orderliness. The motifs themselves, within these borders, are none the less freely drawn.

In contrast to Schumacher, Henrich Otto decorated more than just Taufscheins. [401]    He supplied Geistliche Irrgartens, [402] Haus-Segens, [403] and even occasional books. One of the latter is owned by the Schwenkfelder Historical Library (dated 1772) and in its lettering bears close relationship to Dock's work, because of its purely penmanship approach. The use of dots and interlaces to fill in spaces around the letters suggests this same background, although the designs which appear are strictly Otto's own.

Otto's individual free-hand drawings are masterpieces of flowing penmanship and decorative brushwork. Most of these Fraktur drawings are finished off at the bottom with a kind of undulating groundwork, as if they required some support for their existence. [404] This idea was adopted by at least two contemporaries of Otto: Friederich Speyer and Friedrich Krebs.

The relationship between Otto, Speyer, and Krebs is so close that it is tantalizing to suggest possible explanations. Lacking documentary evidence to prove these explanations, however, their proximity in Lancaster and Berks County seems the only satisfactory answer. The transfer of motifs is so direct that they must have been quite aware of one another's work, although Otto does not seem to borrow from the others. Together, these three occupy the pivotal position in late 18th century Fraktur, between the hand-drawn and the printed certificate

---

[400] See figure 289.
[401] See figure 188; also Color Plate IV.
[402] See figure 189.
[403] See figure 190.
[404] See figures 187 (upper and lower right) and 289 (lower left and right).

forms. The *earliest* of these forms came from Otto in Ephrata about 1784, and the *largest quantity* from the numerous presses in Reading beginning about 1790.

GEORG FRIEDERICH SPEYER, like Otto, decorated Irrgartens, Haus-Segens, Adam and Eve broadsides, and other printed forms.[405] While his color is brighter and less carefully applied, and his drawing less rhythmic and fluent, he nevertheless achieved Fraktur decorations of great strength and primitive charm. Making no attempt to imitate Otto's superb lettering style, Speyer limited his borrowing to flower designs, birds, lions, mermaids, angel heads, and crowns. To these he added several motifs of his own introducing the human figure, notably (1) *pairs of angels* bearing flowers in one hand and palms in the other, and (2) *pairs of women* wearing bonnets. [406] The second of these may be borrowed from the "Cross-legged Angel Artist" whose figures they closely resemble, and who was quite active in the same community about the same time. Speyer occasionally introduced one of these cross-legged angels which he had borrowed from this very source. [407]

In contrast to Otto, and to Friedrich Krebs, Speyer does not seem to have produced any great number of independent Fraktur drawings. He did decorate an *Adam and Eve* broadside in which a simple block of type provides the excuse for his decoration. Several half-size Haus-Segens not employed by other Fraktur writers contain the same square block of type around which Speyer placed his motifs.

FRIEDRICH KREBS, [408] in contrast to Speyer who evidences no particular development in his illuminated style, shows four quite different methods of Fraktur decoration. Fortunately, by virtue of the fact that he engaged so actively in the decoration of printed Taufscheins, it is possible to assign these otherwise unrelated styles to him. And it is possible also to attribute to him many pieces which otherwise would have lost their identity.

If we include the many stamped, printed, and applied Taufscheins he "completed," Krebs is by all odds the *most prolific decorator* in the

---

[405] See figures 191-194 and 288.
[406] See figures 192 and 248.
[407] Compare figures 193 and 248 with 204.
[408] Krebs' first name is spelled Friedrich, rather than Frie*d*e*r*ich, only on his earliest "dot and dash" pieces.

field of Pennsylvania German illumination.  Although most of these bear Reading imprints, Krebs apparently did not live there. [409]  His period of activity would extend at least three decades — from about 1780 to 1810 — and he would be responsible for some of the poorest as well as some of the best Frakturs.  His rapid artistic progress over this period would be hard to believe, were it not that his four techniques distinctly overlap, each displaying the same bold approach to his material and the same general color scheme.

STYLE I might be called Krebs' "line and dot" technique. [410]  It takes the form of a very simplified border design consisting of a wavy line in one color weaving in and out between a series of comma-like dots in a contrasting color.  Presumably this simple motif belongs to the early 1780's, if not earlier.

STYLE II is a further development of this linear treatment and was employed by Krebs to emphasize the shape and outline of his printed forms. [411]  It is brushed in very freely in two colors and occasionally is augmented by early block stamps or cutouts as in Fig. 197.  He began to employ this technique about 1790, in connection with the new Reading heart-shaped certificate, which remained popular for so many years thereafter.  Later, Krebs reenforces this linear pattern ofttimes by using a faint background tone over the major portion of the certificate, thereby achieving a somewhat three-dimensional effect.

---

[409] Shoemaker, Alfred L., 'Notes on Frederick Krebs, the Noted Fractur Artist', *The Pennsylvania Dutchman*, III, 11 (November 1, 1951), p. 3:
   "From an entry in the Reading *Adler* account books, we learn that Frederick Krebs hailed from Dauphin County.
   The earliest *dated* Krebs taufschein is 1790   (His name for some reason does not appear in the 1790 census).  In 1796 he bought a property between Harrisburg and Hummelstown.  The assessment list for Swatara Township for the year 1805 lists Frederick Krebs as a *schoolmaster*, owning three acres of land. . .
   Frederick Krebs died in the year 1815.  His estate was appraised on July 29, 1815.  The appraisement contains the following revealing entries:
   'By a lot of picters and clean paper.
   By a third lot of clean paper and paper for birthday.
   By a lot of papers picterd and papers for birth Dayes.
   By a lot of paper picterd.'
The "paper for birth Days" obviously refers to taufscheins (birth and baptismal) paper.
   Frederick Krebs' most active year, judging from the *Adler* account book, was 1804.  In this year he had three printings run off: January 3rd, 287; June 21st, 700; and October 31st, 1,000, or a total of 1987 copies.
   Between September 16, 1801 and July 8, 1813, the Reading *Adler* printing office printed *6,974 taufscheins* for Krebs. . ."
[410] See figure 195.
[411] See figures 196-197.

STYLE III was no doubt developed by Krebs as a hand-drawn technique. Venturing beyond the purely decorative approach, he first secured a woodcut of a single bird and tulip motif borrowed from Otto's famous block border. [412] Imitating free-hand with pen and ink the heart-shaped outlines of a printed certificate, Krebs introduced in the lower left and right corners his *woodcut* copy of the Otto bird and in the upper corners a floral motif. To bring these together, he borrowed Otto's "leaf chain" and developed a free-hand formula of his own. While there are no means such as imprint dates for checking just when he developed this technique, it appears that he was occasionally employing it even before the year 1790.

STYLE IV represents the logical synthesis of all these techniques into a homogeneous style, yet retains elements of each of the four. Krebs no longer uses his woodcut of the bird and tulip, but now sketches in the birds, tulips, and sun and moon *by hand,* connecting all of them with his vine motif. [413] Remnants of Style I can still be recognized, however, in the heavily outlined hearts, heavy border line around the certificate, and triangular forms which now fill the upper corners formerly occupied by the painted or stamped flower motifs. From 1790 onwards, most of his certificates are decorated in this style, which became his trademark and easily identifies his work.

Krebs' more spectacular Fraktur drawings of religious and secular subjects follow the two later styles, III and IV. Examples like the Horseman, [414] and the Crucifixion, [415] follow the heavier character of Style IV, while lighter and thinner specimens like the Prodigal Son or the Seven Swabians, follow the Spencerian character of Style III. While not as careful or competent a draftsman as Otto, Friedrich Krebs nevertheless succeeds in endowing his subjects with remarkable vigor and charm.

The height of Krebs' Taufschein decoration is attained by the addition of applied bronzed cutouts over the top of all four of his styles. [416] To him no doubt should go the credit for originating this new idea, for *every specimen* that has appeared to date using this method, has been a

---

[412] See figure 34; also Color Plate IV.
[413] See figure 198.
[414] See figure 199.
[415] See figure 200.
[416] See figures 90, 91, and 249.

Krebs work! While Krebs' printed works have thus far outshone his hand-drawn Frakturs, it is only because the latter have not until now been recognized as the products of his hands. There may be equally significant facets of his career which still remain unknown and, hence, unappreciated.

Because of Friedrich Krebs' close association with both Otto and Speyer, it is logical to consider his work at this point, even though his activity extends *past* the end of the 18th century. His large production of Taufscheins, their various levels of artistic merit, and his entrance into the field of Folklore subject-matter, all indicate the advent of the professional Fraktur penman of the 19th century.

JOHANN VALENTIN SCHULLER, whose Certificate forms were also printed in Reading, would be the completion of this transition from the late 18th century Fraktur decorator to the 19th century scrivener who simply filled in the printed forms. The course of this new development will be studied in the next chapter devoted to the Certificate Printers.

### *19th Century Taufscheins*

The period from 1800 to 1835 witnessed the greatest development of Fraktur writing and the largest number of individual artist-illuminators. Normally one would expect that the mass-production of printed Taufscheins in a center like Reading would be reflected in a corresponding decline of hand-written examples. This *did not* happen. Instead, the competition of printed forms only encouraged increased activity on the part of the individual illuminator and, for several decades at least, he met this competition on fairly equal terms.

The degree to which these artists met the competition of printed forms is the more remarkable when we consider the variety of techniques prevalent at the time. Printed forms with colored backgrounds, applied gilt-paper cutouts, and the first stipple-engraved Taufscheins all flourished side by side with hand-written certificates. Perhaps it was the very fear of the popularity of printed forms that spurred the artist on to explore new possibilities, but it is certain that the first third of the 19th century was a most productive one for hand-drawn Pennsylvania German illumination. It should be noted here that both the Mennonite and the Schwenkfelder Fraktur schools reached their zenith in this period, so that the subject-matter of the time was by no means limited to Taufscheins. The Mennonite Vorschriften and Songbook Title-pages began to "thin out" considerably by 1835 and, although Schwenkfelder decorators continued beyond this date, they never again achieved the richness and quality of the Hübner and Kriebel work of 1800-1815.

Not that the work of the early 19th century Taufschein writers was inferior to these. On the contrary, equally expert illumination was at times achieved by these unknown artists as by the Mennonite or Schwenkfelder artists. Taken as a whole, however, there is a distinct loss in quality, color, draftsmanship, and calligraphy in this school. The Taufscheins often seem casually planned, the designs loosely drawn, and the texts poorly written. In the work of some decorators, of course, this greater freedom of treatment resulted in more rhythmic and more decorative effects, but in others it presages the subsequent disintegration of the whole Pennsylvania German Illuminated Style.

It is perhaps unfair to compare the quickly-turned-out Taufschein to the carefully-planned Vorschriften of the more highly cultured religious groups, especially since their aims and backgrounds were so different. The Vorschriften, after all, were intended as *writing copies* to be followed by students, and much more care and thought went into their creation. They were primarily the work of a limited number of highly educated ministers and schoolteachers. They embody much pride on the part of the writer as well as the owner, hence the frequent appearance of *their names* on these Frakturs. The Taufscheins, on the other hand, were in most cases the achievements of numerous *unknown* illuminators, who turned them out as rapidly as possible and who did the best they could with what limited talents they had. They were not trained artists, nor were they working quietly in a cloister or school. On the contrary, many of these Taufscheins were done "on the road" and often, no doubt, under rather trying circumstances. It is most unlikely that we shall ever find signed pieces revealing the identities of very many of them.

The classification of their work, therefore, becomes a rather difficult problem. For every example signed by H. Seiler, Karl Münch, Abraham Huth, Martin Brechall, or Durs Rudy, there are hundreds of unsigned specimens. These can most easily be grouped by the motifs employed in their borders or by their place of origin, and it is on this basis that the present designations have been created. It is difficult even to specify beyond question the county in which they operated, because they moved about so freely. In most cases, however, one county or township predominates over the others, and it is this system which has been used in labeling the illustrations of their works.

The transition from the 18th century into this Folk Art style of the 19th century was made by artists like the schoolmaster C.M.,[417] H. Seiler,[418] and Karl Münch[419] in *Dauphin (or Lancaster) County;* the Reading-Berks,[420] Cross-legged,[421] and Wetzel[422] Artists in *Berks County;* the Ehre Vater Artist[423] in *Bucks County;* and the Flying Angel[424] and Easton Bible Artists[425] in *Northampton County.* The works of this group fall generally between 1790 and 1815, and they still maintain much of the feeling of 18th century work in their composition, methodical arrangement of motifs, and artistic qualtiy. The nervous and scratchy character of 19th century Fraktur is only foreshadowed in their productions. Strong influences of Otto may be observed in the Lancaster and Berks County pieces, with their parrots and stylized flowers.

Most active of this group is the Flying Angel Artist who, next to Krebs, is the most prolific certificate decorator. While active chiefly in Northampton County, he also worked in Lehigh and Berks. His Frakturs lack the refinement of those of other artists, but they are quite vigorous and extremely decorative. His circular center for the text had considerable influence and was imitated by many other artists of his period. His vocabulary of decorations included a variety of birds, swans, and flowers which, though the two angels at the top of the certificate remained unchanged, were constantly shifted from their positions to create a new design.

The full impact of the early 19th century spirit may best be seen in the Weak Artist,[426] Flat Parrot Artist,[427] Martin Brechall.[428] Abraham Huth,[429] Flat Tulip Artist,[430] and Springing Deer Artist.[431] Their

---

[417] See figure 201.
[418] See figure 202.
[419] See figure 232.
[420] See figure 203; also Color Plate V.
[421] See figure 204.
[422] See figures 62 and 205.
[423] See figure 206.
[424] See figure 207.
[425] See figures 46, 49, and 208.
[426] See figure 209.
[427] See figure 210.
[428] See figure 211.
[429] See figure 212.
[430] See figure 213.
[431] See figure 214.

individual styles remained sufficiently unaltered over several decades so as to make it unnecessary to illustrate more than one example of each. Whereas Martin Brechall signed about half of his certificates, only one signature of Abraham Huth has appeared and of the remainder of these Fraktur writers, none. Brechall, who was active chiefly in Northampton County, naturally shows reminiscences of the Flying Angel Artist, while Abraham Huth, the Flat Parrot Artist, and the Springing Deer Artist show influences of the Lancaster County work of Henrich Otto and the early printed Taufschein forms of John Bauman.

As if from a reaction to the loose technique of these masters, several artists of the 1820-30 period resorted to using the rule and compass for better results. The Mount Pleasant Artist, [432] who definitely dated one of his certificates 1828, is one good example of this and Johannes Bard, 1824-29, another. [433] Not only are flowers and leaves drawn by compass, but even human figures. The Mount Pleasant Artist's form (frequently including the clock at the top of the certificate) was continued by Henry Lehn into the 1840's, [434] when it is much more refined and includes all the motifs of Joseph Lehn's later decorated woodenware.

To these later artists of the 1800-1835 group should be added four others who, like Georg Teibel, Christian Peters, the Sussel Artist, and Rev. George Geistweite in the late 18th century, display a distinctly *European* character. Their work is, in each case, apart from the normal Pennsylvania texts, techniques, and subject-matter, and really deserves special study. The first of these is *Ludwig Crecelius,* whose name suggests European background and who produced several outstanding *Familien-Tafel* of extraordinary quality. Among them is the signed and dated Miesse *Familien-Tafel* of 1830, [435] giving the full record of the Reading engraver's family. It should be noted that the very form itself is unusual in Pennsylvania Fraktur. The second artist may be called the *Haus-Segen Artist,* since his illuminations fall mostly into this category. [436] All of them date from 1828 through 1831 and follow European lettering and motifs. Their strong color and "busy" composition cover virtually the entire paper surface. The third artist of this group is *John Zinck,* whose works date

---

[432] See figures 220 and 222.
[433] See figures 219.
[434] See figure 221.
[435] See figure 236.
[436] See figure 235.

from 1828 to 1834 and who obligingly signed his name to one of them. [437] They are characterized by two full-length figures of a man and woman in European costume and between them a block of text in much abbreviated form. The man wears a high hat and the woman a large bonnet. Above and below them are groups of floral motifs lifted from printed Frakturs and Pennsylvania German embroidered "show" towels of the period. The names of the subjects as well as the motifs and colors, identify their source as Lancaster County. The penmanship of these pieces is delicate and the writing extremely carefully done. Most of Zinck's Frakturs are quarter-size and still in their original frames. Lastly, there is the mysterious *Durs Rudy*, whose Fraktur drawings and Certificates show considerable European flavor. [438] An initialed and dated Adam and Eve in the late Claude W. Unger's collection is outstanding, as well as other subjects such as the Crucifixion, Christ Preaching, a Baptismal Scene, and a Memorial to General Washington. His dated pieces range from 1804 to 1842, thereby taking him into our last Fraktur school.

## Late Fraktur, 1835-1860

In this period of Fraktur, the effect of the printed forms upon the hand-written types is seen. Few, indeed, are the artists whose manuscripts stand out above the masses of printed specimens. Particularly is this true near to the centers where these printed forms were published. Easton, Allentown, Reading, and Harrisburg examples are notably scarce, although in Lancaster and York Counties as well as in the newly-formed counties to the west of Harrisburg, Fraktur writers continued to travel the countryside. From this period on, we are much more apt to find Centre, Union, Cumberland, Franklin, or Westmoreland County certificates than those of the eastern counties.

The Lancaster County tradition continued in the work of *Henry Lehn* into the 1840's, and the York County style in the works of *Daniel Peterman* — who signed all of his certificates. Although he lifted his motifs for these from the printed forms, [439] he developed a composition that is distinctly his own. Some of his certificates bear dates as late as 1857 and 1858, and those discovered thus far all come from Manheim and Shrewsbury Townships in York County.

---

[437] See figure 237.
[438] See figure 233.
[439] See figure 217.

*Francis Portzline,* the very first Fraktur artist ever to be identified or to receive any great attention, produced hand-written Taufscheins bearing dates as early as 1800 and as late as 1847. From the earliest to the latest these were issued mainly in Union County and show great similarity of style. Like Peterman, he lifted some of his motifs from printed certificates, but rearranged and added to them as he saw fit. [440] The decorative feeling with which Portzline organized his Taufscheins gives them the impression of being much earlier than they really are, nor does his lettering belie this feeling. His sense of good color, fortunately, reenforces his very pleasing designs of birds, flowers, interlaces, and human figures. It is interesting to note that in most cases his compositions are "grounded" much in the way Henrich Otto was accustomed to do. [441]

The last major step in this long series of Taufschein forms, represents the final conquest of Fraktur designs over lettering. In the 1820's, an unknown illuminator developed four medium-size vertical pictorial Taufschein compositions which eventually enjoyed great popularity. The *simplest* of these forms contained the text written within a small heart at the center of the page, above which appeared a smaller heart flanked by two birds on tulip branches, and at the very top a pair of eight-pointed stars flanking the inscription "Gott allein die Ehre." [442] On either side of the main heart are a pair of roses (similar to those on King's Rose china) and at the lower point of the heart another pair of confronted birds.

The *second step* in the development of this form moved the Birth Text up between the two stars at the top and substituted for the central heart the standing figure of a woman holding in her outstretched hand a bouquet of flowers and in the other a small basket. [443] To her right and left the rose design still appears, and the Baptismal statement is inscribed at the bottom of the page. On other occasions, the single figure of a man appears instead of the woman.

In the 1830's, a *third step* in this pictorial composition was taken which replaced the single figure of a man or woman by those of *both* a

---

[440] See figure 218.
[441] See figures 187 (upper and lower right) and 289 (lower left and right).
[442] See figure 224.
[443] See figure 225.

man and woman, with a small candlestand or table between them on which rests a decanter. [444] In the upper right and left corners, red and blue eight-pointed stars appear and between them the inscription of birth. In this third type of design, the man holds a wine glass in one hand and with the other clasps the hand of the woman.

In a *fourth variation* of this composition, which takes place in the late 1840's and early 1850's, the wine glass in the man's hand is replaced with a bouquet of flowers, the decanter on the small table becomes a handled cup or beaker, [445] and the red and blue stars are either greatly reduced in size or have disappeared completely. In the very latest Taufscheins of this type, which invariably originate from Centre or Union Counties, the proportions of the page become narrower and higher, the human figures become more grotesque, and we find the illuminator employing ordinary ruled paper of poor quality. The text of these late examples is almost always given in English. Despite their ineffectual drawing, however, these last appearances of the once proud Birth and Baptismal Certificate still have a great deal of style.

In contrast to the creative hand-drawn forms, the printed Taufscheins had developed along totally different lines and by this time were already suffering from the competition of yet another printing technique — *lithography*.

## PRINTED TAUFSCHEINS AND TAUFSCHEIN PRINTERS

Long recognized as one of the most extensive (if not *the* most extensive) phase of Fraktur production, the printed certificate has received only summary treatment. While various other printed forms are to be found, the Birth and Baptismal Certificate or *Taufschein* had little competition from them. In fact, it far exceeds in quantity the total of all the others put together. It was the widespread use of printed certificates which soon led to standardized forms and texts for these records of birth and baptism, to the end that common usage today ofttimes uses the words "Fraktur" or "Birth Certificate" or "Taufschein" interchangeably, although in reality the two latter ones constitute but one segment or type within the former, as we have already seen.

---

444 See figure 226.
445 See figure 227.

It is the tremendous genealogical value of these certificates which, until now, has constantly been stressed   Actually, they are of as much interest to the bibliographer and art historian as they are to the genealogist.  Since many of them bear full imprints and dates, or can on the basis of internal evidence be assigned to definite periods, a continuous history of their printing can be developed from the information thus supplied.  For the student of the early German press in Pennsylvania, this has unusual interest since this story corroborates and supplements the facts more readily available in the innumerable books, pamphlets, and broadsides issued by these same printers.  In all, more than 250 imprints from over 100 different presses have come to the author's attention, and no doubt many more still await discovery. [446] Of this vast body of material, only the most significant and representative examples will be cited here.

For the art historian, the printed forms have special value because of what they reveal of artists' styles.  In the vast mixture of artists' styles and regional forms awaiting classification, the information supplied in these imprints not only helps establish the identity of the artist, as has been shown in the preceding section, but places his field of activity beyond any question in the region named in the imprint line.  In cases where similar designs are found in neighboring regions, it is ofttimes possible (because of the dates given in the imprints) to establish priority as to the use of the designs in question.  Nor are these advantages limited to the field of Fraktur alone, for these same yardsticks can be applied to decorated furniture employing the identical motifs, designs, or compositions as in Figs. 287-292.

Because these certificates were mass-produced, they exerted a tremendous influence in several directions.  Not only did printer copy printer, but printer copied hand-drawn and hand-drawn copied printer. And not only did one printer copy another printer, but in some cases it would appear that the engraved wood blocks themselves were actually handed over from one printer to another, much as they had been in Europe in late medieval times.  While these forms were sometimes reprinted with the blocks in the same arrangement, they were also occasionally shifted from a horizontal to a vertical composition.  In their rectilinear form, as we shall see, the earlier Pennsylvania printed forms bear a close relationship to their European prototypes.

---

[446] See Appendix B and C.

Altogether, the relationship of this whole subject to that of imprints is far closer than most people have recognized.  Since most of the printed forms were actually produced on the very same presses as the early religious books, this fact should come as no surprise.  Thus far, only one bibliographer has acknowledged this in concrete form by listing these printed certificates along with the other productions of the county presses. [447]

These same printers also turned out other broadsides popular among the Pennsylvania Germans such as Spiritual Labyrinths, Haus-Segens, Religious Broadsides, and Folk Ballads.  Over the years many interesting changes took place for, whereas there seems little doubt that some of the earliest Certificates, Labyrinths, and Haus-Segens were printed on the Ephrata Press itself, in the late period one finds them coming from newspaper presses like the "Eagle Buchstohr" at Reading, the "Friend Office" at Hanover, the "Welt Bote" [448] Press at Allentown, and even later from Church presses.

The imprints on these forms must be carefully read if we are to avoid confusing the names of decorators and printers.  In some imprints, as a matter of fact, it is difficult to tell which is which because no distinction is made.  Actually, unless the words "Gedruckt bey" or "Verfertigt von" appear, one cannot be certain.  On several occasions when only the printer's name is given, the illuminator took the precaution of writing his own name *in script* immediately beneath the imprint line. [449]  As a general rule, one is more apt to find the illuminator's name printed in the earlier examples (before 1805) than in the later.  For in the 19th century, as the handwork in the borders becomes less and less, and certificates are produced in ever-increasing quantities, the illuminator as an individual is soon lost sight of.  Those earlier imprints which give the name of the decorator, however, have been invaluable in isolating beyond any question the styles of certain artists.  These imprints, plus the similarity of the artist's handwriting, are infallible bases for attribution.

The text of the certificates has already been discussed with respect to its contents and its development from earlier European prototypes.

---

[447] Shoemaker, Alfred L., see Bibliography under Printed Taufscheins.
[448] See figure 260.
[449] See figures 254 and 256.

The transition from the European format to the standard Pennsylvania form has yet another significance — composition. As a rule, the earlier Pennsylvania printed forms carry over the horizontal, rectangular form of these foreign prototypes and one does not find the vertical rectangle until after 1815. [450] Then for some reason which is difficult to surmise, taste changed very rapidly and the vertical certificate superceded the horizontal.

Nor did the printed certificate form ever quite recover from this vertical stratification. Even the arrangement of the text followed this new pattern. The rectangular text-block of the 1780's, which had been superceded by the heart-shaped form at Reading for the first time in the 1790's as well as subsequently at Ephrata, Lebanon, and Hanover, was brought back again in the early 19th century, but this time in vertical form. As will be observed from the illustrations, the horizontal certificate form never seriously challenged the vertical after the period 1815-20.

Once this standardization took place, the problem of the chronological sequence becomes even more complicated. The imprint lines become more and more simple, dates are frequently omitted altogether, and the same woodblock designs are used by several printers in different locations. On occasions, one printer will pirate the designs of another and only minute variations in the woodcuts themselves or slight re-arrangements of the position of the cuts on the certificate, will reveal that they originate from different presses. The appearance of the same ornamental borders or small decorative details will ofttimes help in checking the production of various presses.

In the last analysis, the only guide to a chronology is the listing, spelling, and punctuation of the printer's names as given in the imprint line. And in some cases, as may be seen in the *List of Printers*, [451] the firm-name changed so rapidly that it is difficult to keep up with all the variations. Even these variations, however, follow a general pattern that is worth noting because it reflects the spirit of the time so completely. As the Pennsylvania Germans were exposed more and more to the English language, their printers about 1820-25 soon felt the need for issuing Taufschein forms in English, as well as in German. Not to do so

---

[450] See figures 254-262.
[451] See Appendix C.

would be not to keep up with the times; and with the ever-increasing demand for printed forms, it would simply be bad business not to supply them. Changing the language of the text automatically necessitated additional changes in the imprint, and it is these that are of special significance in developing our chronology. We find Johann Ritter changing first to John Ritter and then simply to J. Ritter; Henrich B. Sage changes to Heinrich B. Sage and then to Henry B. Sage. The expression "und Companie" is condensed into "und Comp.," then "u. Comp.," and finally to "& Co." While these name changes or their sequence are not invariable, they clearly indicate the trend.

It is at this particular point that a careful checkup of these names with those which appear in the books and pamphlets issued by these same early Pennsylvania presses becomes invaluable. With minor reservations, this is a reliable yardstick to use in working out some of the more detailed chronological problems. [452]

Having thus defined in a general way some of the salient features of the printed Fraktur forms, the following chronological account will be more easily understood. As has been stated, although the sequence is generally from hand-drawn borders and individual stamps to the completely printed forms, occasional readjustments are made necessary by the appearance of imprint dates that cannot be doubted.

The printed Taufschein field is so extensive and the variations between some of the more common forms so infinitesimal, that we shall only deal with major types here. The variety of imprints issued from any single town and the names of individual printers who were active there, can be secured from the geographical list given in *Appendix C.*

Suffice it to say that, whereas the Ephrata and Reading Taufscheins dominated the field prior to 1825, and the Harrisburg and Allentown ones dominated it after that date, not all the early printing centers were so active in this field. Lancaster, to pick the most obvious example, seems to have virtually ignored it!

For every Lancaster imprint that has come to the author's attention in the past 20 years, there have been perhaps a hundred Reading, Harrisburg, or Allentown ones. While no obvious explanation for this situation presents itself, two factors may have contributed towards it.

---

452 See Appendix C.

First of all, the nearby Ephrata press certainly supplied sufficient forms in the earlier period so as to make a large issue at Lancaster unnecessary and, secondly, the preponderance of Mennonites and other Sects in the area no doubt favored the production of Vorschriften over Taufscheins. [453]  Although it could be argued as a possible third explanation that the Lancaster Taufscheins may not bear an imprint, this would be most unlikely, especially in the late 18th century or early 19th century period.  As a matter of fact, there are relatively few printed Taufscheins of any period that lack imprints, so that there are only a limited number of possibilities to choose from.  It is odd, however, that with the large number of books and pamphlets issued in Lancaster during the early period, there are not more Taufscheins known.

Easton and York, on the extreme peripheries of the Pennsylvania German region, offer similar problems.  Whereas a fairly large quantity of printed Taufscheins was produced at nearby Hanover in the 1790's, only a single dated York imprint has come to the author's attention and that is a very late one.  A number of unmarked certificates for persons born in Dauphin and Northumberland Counties defy classification thus far.

### The Formative Period, 1784-1800
### Ephrata and Reading

The earliest printed Taufschein forms are of special interest for the study of Fraktur because of their close associations with the first hand-illuminated pieces.  As has been pointed out, they actually flourished side by side and the work of early decorators like Otto, Speyer, and Krebs is seen far more often on these early printed Taufscheins than by itself.

In this Formative Period, in fact, it is not always possible to distinguish between printer and decorator, so intimate is their relationship.  And since the expression "Verfertigt von" was not introduced until about 1790, the appearance of a printed name on the certificate cannot be identified beyond question as either that of the decorator or printer.  Hence, while we can work back from the motifs and styles of decorators like Otto, Speyer, and Krebs as they are found in later certificates, the identity of Henrich Dulheuer is less easily explained.

------

[453] H. W. Villee apparently produced Taufscheins but not in great numbers, as they only appear rarely in the collections studied.

HENRICH DULHEUER's Taufscheins are composed of the same border blocks that appear in Otto's, and the dates of his subjects are in the same period. The only early mention of Dulheuer to date is that in 1786 he was described as a newspaper printer in Baltimore. [454] Whether his Taufschein forms were issued before, during, or after this time, is not clear. [455] They certainly are not found as frequently as Otto's, only a half dozen having come to the author's attention. In view of the great preponderance of Otto's Taufscheins and his early activity as a decorator, the writer has been inclined to accept him as the originator of the famous border blocks, and Dulheuer as an imitator. All of the examples which have turned up with the Dulheuer imprint are Birth and Baptismal forms of this one type, whereas Otto's name appears on three different varieties.

HENRICH OTTO's woodcut border blocks, which are the trademark of his printed Taufscheins, Irrgartens, and Haus-Segens, exerted a tremendous influence upon both printed and hand-written Fraktur. Although their earliest dated appearance seems to be in 1784, Otto's bird blocks were imitated by printers down into the 19th century, and his famous "parrot on a tulip branch" became the favorite motif of subsequent Fraktur decorators, both hand-drawn and printed. His "textile" block was less popular and has appeared only on forms decorated very simply by Friederich Speyer. On occasion, he himself employed *only* this textile block, and filled in the remaining three borders *by hand* in his characteristic bird and flower style.

For the most part, however, the Otto style is a printed style, and far outnumbers his hand-written examples. A few of his printed forms, such as that of his daughter, Anna Barbara, show his typical writing and schnörkel in red ink, and even employ enlarged capital letters for

---

[454] In the *Maryland Journal and Baltimore Advertiser* for June 16, 1786, reference is made to Henry Dulhaier [sic], who published a Baltimore *Deutsche Zeitung*. According to Clarence S. Brigham in his monumental two-volume *History and Bibliography of American Newspapers, 1690-1820*, (1947), "no copy of this paper has been located, nor is its name known." It would appear, however, that Dulheuer did publish the first German language newspaper in Baltimore, Maryland, and the second in that state.

[455] See figure 33. Also Shoemaker, *op. cit.*, on Dulheuer. Cunz, Dieter, *The Maryland Germans, A History*. Princeton, N.J.: Princeton University Press, 1948. Pp. 167-168. More recently, Shoemaker, in the *Pennsylvania Dutchman*, III, 17 (February 1, 1952), 1, stated "Henry Dulheuer was the first printer in America who imprinted his name on his *taufscheins*," but this could not be proved at the present time.

the names of the subjects. [456]   When the textile block is missing at the
bottom of a certificate, Otto frequently finishes off the piece with the
same "ground work" we found in his hand-drawn Frakturs.

Only two printed dates have appeared on these Otto Taufschein
forms: 1784 and 1786.   Corresponding Geistlicher Irrgartens with Otto
borders were printed in 1784 and 1785, [457] as well as in 1788; [458] Christlicher Haus-Segen forms were issued in 1785. [459]   Several of his Taufscheins also have the birth-date figures 178- printed, so that Otto's forms
can unquestionably be assigned to this decade.   Whether any were actually
issued in the 1770's cannot be proved although, as we have seen, he decorated a book in 1772 and published a poem in the same year. [460]

Otto's name appeared in three different places on these Taufscheins. [461]   At first it supplanted the date 1784, just above the textile
block in large type with the word "Von" just above it.   When the textile
block was transferred to the top of the page, his name was printed in
smaller block type in the lower right corner between the Baptismal hymn
and the floral border.   Finally it is found in the lower right margin
in even smaller type either with or without the "Von."   In some of these
the textile block has vanished completely, in others it is replaced by
an angel's head, and in still others both of these Otto motifs have disappeared leaving only the two right and left border blocks.   In one or
two of these latter examples, the missing top and bottom blocks have
been filled in by Krebs, Speyer, or other decorators.

The last appearance of this Otto Taufschein form took place in the
late 1790's and early 1800's, although the name of the printer is unknown to us.   Copying Otto's bird blocks just as they occur on the certificate, this later Taufschein shows each of the birds reversed from right
to left.   As a result of this alteration, instead of facing inward towards
the text of the certificate, they face outwards away from the text. [462]
The blocks are poorly executed and very crude imitations of Otto's or-

---

[456] See figures 188a-b, 238; also Color Plate IV.
[457] See figures 189 and 38.
[458] See figure 131.
[459] See figure 190.
[460] Evans, Charles, *American Bibliography* (1903), p. 328, "Ein geistlich Lied
auf Paul Springs Selbstmord. . . (*Philadelphia:* gedruckt bey Henrich Miller,
1772).
[461] See figure 188; also Color Plate IV.
[462] See figure 239.

·iginals. In the place of the textile block at the top, a crude angel head
·or Sophia is introduced in large size, or else an American eagle. The
latter is a remarkably early use of this patriotic device on a certificate,
for the numerals "17—" are actually printed with the text. One example
with the Sophia head, by contrast, has the date "18—" printed on it.
With one exception, and this should be carefully noted, these pseudo-Otto
·certificates were all filled out in Friederich County, Marland [sic]!

An occasional vertical Taufschein with similar crudely executed
·woodblocks turns up now and then from York County, suggesting the
transfer of Otto ideas from Lancaster County *westward* towards the
·Susquehanna River and *southward* into Maryland.

Taufscheins with simple, rectangular text-blocks at the center were
also the earliest form issued from the Reading presses. [463] While it is
impossible to date these accurately because no imprint dates occur, the
·decorated borders by Speyer and Krebs suggest that they must have
followed the Ephrata ones by a few years. They are printed in finer
type and enclosed within a very delicate border. [464] While many of
these are not signed, quite a few have the names of Friederich Speyer or
Friedrich Krebs printed just inside the lower right corner. Two examples signed in Friederich Speyer's handwriting have come to the
author's attention, [465] but none signed by Krebs. The borders seem to
be decorated either in Speyer's usual style, or in Krebs earliest "line
and dot" technique. One by Speyer employs hand-written imitations of
Otto's bird blocks on either side and another by Krebs, of later date,
shows one of the first appearances of the large confronted parrots so
characteristic of his later period. His use of this motif here is awkward,
·because it was designed to fill the larger spaces available on the "Heart
form" Certificate which had already been developed at Reading about
1789.

Rectangular text-blocks, with bordering woodcuts reminiscent of
·Otto, continued in favor at Carlisle as late as 1812, [466] as well as at
·Chambersburg to the West. Simple rectangular text-forms similar to
·those produced in Reading for Johann Valentin Schuller appeared at

---

463 See figures 191 and 195.
464 See figures 191 and 195.
465 See figure 191.
466 See figure 242.

Frederick, Maryland, under the imprint of C. T. Melsheimer, [467] while in Lebanon, Pa., Joseph Schnee and J. Hartman were reducing the text-area even smaller to make way for bold woodcuts of kneeling Angels, Saints, butterflies and fruits in the borders. [468] One of the latest of these horizontal forms to appear, was published at Hanover in 1825, by D. P. Lange, but by this time elsewhere the simple rectangular form had already passed away as well as the heart-shaped horizontal form. From now on, the vertical Taufschein was the thing, even when it still contained reminiscences of Otto's 18th century blocks and was published by William Gunckel at Germantown. *Ohio!* [469]

### Heart-Shaped Taufscheins

The second step of major importance in the development of the printed Taufschein took place in Reading about 1789 with the creation of the *heart-shaped form*. This new idea took hold immediately and was taken up not only by the printers in other locales, but by the manu-script decorators as well. These heart-shaped certificates were published in large quantity during the 1790's and held their popularity down into the 1830's and 1840's. With their large central heart containing the text and two smaller hearts holding baptismal hymns, they provided an ideal composition for the *horizontal* Taufschein and allowed sufficient space for the addition of attractive border motifs, whether hand-drawn, stamped, applied, or printed. This format was so pleasing to the Penn-sylvania Germans that only the development of the 3rd printed Tauf-schein form about 1820, the "Angel Taufschein," with its return to vertical shape and fully-printed borders was able to supplant it.

The Reading printers completely dominated this second phase of the Taufschein story and their most famous decorators, Speyer and Krebs played prominent roles. While it is true that Reading forms were also decorated by other Fraktur artists, they are few indeed in comparison to the large numbers supplied by Krebs particularly. About nine out of every ten Reading certificates issued between 1790 and 1810, regardless of printer, are "Verfertigt von F. Krebs." One wonders, in fact, how it is that so little has been known about Krebs as an individual when his work was so popular. Certainly the variety of techniques he

---

467 See figure 243.
468 See figures 244-245.
469 See figure 247.

developed to meet the constantly increasing demand for Taufscheins shows no want of originality. And since some of these printed forms showed only Krebs' name, one might even wonder if he could have printed some of these *himself*. But, as we have seen, the *Adler* Press in Reading, according to their account books, did supply him with tremendous quantities of printed Taufschein forms [470]

Krebs' Taufscheins during the 1790's were produced under four different firm imprints: (1) Barton und Jungmann, (2) Jungmann und Gruber, (3) Gottlob Jungman, and (4) J. Schneider u. Co. The sequence of these is typical of what we shall find much more commonly in the 19th century, where a firm name will change six or eight times, and the wording of its imprint line even more often  This sequence of printers does not seem to have bothered Krebs in the least, however, for he worked with each of them in his various styles. One finds some of these imprints with his simple early style, others with his bird or mermaid stamps reminiscent of Otto, and still others in his mature Fraktur style. Although most of his applied and tonal background pieces date after 1800 when only Krebs' name and the imprint date appear, [471] one tonal example dated 1797 from J Schneider u. Co, has come to the author's attention. During the period from 1800 until 1810, Krebs continues his main styles of Fraktur illumination and since a great many Taufschein forms subsequently bear only his name and no date, it is possible from the birth and baptismal dates on these that he might have continued producing these right up to his death in 1815. Only Krebs' initials "F.K." appear on some of the later Taufschein forms decorated by him. Several other Berks County decorators of this period are identified only as Ph. Meng (1800), J.H. (1803), and F.B. (1820).

Krebs' close associate in the decoration of Heart Forms in the Berks and Dauphin County area was Friederich Speyer. His chief motifs — flowers, parrots, lions, mermaids, crowns, and angel heads — show the influence of Otto pieces although he added to them his own figures of a pair of Angels or Women [472] While not as frequently seen as Krebs' works, they are more primitive in their drawing and rely heavily on the primary colors. The fact that some of them have two numerals of their dates printed in, 17—, suggests that the remainder very

---

[470] See foot-note 409.
[471] See figure 91.
[472] See figures 192 and 248.

probably date after 1800. While no printer's name is imprinted on any of these, the later ones have the name "Friederich Speyer" printed at the bottom of the heart.

The Heart Form developed so effectively at Reading, was soon adopted by printers in Easton to the east and in Ephrata, Lebanon, Lancaster, and Hanover to the west. Through the first two decades of the 19th century, the Heart Form held the spotlight in the Taufschein field, and the printers of each of these forms developed his own individual designs. Although the Easton printers, C. J. Hütter and H. und W. Hütter, followed very closely the Reading ones which left the borders free for hand-drawn decorations, the Ephrata, Lebanon, and Hanover printers filled the entire border with flower and bird woodcuts. Each of them developed a form that is different from the others and which can readily be identified without even reading the imprint line. Both technically and aesthetically, these all-printed forms have much to commend them.

At Ephrata, John and Samuel Bauman produced most attractive and beautiful Heart Taufscheins. By 1800, and probably earlier, John Bauman was printing on a large scale Heart Taufscheins which featured a pair of parrots at the top and two pairs of robins at the bottom. [473] Occasionally these turn up printed in *red and green* inks rather than black, and in this form provide one of the most attractive of all printed Fraktur specimens. These bird and flower blocks are boldly cut, and their capital initial "D" as well as the "ground-line" on which the robins stand, still echo the best traditions of Otto's hand-written Fraktur.

During the first decade of the 19th century, John Bauman altered his "robin" form and produced still another composition with "springing deer." [474] It was this Taufschein form which became the trademark of Samuel Bauman and which was evidently extremely popular in Lancaster County down into the 1820's. Fraktur decorators constantly borrowed ideas for their hand-written certificates from this "springing deer" composition, and even as late as 1852 we find John A. Landis suddenly employing Samuel Bauman's bird-on-branch motif. [475]

At Hanover, as early as 1798, W. Lepper and E. Stettinius were producing Heart Forms of great charm and originality. The lobes of

---

[473] See figures 86 and 250.
[474] See figure 251.
[475] See figure 223.

the large heart are slightly squared and the texts of the two smaller
hearts are printed diagonally. [476]   The side borders and top each consist
of a single woodblock, in a manner reminiscent of Otto's printed forms.
The luxuriant leaves, flowers, and urns create an effect of great richness,
particularly because so much of the paper background is covered.   On
occasion, bits of handwork are also introduced.

Of the heart-shaped Taufscheins, the Lebanon imprints of J. Stöver
are perhaps the latest.   In general effect, they are somewhat similar to
the Hanover forms, but the two could never be confused.   In contrast to
the solid woodcut of the Lepper & Stettinius Taufscheins, Stöver's are
thin and show a great deal of background between the vines. [477]   Although three different Stöver types have come to the writer's attention,
they all contain the usual flat-top Heart shape which was peculiar to Stöver,
and they differ only in very minor rearrangements of the text-blocks.

It should be noted that F. W. Schöpflin at Chambersburg also produced a few Taufscheins with heart centers, but the heart is so small
and the shape so pointed that they really belong (as far as the accompanying motifs are concerned certainly), to a still later period.   Their
composition and individual woodcuts are entirely representative of the
last phase of the printed Taufschein, the "Angel Certificate."   In fact,
the corner blocks of angels and fruits are borrowed from a vertical Hanover certificate of the Angel type.

### Angel Certificates

Just as the *horizontal* Taufschein with rectangular text-block dominated the last two decades of the 18th century and the *heart-form* the
first two decades of the 19th century, so the vertical Angel-type dominated the period from 1815 to 1875.   Even the subsequent development
of the stipple-engraved certificate and the Currier lithographed forms
had no appreciable effect upon its popularity.   The Angel-type, in its
manifold forms, represents the highest point in terms of production of
the printed Fraktur, and it is strange indeed that no detailed study of
them has ever been made.   For although they were mass-produced, their
wide variety offers ample field for serious investigation.

---

[476] See figure 252.
[477] See figure 253.

Whether the whole idea originated from the hand-drawn angels of illuminators like Speyer, or whether it developed independently, is not clear. Suffice it to say that about 1815, we begin to observe a complete change in the printed Taufschein. In the first place, the horizontal composition of the heart-shaped forms is supplanted by a new vertical composition. Secondly, the birds and flowers which dominated both the horizontal and heart-shaped forms are replaced by the motif of a pair of confronted angels. Thirdly, although most of these Taufscheins bear an imprint and date, the illuminator or decorator is rarely mentioned. This does not mean that these forms were no longer colored by hand, but simply that the decorator no longer played the important role he once had. G. S. Peters at Harrisburg even resorted to the application of colors by using *color-stencils* on his Angel Taufscheins, but he seems to have been one of very few printers who employed this method.

The quantity of these Angel Certificates and the variety of Angels represented, is surprising indeed. As the writer proceeded to record some of the larger collections of printed Taufscheins, he was forced to enlarge his original classification of Angel-types from four to seven. This is not surprising when we stop to consider that they were produced over a period of more than 60 years by printers in almost every large town in the Pennsylvania German area. The characteristics which identify these seven types are best seen from the illustrations and need not be described in detail here. Each of them is distinct, and adequately expresses the spirit of its time. As the Victorian style took hold more and more, the gradual loss of vigor from the old Pennsylvania German motifs is nowhere more graphically seen than in these representations of Angels.

It is interesting to observe the development of new printing firms in other towns. We have seen how Ephrata and Reading were reenforced by Easton, Lebanon, Lancaster, and Hanover. These, in turn, are now dominated by very active presses in Allentown and in Harrisburg. While Reading, Allentown, and Harrisburg played key roles in the mid-19th century, a glance at the list of printers in *Appendix C* will show what happened after 1830. And with this rapid expansion extending even beyond the boundaries of the State into Maryland and Virginia, Ohio and Indiana, the force of the printed Taufschein was gradually spent.

For the sake of clarity, an example of each type of Angel is illustrated and the general style characterized. It is difficult to assign most of them to a single locale, however, since the woodcuts not only were copied by other printers, but the printers themselves moved from one town to another. It is not at all unusual to have a Taufschein form cease production abruptly in one town and begin just as abruptly in another, or, to have a certain form appear in one town and then be pirated for the next 10 years by printers in adjoining towns.

### Angel I — Reading — Ritter

Reading, the source of so many innovations in Fraktur history, seems also to have been the first to introduce the Angel Taufschein. Having popularized the Heart-shaped Taufschein with so many technical improvements, it now took the lead over Allentown, Lancaster, and Harrisburg in the new vertical Taufscheins. Priority for Reading appears to be established by a certificate that recently came to the author's attention in the Elie Nadelman Collection, which bears at the bottom the inscription "Verfertigt von Gottfried Miller bey Bethlehem *1814*," but the Taufschein is a Reading Angel I form. [478] Henrich Ebner's similar Allentown forms are dated 1817, 1818, 1820, and 1821; H. W. Villee's Lancaster forms are undated, but have Gabriel Miesse's Angel blocks (he was only born in 1807); Gleim und Wiestling's Harrisburg forms are undated and Johann S. Wiestling's bear the dates 1824 and 1826. In the latter the angels are shifted from right to left, both as regards the bird and wreath in their hands as well as the shading of their garments, thereby suggesting the possibility that they may be later copies.

The chief producer of these Reading forms was the firm of John Ritter Throughout its lengthy activity, the angel with the bird was constantly on the left side of the Taufschein and apparently Johann Walter and A. Puwelle, who also printed some of these, followed Ritter's form very closely. Only a minor change in a border design or a small vignette block reveals any development in this design, whether Ritter. Walter, or Puwelle. Even Gleim und Wiestling's first productions at Harrisburg show only the enclosure of the two upper baptismal verses in heart-shaped rather than rectangular blocks.

---

478 See figure 254

Next to Angel IV — the Moser and Peters type from Carlisle and Harrisburg — this Reading Angel is the most commonly-seen printed form. It is easily distinguishable by the brilliant colored patterns which frequently appear on the angel's costumes, around the putti at the top, and on the foliage of the two bird blocks at the bottom. When attractively colored, it is one of the most pleasing of the printed Taufschein forms.

### Angel II — Hanover — Lange

These Angels are quite different from all those used elsewhere in that they are a *matched pair* of figures holding wreaths; the other figure holding a bird does not appear. The writer has always referred to them as the "graceful" angels, for they almost seem to dance quietly across the certificate and their delicate figures, in contrast to the heavier "Dutch" ones of the other Angel forms, seem doubly graceful by comparison. [479]

Angel II was introduced as early as 1817 at Hanover by Dan. Phil. Lange, who issued them in German in 1818, 1819, and 1822. In 1825 he issued a late horizontal one in German with these same motifs [480] and the following year, 1826, another similar one in English. Lange's vertical forms were taken over by John S. Wiestling in Harrisburg and re-issued with a complete change of border blocks. As in the case of Angel I, Wiestling enclosed the baptismal verses in heart forms; Lange's eagle block at top center is remodeled, one of his two small putti is moved from the top-right side of the certificate to the bottom-right side, and the other to the center of the certificate; and Lange's two birds at the bottom are replaced with fruit designs. Instead of Lange's six blocks of type, there are now only three: two small ones at the top, and the main Taufschein textblock. Wiestling's changes did not alter Lange's form radically and the original charm of the graceful angels remains unimpaired.

### Angel III — Reading — Sages, Roths

With this Taufschein form, developed at Reading by the Sages, we return once more to the confronted angel figures with wreath and bird. The bird is now in its more common position at the right and the wreath

---

[479] See figure 255.
[480] See figure 246.

at the left has become a spray of flowers. Angel III is a logical advance from the more simplified form of Angel I. The Angels are more angular in their treatment and they are now supported by other decorative designs of great interest. [481] At the top center, an excellent woodcut of the Baptism of Christ signed by "Smith" appears. This is the only appearance of his name known to the author, but it is quite possible in view of the unity of all of the woodcuts on this Taufschein form, that all of them are by Smith. Of equal interest on this Baptism scene is the Pavilion-and-Statue woodblock in the center of the certificate. Even the single bird motifs in the lower right and left corners have been simplified in a very original way. At any rate, this Taufschein form has a most interesting assortment of woodcuts and, with the addition of occasional decorative borders, is one of the most attractive and unusual forms produced.

Angel III seems to be very closely limited to the Reading presses of Henrich (Heinrich) B. Sage, G. Adolph Sage, and Daniel Roths. As far as can be ascertained, none of these interesting new woodcuts has ever appeared elsewhere on printed Taufscheins.

### Angel IV — Carlisle — Moser u. Peters

With this Taufschein form, we reach the zenith in mass production. Of all the printed forms, this is the one *most commonly seen* and for two very good reasons. In the first place, once Moser and Peters had developed it at Carlisle, they employed color stencils to apply the two colors they required for completing it: red and yellow. Secondly, once they put a large number of these Taufscheins into circulation, this design was imitated and promoted by three or four other printers with the result that it became extremely popular. Since some of these were to the west of the Pennsylvania German area and others to the east, Angel IV thoroughly permeated the whole eastern Pennsylvania region.

Like Reading Angels I and III, this design presents two confronted angels between which is the vertical textblock of the Taufschein. [482] The angel holding a bird is at the right and the one with a wreath is at the left. Beneath each of these is a woodcut with two birds and these, too, face one another. Between them are three small bouquets of flowers

---

481 See figure 256.
482 See figure 257; also figures 94, 95, and 292.

surmounting two baskets of flowers. An ornamental border finishes off this very neat and compact design.

Whereas G. S. Peters' Harrisburg press was the chief center for the production of these in the west, the Allentown firm of Blumer took up Angel IV and produced it for more than 30 years. Moser and Peters introduced it in 1825 and 1826 at Carlisle, and when Peters moved to Harrisburg, he took it up in earnest, issuing it many times in English as well as in German. Some of Peters' Taufscheins bear the dates 1829 and 1830. When Blumer at Allentown took it up in the early 1830's, he enlarged and dramatized the eagle block at the top by introducing a sunburst effect as a background. he added a heavy ornamental border around the text, and he moved the baptismal verses into a central block at the bottom to replace Peters' bouquets and baskets of flowers. As Blumer issued and re-issued his Taufscheins. and as his firm changed again and again, he occasionally altered the outside border of the certificate and exchanged the angels from side to side, so that they face away from each other and away from the central block. The birds at the bottom, however, always remained the same.

Later in the same decade, this identical Angel IV was issued at New-Berlin, at Bath (1838), and at Millgrove, with occasional changes. In those printed by G. Miller at New-Berlin, the composition of the Taufschein remains substantially the same. the woodcut at the top center being the only noticeable addition. Those forms produced by S. Siegfried at Bath in 1838 and by Sam. Siegfried at Millgrove. on the other hand, show major changes. A new woodcut of Love. Hope, and Faith, replaces the eagle at the top center and, in the work of the latter printer, a large woodcut of the Baptism of Christ appears in the bottom center, with text on either side. In all of these variations of the original Moser and Peters Angel IV, however, the one angel with bird still appears at the right side and the other, with a wreath, at the left

A change of technique also distinguishes the early western productions of Moser and Peters at Carlisle and of Peters at Harrisburg from the farther-east forms of the Blumers at Allentown. of Miller at New-Berlin, and of Samuel Siegfried at Bath and at Millgrove Whereas the former used *color stencils* almost exclusively, the latter printers did all their *coloring by hand*. And the Allentown forms, with bold horizontal patterns painted across the skirts of the Angels and blazing top

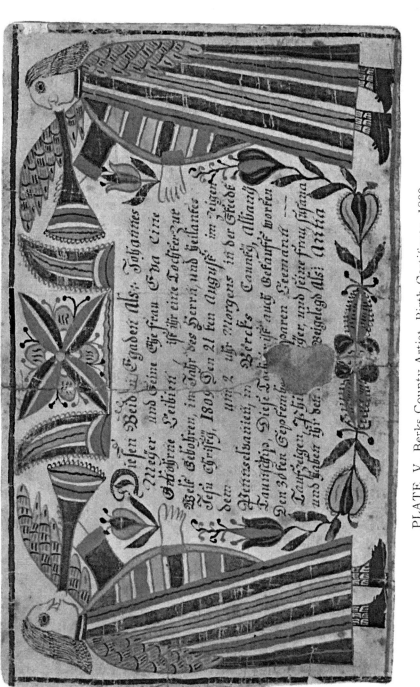

PLATE V. Berks County Artist, Birth Certificate, 1809
*Edward W. Schlechter collection, Allentown, Pa.*

feathers on the birds, carry one step further the color work of Reading Angel I, thereby providing one of the most startling phases of later Fraktur decoration.

### Angel V — Reading Grotesque — Baab und Döbler

Always ready to supply a new Taufschein form or remodel an old one, Reading was not content to rest on her laurels after creating Angels I and III. Angel I had enjoyed tremendous popularity, it is true, but even before the end of the third decade of the 19th century a new Angel form had been created in Reading which, while it is not attractive aesthetically, was copied by printers of other localities. Certainly its grotesque, hatchet-faced angels could not be confused with any of our other varieties.

Angel V follows the plan of the confronted angels and seems to have been issued by Baab and Döbler about 1830. Single birds seated on branches beneath these two figures face one another and at the top, a large seated figure of a woman holds a large heart in her outstretched hand. [483] Aside from the fact that the two angels now bear different symbols and the ornamental borders change from time to time, this Taufschein remained fairly intact even after being copied by printers of Lancaster, Orwigsburg, and Pottsville.

Why Baab and Döbler's rather unattractive Reading Taufschein should have enjoyed such popularity, is difficult to understand. Nevertheless, it was copied in Lancaster by H. W. Villee, in Orwigsburg by Jacob Thoma and by Thoma and May, and in Pottsville by J. T. Werner and John P. Bertram. Werner, as a matter of fact, issued it in English as well as in German. In the English version, Werner adopted a different woodcut for the top center place and this same subject was employed by John P. Bertram in both his Angel V Taufschein forms. The relative thinness of the design of this Taufschein and the delicate character of the ornamental borders are indicative of its late origin.

### Angel VI — Reading — Ritter, Kessler

Last of the Angel types to originate in Reading is this Taufschein with the Angels facing outwards, the right one holding the usual bird

---

[483] See figure 258.

and the left one a wreath. The normal double-bird motif appears in the lower left and right corners and at the top, the favorite Reading putti is turned from left to right. [484]

Angel VI is definitely a transitional form, for while employing the format and motifs of the earlier Reading Taufscheins, it has completely lost its angular Folk Art character. Not only are the figures of the Angels softened with a kind of Victorian glamour, but even the double birds and the putti have lost much of their original strength. Typical of the entry of Victorian flavor into the Taufschein is the very literal introduction of the motif of the open Bible with the dove above it.

.    Oddly enough, John Ritter, who is responsible for those very strong Angel I Taufscheins, seems to have introduced this last of the great Reading forms. This accounts, no doubt, for the double bird motif at the lower corners rather than the single. Carl Kessler and the "Eagle" Buchstohr seem to be the chief source of this type of Taufschein, however, only very few Ritter forms having appeared to date. The "Eagle" Buchstohr was by far the greatest producer of them, for even an English version was finally published.

Most of the Angel VI Taufscheins that have turned up bear dates in the 1860's and 1870's.

### Angel VII — Allentown — Leisenring

The last and most Victorian of the Angel types was produced by E. D. Leisenring and Co. at Allentown, Pa. While the two large figures of angels at either side are still retained, instead of holding the usual bird and wreath, they now display between them a huge scroll on which is inscribed the main text of the Taufschein. [485] While three stanzas of the baptismal hymn may still be found at the bottom center and birds appear in upper right and left, the whole spirit of the Certificate has changed. A realistic representation of a contemporary Baptismal Scene occupies the top center of the certificate and smaller scenes of the Baptism of Christ and the Holy Kinship fill the lower left and right corners respectively. The introduction of a series of columns and arches to create an architectural setting, and the richness of textures in the various costumes both reveal the late origin of this Taufschein form.

---

[484] See figure 259.
[485] See figure 260.

The production of this certificate seems limited to Allentown, the earlier ones bearing the imprint of E. D. Leisenring and Co., and the later ones Leisenring, Trexler and Co.'s "Welt Bote" press and Trexler & Hartzell. There is little doubt that they must date from the 1860's and 1870's. Only German texts have appeared thus far.

Additional Angel forms exist, such as those of A. H. Senseman at Easton, but they do not seem to exist in large quantities. Of if they do, they are very closely held by families. They apparently date from the mid-19th century.

### Miscellaneous Taufscheins

Other vertical Taufscheins, like the Pottsville, Stroudsburg, Sumneytown, and York examples, but *without* Angels, were also issued in the 1830's to 1860's though they are only rarely seen. For the most part they are "thin" in design and retain little of the real Taufschein flavor. Possible exceptions to this are a fine H. W. Villee form issued at Lancaster, and an elaborate four-color form produced by Theo. F. Scheffer at Harrisburg.

The Villee form, [486] with its heavy ornamental border and large color areas around the central textblock, introduces a whole new set of motifs of which the *Baptism of Christ* is the only familiar one. None the less, it retains much of the character of the earlier forms.

The Scheffer form, [487] by contrast, is a complete departure from all previous designs. An almost theatrical composition is achieved by placing large figures of Prophets within niches at each side where Angels previously were used, and a galaxy of smaller figures of Saints and Apostles at the top. A flat, tracery-like geometric border betrays the mid-19th century character of the form. By contrast with the Villee form also, which appears only rarely, the Scheffer form is most common and ranks second only to the Moser and Peters Angel IV forms in popularity.

The vertical Taufschein, as we have seen, dominated the printed Taufschein field from about 1815 to 1865, and extends the story of printed Fraktur forms well down into the late 19th century. That it did not have the entire field to itself, however, will be clear from the number of Tauf-

---

[486] See figure 261.
[487] See figure 262.

scheins executed in two other contemporary techniques: *stipple-engraving* and *lithography*. The story of the development of these two varieties of illumination will complete our panorama of the Fraktur style in eastern Pennsylvania.

## STIPPLE-ENGRAVED TAUFSCHEINS (c.1820 - c.1845)

We have already seen from the quantity of Printed Certificates issued from the city of Reading and the large number of individual printers who produced them, the great pre-eminence of Reading as a center for Fraktur work. Granted the advantage of mass production via the printing press, considerable handwork continued to appear in the borders of these forms, so that Reading could easily claim the distinction of being the *most active* Fraktur center, whether printed or not. A sample survey of Counties and Townships represented amply confirms this fact, especially since the author's photographs do not include anywhere near the full quantity of printed forms seen.

Even before the fullest height of the printed production was reached, Reading contributed another new technique to the field of Fraktur: *stipple-engraving*. This medium, moreover, seems never to have been employed elsewhere. Though a completely different technique, it is a step beyond the stamped, applied, and cutout types developed there and is a logical further refinement of the printed Fraktur. The author has already referred in previous publications to the stipple-engraved certificates of the chief proponent of this school, *Carl Friederich Egelmann*, as culminating items "in point of artistic development and technique." [488] Although engraved, the flowing hand of Egelmann recaptured in many ways the refinement of the finest hand-drawn Fraktur. In the works of *Gabriel Miesse*, the second member of this same stipple-engraved school and probable pupil of Egelmann, this refinement is replaced by a faltering and somewhat crude technique. Miesse's technical shortcomings and choice of subject-matter, as a matter of fact, led Rudolf Hommel to characterize him as a "copyist." [489] Additional facts to support this contention became apparent as the author developed and enlarged the list of Miesse's known engravings given in the following pages. Oddly

---

[488] Shelley, *op. cit.*, p. 101.
[489] Hommel, Rudolf P., 'Gabriel Miesse, Copyist', *Antiques* (May, 1943), p. 225.

enough, neither Egelmann nor Miesse are familiar to students of engraving, so that a résumé of their known works is in order here.

CARL FRIEDERICH EGELMANN (1782-1860), engraver and teacher
has, until recently, scarcely been known. [490] We lacked the simplest biographical facts of place and date of birth, such as we had in Miesse's case
18 years ago. The only mention of Egelmann in lists of engravers was
in the biographical portion of Stauffer (1907), [491] where he was identified as "C. F. *Eng*elmann." [492] Stauffer cited Egelmann's later *Last
Supper Certificate* in English [493] and characterized it as "an elaborate,
curiously designed, and crudely engraved Birth and Baptismal Certificate,
published about 1814 . . ." He went on to say that "the design follows
closely similar works emanating from the community of Seventh Day
Baptists, at Ephrata . . ." a comparison which was far-fetched to say the
least, except for the pictorial subjects contained in the *Christian ABC
Book,* which was after all a special case and can hardly be called characteristic of the Ephrata work as a whole.

In Mantle Fielding's *Supplement to Stauffer* (1917), the first and
only list of Egelmann's work appeared. [494] The following account of
his engraved Fraktur is based upon that list supplemented by additional
information gleaned from examples seen or photographed by the author.
Those three items described by Fielding in 1917 are so marked.

That Egelmann was active in Reading was suggested to the author
by the fact that the examples found in the first Fraktur collections photographed in 1937-38 were chiefly Birth and Baptismal Certificates filled
out in Berks County. This supposition was strengthened by his engraved *Copybook* which, although no place of printing is mentioned on
the Titlepage, contains a sample Promissory Note form marked "Reading," and it was subsequently confirmed by his later Certificate form
which bears the legend "Eng'd and sold by C. F. Egelmann on Pennsmount near Reading." [495]    As we shall see, he also engraved the illus-

---

[490] *Historical Review of Berks County,* XIII, 4 (July, 1948), 99; also see XIV,
2 (January, 1949), p 46 for portrait of Egelmann.
[491] Stauffer, D. McN., *American Engravers upon Copper and Steel,* I (1907),
p. 80.
[492] Drepperd, Carl W., in article on Miesse, *Antiques* (October, 1942), spelled
it Egel*man.*
[493] Stauffer, *op. cit,* I, p. 80.
[494] Fielding, Mantle, *American Engravers upon Copper and Steel.* Supplement
to David McNeely Stauffer's *American Engravers.* Philadelphia, 1917, p. 105.
[495] Mt. Penn, now a suburb of Reading itself, see also figure 271.

trations for at least two books printed in 1824 and 1830 by Johann Ritter, perhaps Reading's greatest Taufschein printer.

Aside from Egelmann's location in the city of Reading which had been the center of production for printed Taufscheins, another feature of his work is noteworthy. Like Ritter, the Baumanns at Ephrata, Blumer at Allentown, and G. S. Peters at Harrisburg, Egelmann found it to his advantage to supply certificate forms in *both* German and English. His *Copybook* of Fraktur writing contained instructions not only in German and English, but also occasional admonitions and proverbs in *French!* The reasons for Egelmann's bilingual nature are easily explained now that more information about him is available.

According to the biographical sketch published in the Bicentennial Issue of *The Historical Review of Berks County* (1948), [496] Carl Friederich Egelmann was born May 12, 1782 in the then Osnabrueck Duchy of Lueneburg, of which King George III of Great Britain was Duke. The Reading engraver's grandfather was sent by England to Holland as ambassador, and Egelmann's father was born there; his mother, Van Der Heide by name, was a Flemish woman. With this language background, and with both parents from titled families, Egelmann's later success in Reading, Pa., as a teacher, musician, astronomer, and mathematician should come as no surprise.

Young Egelmann received a good education, including the study of music, and at the age of 17 was first engaged as a secretary to the Chamberlain of England, then as private secretary. The deaths of his own family, and ultimately of his employer, forced him to seek his fortune elsewhere, and he landed in America in October, 1802.

For two or three years he worked in Baltimore as an apprentice to a coachmaker, while spending his spare time in learning copperplate engraving. In 1808 he married Maria Schoepke and the following winter (1809-10), according to family data, we find him in the role of furniture maker with a "sub-contract to make a dozen chairs for President Madison."

From this time onwards, however, emphasis is rather on teaching and music, and on printing, mathematics, and astronomy. He first taught

---

[496] Based on a Paper by E. E. Hafer, *Charles F. Egelman*, read before the Historical Society of Berks County on December 12, 1922, upon the occasion of the presentation of a portrait of Egelmann by Mrs. Wm. H. Luden.

school in English at Chester in 1810, then he came to Hain's Church, Heidelberg Township, Berks County "to teach German in the parochial school, and to be organist and choir leader. Later, about 1815, he went to Spies' Church in Alsace Township, Berks County, where his duties were the same. While there he made his first almanac calculations."

Shortly thereafter he must have moved to Reading, for in 1821 the first edition of his Fraktur *Copybook* appeared, in 1824 the Ritter *Surveying Book* with his engraved plates, in 1825 his *Southeast View of Reading*, in 1830 the Ritter *Astronomy Book* with his engraved plates, and in 1831 the second edition of his Fraktur *Copybook*.

"From 1834 to 1838, he and a son published a German newspaper, the *Berks County Adler*. About this time he was organist of Trinity Lutheran Church, Reading. Later he sold the newspaper and printing business and quit all business except making almanac calculations, [497] which he continued during the remaining 41 years of his life, until his death which occurred November 30, 1860."

The success of Egelmann's stipple-engraved Fraktur Certificates (c.1810-c.1845) can be measured from the number which have been preserved, which is not large. And copies of his *Copybook* are excessively rare, perhaps only a half dozen have appeared to date. Certainly this mediocre degree of success cannot be blamed upon their artistic quality, for as a draughtsman and composer he was highly gifted. His handwriting, his figure drawing, and his designs as a whole are well beyond any criticism. Several possible explanations come to mind. Is it possible that the Pennsylvania Germans were becoming conscious of a great loss in Egelmann's more sophisticated engravings — loss of much of the Medieval flavor of their block-printed Certificates which they loved so well? Perhaps they also missed the strong, vibrant colors of the block-printed Certificates in Egelmann's stipple-engraved ones, few of which ever seem to have been colored. Or could it be that they found the decidedly European flavor of the Egelmann forms less appealing then the hearts, flowers, and birds, of the more common Pennsylvania German Certificate forms?

Whatever the reason may be, it is safe to say that Egelmann's work has never received the attention it merits, due, no doubt, to the limited

---

[497] Besides being a noted astronomer, he was an expert mathematician and an honorary member of the New England Society of Mathematicians.

quantity available. Its ever-increasing pictorial character, however, prophecies the future development of Taufschein forms which, within two or three decades, in the lithographs of N. Currier, Ig. Kohler, and others, became wholly pictorial.

All of the items in the following list betray strong European influences in their motifs and in their conception, as has been pointed out previously by the author. [498] As is quite apparent from the preceding discussion of motifs and designs, subjects such as the Baptism of Christ, the Ascension, the Last Supper, Paradise Lost and Paradise Found, are not common ones in the Pennsylvania German field. Just what the models were for these Egelmann themes, or for those of Miesse who followed him, is not clear but their ultimate origin in Europe cannot be doubted. The issuing of Egelmann and Miesse Certificates in several varying states also has European connotations:

(1) BIRTH AND BAPTISMAL CERTIFICATE ($11\frac{3}{4}$ x $9\frac{3}{4}$ in.)
Inscribed: "Gezeichnet und gestochen von C. F. Egelmann."
*(Fielding #428)*.

> In the *first state* this form appears without clouds in the sky and without the two seals "LS," but in the *second state* both have been added. [499]
> Although I first dated this Certificate as c.1840, [500] it is no doubt much earlier, probably about 1820, if we can judge from the manuscript dates which appear upon them. Of this handsome design, very few have turned up in full color.

(2) ENGRAVED COPYBOOK FOR THE INSTRUCTION OF YOUTH
Inscribed: "Aufgesetzt und gestochen von Carl Friederich Egelmann." *(Fielding #430)*.

> Like the preceding Certificate, this unusual booklet appears in several states, the first two dated 1821 and a later one dated 1831. This chronology is based upon the engraved dates on the Promissory Note forms given in the book. In the first state, there are less designs on the *Title-page* and 12 pages of text; in the second, the *Title-page* is much more elaborate [501] and four pages of text have been added. A third state contains a total of 21 pages.
>
> Of particular interest is the engraving of the *Scriptorium,* with full instructions how the Fraktur writer should sit,

---

[498] Shelley, *op. cit.,* p. 101.
[499] Compare figures 101 and 270; also Color Plate VI.
[500] Shelley, *op. cit.,* p. 105.
[501] See figures 267-269.

and the correct manner of just how he should hold both his pen and his sheet of paper. [502]   It is interesting to note that half of this page is in German and half in English; a French maxim appears at the bottom.   Actually, the number of pages in each language is nearly equal, with German predominating slightly, of course.

Egelmann even contributed a poem of his own — in English!   This appears in the 1831 second edition only, along with a sampler page of cross-stitch designs.   Neither of these occurs in the 1821 first edition.

While the sequence of pages differs in the various copies examined by the author, each copy includes the following pages:

(1) Titlepage
(2) Ermahnung an die Jugend (instruction)
(3) Fraktur Alphabete
(4) Raum und Zeit
(5) Vom Loewen
(6) Vom Elephanten
(7) A Common Note — A Receipt

The second edition (1831) adds two more engraved subjects:

(8) On the Heavenly Bodys
(9) Sampler Page with Alphabet and Numerals

This Copybook is particularly interesting because, aside from being one of very few printed in Pennsylvania, it not only presents the theoretical teachings of a professional illuminator and teacher, but also presents examples of his theory in completed state.

(3) Surveying Book Illustrated By Egelmann, *1824*
    *Der Bauer als Landmesser,* although published by H. W. Villee at Lancaster, was actually printed in Reading by Johann Ritter in 1824.   Ritter brought in Egelmann to engrave the six diagrammatic plates of instructions inserted at the back of the book.

(4) South East View Of Reading, July *12, 1825* [503]
    (c.14 x 16 in.)
    "Map of Berks County surveyed by H. M. Richards"

    Lower right: "Engraven printed and sold by C. F. Egelman on Pennsmount near Reading."   View appears in upper left corner as vignette for the map.

---

[502] See figures 70 and 71.
[503] Illustrated in the *Historical Review of Berks County,* XIII, 4 (July, 1948), p. 99.

**(5)** ASTRONOMY BOOK ILLUSTRATED BY EGELMANN, *1830*
*Vollständige Erklärung des calendars mit einen fasslichen Unterrichte über die Himmelskörper* by E. L. Walz, printed by Johann Ritter and illustrated with six engraved plates by Egelmann.

How many such volumes as this and the preceding *Surveying Book* were illustrated by Egelmann is difficult to say at this point, but it is interesting to note that the publication of his own *Calendar* with all its calculations begins in this same year and continues until 1839 when he is joined by his son, and thence until his death in 1860.

**(6)** ORIGINAL COPPER PLATE OF POLITICAL BROADSIDE, *1836*
(3 x 5 in.)

"Praesidenten Wahl 1836."
Two groups of supporters, each holding banners reading at left: "Jackson van Buren/ & No Bank" and, at right, "Harrison/ & Equal Right"

**(7)** EGELMAN RECEIPT, APRIL *4, 1837* (5 x 6 in.)

"Received of William Lanks on the/ Subscription of the Berks County/ Egle payment up vollum 11, 44/
Charles F. Egelman"

**(8)** LAST SUPPER BIRTH AND BAPTISMAL CERTIFICATE, *c.1840-50*
Inscribed: "Engd. and sold by C. F. Egelmann on Pennsmount near Reading." *(Fielding #429)*.

The latest of Egelmann's stipple-engraved forms has appeared only in English, no German specimens having come to the author's attention. None has been found in full color, although one specimen printed in dark Prussian blue ink rather than black has appeared. [504]

The *Ascension scene* at the bottom of Item #1 [505] has been moved to the top of this Certificate and a full-sized *Last Supper scene* (the only one I have seen in Pennsylvania German Folk Art), now occupies most of the lower half of the composition. [506]

This Certificate form again seems limited to Berks County. Two states exist, one showing a *plain* tablecloth in the Last Supper scene, and a later one showing a *dotted and shaded* tablecloth.

---

[504] In collection of the Reading Public Museum and Art Gallery.
[505] See figure 270.
[506] See figure 271.

More dramatic angels, the ambitious *Last Supper scene,* and the tablets with *Paradise Lost* and *Paradise Found,* all betray the exaggeration and overstatement of the later period. In the enlarged scale and crowded composition, one misses the delicacy and Fraktur nature of Egelmann's earlier Birth and Baptismal Certificate.

(9) VERBESSERTER CALENDAR, *1843* ( 8 x 6 in. )
    "Gedruckt und zu haben bey J.C.F. Egelman*n,*
    Berechnet von Carl Friderich Egelma*n*
                             Reading, Penn."

(10) LOTTERY TICKET (1½ x 3 in.)

(11) PERPETUAL CALENDAR (12 x 10 in.)
    Printed from the original plate by Egelmann.
    Upper right: "C. F. Egelmann fecit."

(12) ORIGINAL COPPER PLATE OF THE VERBESSERTER CALENDAR
    (4 x 4½ in.)
    Not signed or dated.
    Labeled at top: "Egelmans Improved Almanac."

(13) BUST PORTRAIT OF GEORGE WASHINGTON *(after Peale)*
    Not signed or dated.   Hand-colored engraving.

GABRIEL MIESSE (1807-1886), on the basis of what has survived at least, may have been a more versatile, but less gifted, artist than Egelmann. While contemporary with Egelmann, his work is certainly less accomplished and the fact that he even copied his contemporary's early Birth and Baptismal Certificate form so closely, suggests the possibility that he might have been a young student of Egelmann's. [507] Although Miesse was re-discovered only in 1942, somewhat more is known of his life and works than Egelmann's. In contrast to the latter, neither Stauffer in 1907 nor Mantle Fielding in 1917 have one word to say about him. The existence of the Fraktur forms he produced, seems to have been unnoticed until Drepperd's article in *Antiques,* [508] where four engraved subjects — only one of them a Certificate form — were reproduced for the first time.

The author was familiar with Miesse's copies after the earlier Egelmann Certificate as early as 1937 when he kept finding impressions of it

[507] Drepperd, Carl W., 'New Delvings in Old Fields, Found: A New Early American Engraver', *Antiques,* XLII, 4 (October, 1942), 204.
[508] *Ibid.,* p. 204.

in the first collections he photographed, but he did not publish this material because he hoped to find more examples of Miesse's work. Oddly enough, if Drepperd knew of these copies in 1942 or Hommel in 1943, neither mentioned them in their respective articles. Further engravings by Miesse including his own bookplate, have been discovered since that time, and now enable us to more than double Drepperd's original list. While most of them exist in the original copper plates rather than early impressions, the latter will no doubt turn up sooner or later.

Although it was Drepperd who re-discovered Miesse in 1942, the first printed biographical account appeared nearly a century earlier in Rupp's *History of Berks and Lebanon Counties* (1844), which was during the engraver's lifetime. This early account, "clipt" from the "Schuylkill Journal" of May, 1839, and the discovery of the Miesse "Familien-Tafel," three copper plates, and one colored engraving in Ohio in 1942 by Arthur Sussel, have been further augmented by family data published by Dr. Oda. [509]   On the basis of these three sources, plus the list of Miesse's engravings which have turned up thus far, it is possible to get a fairly clear picture of his life and work.

The Editor of the *Schuylkill Journal* (1839) says: "A short time since I called to see *Jacob Miesse, Esq.* of Bern Township, Berks County, Pa., who showed me a number of engravings executed by his son, Gabriel Miesse. The young gentleman has an undoubted claim to talents. The first piece of work of the kind he prepared, is surprisingly well done, when it is recollected he had never seen a copper-plate — in fact, not even a graver, for this instrument was constructed by a neighboring blacksmith, according to a pattern furnished by the young man himself . . ."

Apparently Jacob Miesse, his father, also was artistically inclined, an inclination that he passed down to at least one other son besides Gabriel: Jonathan. [510]   Aside from art, Jacob Miesse was interested in many other fields such as medicine, an interest which Dr. Oda says is shown in his support of a booklet by Dr. Daniel Quenaudon, a friend of his and an early advocate of psychotherapy. Although Gabriel was brought up in the Lutheran Church, his brothers who went into the

---

[509] Oda, Wilbur H., 'Gabriel Miesse — Doctor and Engraver', *The Pennsylvania Dutchman*, III, 11 (November 1, 1951), 1; 2 ill.

[510] Drepperd, *op. cit.*, p. 204.

ministry turned to other denominations: Isaac to the Reformed, and Samuel and Henry to the Evangelical.

All of these are listed on Ludwig Crecelius' 1830 *Miesse Familien-Tafel*[511] of Jacob Miesse and Katharina Dundo, his wife, and their eight children, which specifically lists their home as Bern Township, Berks County. This fact confirms the *Schuylkill Journal* account and definitely places the engraver in the vicinity of *Reading* where he would have had access to Egelmann and to Egelmann's published works.

According to Oda, Gabriel the engraver was born near Reading, Pa., on March 26, 1807, and although he very early displayed his artistic talent, his health was very poor.[512] Rupp's *History* states that "In consequence of the development of such promising talents, he was prevailed upon by the liberality of his father, to resort to Philadelphia, and put himself under the care of an experienced artist."[513] Who that artist and teacher might have been is nowhere revealed.

Rupp continues: "But from great constitutional delicacy of frame, he did not remain there more than ten days or two weeks, before he was attacked by a severe illness, which obliged him to return to the country, and abandon those opportunities so congenial to his taste. He continued, however, to amuse himself by engraving a great variety of pieces, among which are plants, flowers, animals, the human figure, &c., executed with a spirit of fidelity, truly astonishing, and turned off by an apparatus wholly constructed by himself, from the stile to the press."

Concerning this same Philadelphia sojourn, Dr. Oda's recent account of Miesse states that "In his nineteenth year he was sent by his parents

---

[511] See figure 236. Drepperd's tentative attribution of the Miesse Familien-Tafel of 1830 to *Jonathan Miesse*, whom he also reported as a skilled artist in Fraktur, was corrected by Rudolf P. Hommel in a subsequent issue of *Antiques*, XIII, 5 (May, 1943), 225, where he pointed out that it is fully and conspicuously signed and dated by *Ludwig Crecelius*, two of whose works have come to the author's attention. Both of these contain the large urn which Hommel thought might have been a silversmith's drawing taken over by a Fraktur artist
The author believes rather that it is simply a decorative form which suggests a silversmith's work because of the engraving-like technique of the artist. Certainly the brilliant coloring has little relationship to silver drawings.

[512] Drepperd, *op. cit.*, p. 204, says that Gabriel specialized in Fraktur, and before he was fifteen years old his work was much in demand. Regarding these same years, Rupp says: "He was confined to his bed from the time he was eight until he became 16, but managed to study Anatomy, Medicine, Music, Drawing, Surveying, Sea Navigation, Astronomy, and his own sickness."

[513] Rupp, I. Daniel, *A History of Berks and Lebanon Counties*. Lancaster Pa.: G. Hills, 1844. Cf. p. 130.

to Philadelphia where, according to one report, he attended class, probably in medicine, for when he left Philadelphia he had in his possession a few surgical instruments and a small stack of medicine." [514]

While these discrepancies regarding the time and purpose of his Philadelphia experience are disconcerting, the difference of opinions regarding his later life is even greater. Drepperd says that "At the age of twenty [or about 1827], Miesse moved to Greenville, Ohio, where he spent the rest of his life. There he did engraving, practiced "pow-wow" doctoring or sympathetic healing, and later became a politician and real estate speculator." [515] Dr. Oda takes issue as to the approximate date of his moving westward by stating that "About the year 1830, Miesse moved to Fairfield County, Ohio. He later lived for seventeen years at Columbus, from which place he moved to Greenville, Ohio, where, in the course of time, he became a wealthy landowner. In the year 1847 he graduated from the Eclectic Medical Institute of Cincinnati, Ohio. Until the year 1854 he had performed almost 1500 surgical operations with almost entire success." Dr. Oda points out that because of Miesse's studying Anatomy and medicine in general at Philadelphia, because one of his great discoveries was a method for curing diseases of the lungs, and because he was bitterly opposed to the older "methods of treatment" by counter irritation, cupping, leeching, and medicine given in the stomach, Gabriel Miesse was more than what is popularly known as a "pow-wow" doctor.

Like Egelmann, Miesse's interest extended beyond engraving and medicine into sculpture and music. A marble bust of his brother in the Ross County (Ohio) Historical Society is said to have been executed by him. That he took his music seriously is indicated by the use of a harpsichord on his Bookplate; [516] several hymns and the music to at least one song were written by him. [517]

At Greenville, Ohio, Gabriel Miesse became a member of the Methodist Church. He died on August 10, 1886 and is buried in the cemetery there.

---

514 Oda, *op. cit.*, p. I.
515 Drepperd, *op. cit.*, p. 204.
516 See figure 275.
517 'Piety better than Beauty', by Rev. A. W. Orwig, in *The Evergreen, Songs for the Sunday School, Sanctuary and Home Circle*, published by Rev. Elisha A. Hoffman, Cleveland, Ohio, about 1873.

As will be observed in the following list, Miesse signed most of his work, and it may be that some chronology or sequence can be developed from his manner of signing. For this reason, the full imprints are given in the list. If his work was so much in demand "before he was fifteen years old" (c.1822), it would be interesting to know which of these were done while he was in Reading and which, if any, after he moved to Greenville, Ohio, about 1827, at the "age of twenty."

It should be pointed out that excepting for the copy after the Egelmann certificate, the copy after the Ritter Haus-Segen, and the H. W. Villee certificate — all of which are German forms — Miesse's work is entirely in English. Two of his productions, the *Moravian Town Battle* (c.1823) and the copy of the *Egelmann Certificate,* moreover, bear price marks — something Egelmann himself never included.

The following list of Miesse's production is based on the impressions and engraved copper plates which have turned up to date. In almost every instance, it should be noted, there is a suggestion that the subject is not original with Miesse but was taken by him from some other source. Although some of his forms were printed for him by the same printers Egelmann worked with, to date no books illustrated by Miesse have appeared:

(1) Copy After Egelmann Certificate (11½ x 9¼ in.)
Inscribed at bottom: "Pr. 37½ Cent" and "Gabriel Miesse Sc." [518]
Issued in two states, both with clouded sky: (1) without price or halo inscription, and (2) with price and with halo inscription.

(2) Birth and Baptismal Certificate (11½ x 9¾ in.)
Inscribed at top: "Engd. and sold by G. Miesse."
Suggests Italian painting in composition. [519]

(3) H. W. Villee Birth Certificate [520]
Putti marked: "G. Miesse S"
Left angel: "G. Miesse" and right angel: "G. M. Sc."

(4) Haus-Segen
Angel at right marked: "G. Miesse Sc."
Hommel believes this is inferior, hence a copy *after* the Johann Ritter form he also illustrated. [521]

[518] Compare figure 272 with 270; also with Color Plate VI.
[519] See figure 273.
[520] See figure 274.
[521] *Antiques,* XLIII, 5 (May, 1943), p. 225.

(5) ADAM AND EVE BROADSIDE
Inscribed at base of woodcut: "G. Miesse"
Illustrated in the *Pennsylvania Dutchman*, IV, 6 (October, 1952), 5.

(6) MORAVIAN TOWN BATTLE
Inscribed at bottom center: "Engraved by G.F.L. Miesse" and at right: "Pr 50 Cent."
The date 1823 on this impression is hand-written, not engraved. Dr. Oda feels this subject may have been copied by Miesse from the frontispiece "Engagement . . . near the Moravian Town" of Henry Trumbull's *History of the Discovery of America,* Boston, 1828, which was engraved by Abel Bowen (1790-1850). In the *Pennsylvania Dutchman*, III, 11 (November 1, 1951), 1, he stated that the engraved copper plate for this subject is now owned by Dr. Norman E. Clarke, Detroit, Michigan.

(7) WASHINGTON PORTRAIT (9¾ x 7¾ in.)
Inscribed bottom center: "Gabriel Miesse Sc."
Faint signature under left side of shield: "Miesse" — Drepperd says first signature at *right* under foliage was burnished out. Miesse's engraving suggests Strickland's treatment of the same subject.

(8) ORIGINAL COPPER PLATE OF WASHINGTON PORTRAIT (4¾ x 4¾ in.)
Inscribed bottom center: "Geo Washington. G.M" and along lower left edge: "G. Miesse No. 1." [522]
Appears to be a copy after the above, since bust is *reversed from right to left* and new background added. Outlines and drawing different, precludes use of same plate.

(9) JACKSON PORTRAIT (8 x 5¾ in.)
Inscribed at right: "G. Miesse Sc"
Letter "a" unfinished, leads Drepperd to say "it is doubtful that any proofs were pulled from either of these plates." (i.e. this one and the following one).

(10) ORIGINAL COPPER PLATE OF MIESSE BOOKPLATE (2 x 2 in.) [523]
Inscribed at center: "Gabriel Miesse" and at bottom: "G. Miesse"
With self-portrait at left and harpsichord at right, and on reverse of plate a clock dial with hands set at 23 minutes to 1 o'clock.

---

[522] See figure 279.
[523] See figures 275 and 276.

(11) ORIGINAL COPPER PLATE OF SWAN (2⅛ x 3⅛ in.)[524]
   Inscribed lower right: "G. Miesse"
      Shows swan swimming towards left with caption above in
      script "Swan." On the reverse is a seated female figure
      with Liberty Hat, spear, eagle, shield, and emblems of
      commerce.

(12) ORIGINAL COPPER PLATE OF TIGER (2⅞ x 3½ in.)
   No inscription or date.
      Shows tiger facing right with borders filled by random
      cross-hatchings.

If we wish to compare the work of these two unusual engravers, Carl
Friederich Egelmann certainly would be far more competent. Gabriel
Miesse's work, though not entirely crude, betrays the incompetence and
inexperience that is perhaps due to his youth. In any case, these two
made a definite and distinctive contribution to the history of Fraktur
through their Birth and Baptismal Certificates. Perhaps their very diffi-
culty of classification and their wavering between German and English
texts, is symptomatic of the fact that the sun had reached its zenith
and Fraktur had begun to lose its Germanic quality.

Occasional influences of the engraver's technique have already been
noted in hand-drawn work. If Egelmann's and Miesse's forms exerted
any influence whatsoever, it certainly is not easily traceable.

## LITHOGRAPHED TAUFSCHEINS (c.1840 - c.1900)

With the "modern" school of lithography, the final chapter of our
history of Fraktur style takes a completely new direction. Not that
these colored lithographs actually replaced hand-drawn or block-printed
certificates immediately, but rather that the lithographed forms provided
more and more competition, and by the last quarter of the century,
there were only a few Fraktur writers who still found it worthwhile to
travel through the countryside in seach of business. The church people —
Lutheran and Reformed — who by this time had formed sizeable con-
gregations in the cities and smaller towns, found it much simpler to purchase the lithographed forms. Due to mass production, they were
inexpensive and, in addition, more attractive to frame and hang on the wall.

---

[524] See figures 277 and 278.

An examination of these lithographed forms which flourished throughout the second half of the century soon reveals why they were more palatable to the general public. Every trace of the Folk Art forms had disappeared from them. The Fraktur script, the characteristic Folk designs, and the vibrant colors have all vanished. Hearts, tulips, and birds are gone and in their place appear the Nativity, the Baptism of Christ, the Last Supper, and most prominent of all are the themes of marriage and baptism, or of confirmation.[525] To most people, naturally, these more *pictorial* themes held greater interest. They neither appreciated nor understood the quaint motifs of rural Folk Art and, in addition, found the angular Fraktur letters difficult to read. The change to early Victorian subject-matter and block-type was to be expected.

The supremacy of the Birth and Baptismal Certificate was now challenged by other forms. First the *Family Register* and then the *Marriage Certificate* became the pièce de résistance. With each of these steps, the pictorial element became more prominent and the theme more *sentimental*. It is this unbridled sentiment which Harry T. Peters noted as characteristic of the national life of the time, and which brought forth a veritable flood of lithographic subjects that were either religious, moral, or patriotic.[526] In areas more distant from eastern Pennsylvania, the *In Memoriam* equivalent of the *Todeschein* was added to this list of themes. N. Currier and Currier & Ives alone published 13 of these *In Memoriam* certificates.[527]

It is interesting to note that the three chief centers for the production of lithographed forms were Philadelphia, Baltimore, and New York — in order of their distance from the Pennsylvania German area. Examination of the forms issued by the various printers in these cities reveals that most of those issued at Philadelphia and New York were in German or followed the German text form, the chief exception being the N. Currier *Family Register* in English; those issued at Baltimore were more apt to be in English and to be *Confirmation Certificates*. These realistic *Confirmation Certificates,* lithographed chiefly in black and white

[525] Wood, T. Kenneth, 'Medieval Art Among the Pennsylvania Germans', *Antiques,* VII, 5 (May, 1925), 266, first called attention to lithographed Confirmation Certificates.

[526] Peters, H. T., *America on Stone*. Special Edition for the Book-of-the-Month Club, 1942. Cf. p. 36.

[527] McClinton, Katharine Morrison, *A Handbook of Popular Antiques*. New York: Random House, 1945 and 1946, p. 164.

and mechanically repeating the interior of the church with altar and kneeling figures, although they represent the last stage of this whole chronological development, actually have very little left to connect them with earlier illuminated forms.    Only the Fraktur heading remains; neither the vigorous color nor the Folk Art motifs have survived.

Katharine McClinton notes that [printed] "Baptismal certificates are not as scarce as marriage certificates.    However, although the printed designs of these certificates are interesting, the coloring is often so crude and so carelessly done that any value attached to the certificate is lost." [528] It should be added in this connection that it is this very "crude" coloring which gives these printed *Birth Certificates* their Folk Art character and which, incidentally, has virtually priced them out of the market today.    As time goes on, they are almost as avidly sought after as the hand-drawn examples by collectors who want to add color and design to their homes.

The appeal of these block-printed certificates with their freely applied colors no doubt explains why so relatively small a number of the less vivid lithographed Birth Certificate forms turn up in Pennsylvania today.    Even though the Currier & Ives forms were as popular as any of the others, the author has still not been able to assemble a complete set of the certificates listed by Harry T. Peters.    And specimens of the various Confirmation forms are only occasionally seen.    In brief, there seems little doubt that the Pennsylvania German population preferred the block-printed and gaudily-colored local certificate forms to those mass-produced city forms.    Though publishing as late as 1924 a copy of the *Way to Eternal Life & Damnation* (at Annville), G. Struphar went out of his way to go back to the Harrisburg and Lancaster block-printed forms of 100 years earlier.

Bearing closest resemblance to the usual Certificate text and to Egelmann s later engraved form, is the type lithographed in Philadelphia by C. L. Rademacher [529] and in New York by N. Currier [530] during the 1840's    Not only do these bear the usual heading, *Geburts und Taufschein,* but they are in German and include some of the stanzas of "Ich bin getauft, etc."    It is in their use of the *Baptism of Christ* and the *Last Supper* that they recall Egelmann's work.    Currier soon afterwards

528 *Ibid.,* p. 164.
529 See figure 283.
530 See figure 281.

published another similar form in German with a wide band of lettering across the top. With this still-vertical example, however, he finished his German work and thereafter limited his production to horizontal English *Records of Birth & Baptism* [531] and *Family Registers,* [532] forms which were continued after the formation of the famous partnership with Ives in 1857.

As early as 1848, N. Currier produced a small *Marriage Certificate* picturing a man and woman in wedding costume before a minister and listing at the left and right respectively the requirements for a husband and for a wife. Similar certificates, with blanks for name, place, and date were issued by Currier & Ives in 1857, 1865, 1875 (small), and in 1877. Even a more active business was carried on by this firm in the field of *In Memoriam* certificates, no less than 13 types having been issued (10 by N. Currier and 3 by Currier & Ives). Following the ready-made formula of earlier theorem paintings with their monument and space for the subject's name, their weeping willows and figures of men, women and children mourning, these occasionally introduced additional subject-matter.

N. Currier used St. Paul's Church, New York, in his two small *In Memoriam* certificates of 1845 and 1847 each, three larger ones of 1846 and two of 1849, and one undated form. An undated Currier even presented Cooke's Tomb. Currier and Ives continued their activity by producing two *In Memoriam* forms in 1872 as well as another undated one. One of the 1849 Currier's was signed by J. Schultz, Currier & Ives artist, an interesting comparison to our printed Pennsylvania German forms. Nothing further needs to be said regarding these various forms produced by Kellogg, Foster & Kimmel, and many other lithographers, since neither their text nor their designs permit them to be confused with Pennsylvania German certificates.

At Philadelphia in 1849, August Köllner (of erstwhile fame as a traveling watercolorist and recorder of the American scene) began producing a different form of lithographed *Birth and Baptismal Certificate.* Like Currier, he issued a *Geburts-und-Taufschein* (using the German hyphen form) [533] and an English *Certificate of Birth and Baptism,* both

---

[531] See figure 282.
[532] See figure 280.
[533] See figure 284.

of which follow the early texts, including the baptismal hymn.  Starting with the vertical composition used by C. L. Rademacher in Philadelphia as well as by N. Currier in his earlier forms in New York, he developed a new design of his own.  Pictorially, Köllner's composition is more Victorian and less virile than their forms: while the pair of flying angels at the top are more reminiscent of the block-printed certificates, within the broken-arch pediment a realistic scene of the *Adoration of the Shepherds* has been inserted; in niches at left and right *St. John* and *St. Peter* now appear, while the *Baptism of Christ* scene (which figured so prominently in Egelman's engraved certificates and N. Currier's lithographed ones) becomes a tiny and rather slight detail at the bottom of an otherwise solid and heavy architectural form.

More prolific than Köllner in Philadelphia was Ig. Kohler, who in 1855 was also lithographing *Birth and Baptismal Certificates* in both German and English.  His two chief innovations were to develop a more delicate, tracery-like border and to replace Köllner's two Saints in the niches on either side of the certificate with even more Victorian subject matter. [534] On the left he pictured a contemporary marriage ceremony, and on the right a correspondingly realistic baptismal scene.  Perhaps this is a natural "throwback" to the ever-present "ehelichen Hausfrau" of earlier days, for Kohler continues to use the regular full text with both Birth and Baptismal information (but without the baptismal hymn), whether the certificate is in German or in English.  Thus far, imprints in both languages for the year 1855 are all that have appeared of Kohler's work.  Harry T. Peters' *America on Stone* [535] dates him from 1854 onwards.

The last step in the Victorianization of the *Birth Certificate* form takes place in the lithograph issued by Schäfer & Koradi at Philadelphia. While continuing closely the German text, the scene depicting the *Presentation of the Child by its Parents for Baptism* has now become the chief feature — in addition to the minister and parents, witnesses or sponsors are introduced here. [536]  Ably supporting this theme are the niche subjects at left and right which now consist of a *Baptismal Scene* and *Christ and the Children*.  Dated 1882 in manuscript, this is a late survival of the old certificate form and is labeled *Geburts-und-Tauf-*

---

[534] See figure 285.
[535] Peters, H. T., *America on Stone*.  New York: Doubleday, Doran, and Co., Inc., 1931.
[536] See figure 286.

*schein.* It should be noted that it was this same press of Schäfer & Koradi which only a few years later (1893) issued Seidensticker's pioneer book on *German Printing in America.* [537]

In this example of the late 19th century lithographed *Birth and Baptismal Certificate* is to be found the fullest expression of the Victorian period which, while holding superficially to the composition and layout of the early 19th century block-printed forms, substituted purely representational and pictorial forms for the quaint and colorful heart, tulip, and bird designs that made this whole illuminated style so definitely an expression of the local craftsman and Folk artist.

---

[537] Seidensticker, Oswald, *The First Century of German Printing in America (1728-1830).* Philadelphia: Schaefer & Koradi, 1893.

# VII. SUMMARY

ROM the vast amount of material examined in connection with the preparation of this monograph, then, it is apparent that Fraktur played a most important role in the development of Pennsylvania German Folk Art. Outside of the boundaries of the State today, it enjoyed considerable popularity as a technique in New England, New York and New Jersey, and in adjoining States on the south and west to which the Germans spread subsequently, although the motifs of the New England examples bespeak a different background.

It is apparent, also, that the European origins of Fraktur as it was practiced in Pennsylvania are much less remote than the medieval illuminated manuscripts as such. European copybooks and local secular manuscripts of the 18th and 19th century provide such immediate parallels, on the contrary, that the Pennsylvania pieces appear more as a transplantation of this late manuscript style.

Not only the technique is transplanted, but the very forms themselves are continued with the local adaptations one would normally expect. No better demonstration than this can be found for the strong and close connections between the Pennsylvania and the German or Swiss Folk Arts. Frequent confusion of native with European-made furniture, glass, pottery, etc., emphasizes this fact. And in the field of Fraktur itself, nearly every period of its development contains several artists or a small group of examples which, though clearly identified as Pennsylvania-made pieces, show very strong European flavor. Despite the mention of County names, however, these might either have been executed abroad and filled in later after the artist had arrived here, or, having arrived in Pennsylvania, the artist at once continued to produce without interruption the same form, and the same texts, he had known in Europe.

In summarizing this study of Fraktur, a fact of chief importance to be carefully noted is the tremendous revival it enjoyed here in America. Once introduced in Pennsylvania, it was enthusiastically received and maintained its popularity throughout most of the 19th century. In the hands at first of educated ministers and schoolteachers, and later of professional itinerant penmen and local artisans, it was developed along new and original lines of great beauty. In this process, the Pennsylvania German Fraktur writers and decorators achieved great homogeneity of form, technique, and motif — so much so that we may properly speak of it as an illuminated "style."

This Pennsylvania German Style of Illumination, which lasted from about 1750 until 1850 and reached its high point between 1800 and 1835, produced some of the finest examples of American Folk Art. These are distinct and apart from any illuminated manuscripts produced elsewhere and fully epitomize the meaning of the term "Pennsylvania German Fraktur" or illuminated style.

It has been demonstrated, also, that this illuminated style can be broken into a number of component schools which produced it. Each of these in turn had its individual artists, forms, and characteristic motifs which can be evaluated within the larger framework of the development as a whole. Each of these schools reflect, as one would expect, the European geographical origin and religious beliefs of the persons making up the group, as well as their aims and teachings here in the New World. As these groups flourished and then faded with the oncoming Industrial Revolution of the later 19th century, and with their ever-increasing contacts with the "outside world," so their hand-illuminated manuscripts blossomed and then perished in the flood of later engraved and lithographed forms. Each of these groups, from the Ephrata Cloister in the mid-18th century down to Currier & Ives' productions of the late 19th century, made some new and characteristic contribution to the development of Fraktur.

We have also noted the fact that the Pennsylvania German Style

·of Illumination had definite connections with, and influences upon, Pennsylvania German art as a whole. Its very continuity from the earliest period of stove-plates, glass, pottery, furniture, and tombstones, down to the latest period of barn signs, buttermolds, and quilts, would insure this. The fact that young children were exposed to it, that via the mediums of both the Church and School it permeated every home, that Fraktur became so popular it was taken up in mass production, gives some hint of the potential influence it must have held. That this influence was ofttimes more than merely *potential* has been demonstrated through comparisons of Fraktur compositions and motifs with contemporary productions in other media.[538] While the priority of Fraktur cannot be established in every case, it is evident in a sufficiently large number to make further comparisons desirable.

Finally, because of this extremely close relationship between Fraktur and other allied Pennsylvania German decorative arts, many of which are *undated* and therefore pose chronology problems, it is possible to use *dated* illuminated manuscripts as a yardstick. With Vorschriften, with signed and dated Certificates, or with Printed Taufscheins bearing imprints, we are on absolutely certain ground and can solve problems of priority and dating quite satisfactorily. This is particularly true with printed forms, since the locale of their origin in turn establishes the area of influence.

Perhaps the most significant and far-reaching result of this monograph in general and of this mode of dating in particular, is the realization that Pennsylvania German Folk Art is chiefly a 19th century phenomenon — certainly a *post-Revolutionary* one   With the exception of the decorated stove-plates and tombstones, the great period of production of slip and sgraffito pottery, of decorated furniture, embroidery, Fraktur, etc., falls between 1780 and 1850.

While in many cases it is the chests, pie-plates, and Frakturs dated between 1780 and 1800 which are best known to the general public, this has been brought about through repetition of illustrations of museum pieces in books and magazines. Actually, in the over-all picture, these

---

[538] See figures 287-292.

early examples are in the minority since in each of these fields many more 19th than 18th century examples exist. The impression of preponderantly 18th century origin has also been stimulated by museums which have labeled and dated their exhibits incorrectly.

As in most fields of Art History, the tendency among the pioneer investigators and collectors of Pennsylvania German Folk Art has been to date the material *too early*. Happily, as the area of study increases this situation is gradually being corrected and, as the study of 18th century Pennsylvania general decorative arts advances, the very strong *English* imprint particularly in Bucks and in Chester Counties is being more accurately appraised. The basic *Germanic* character of the so-called "decorated style" cannot ever seriously be questioned.

# VIII. APPENDIX

A: FRAKTUR ILLUMINATORS
B: FRAKTUR PRINTING CENTERS
C: FRAKTUR PRINTERS

## A: FRAKTUR ILLUMINATORS

Note: Unless otherwise indicated, the dates given below are those of specific examples seen by the author; italics indicate life or activity dates.

*Identified by Signature*

ACHE, H. M.
ANDERS, Abraham (1805)
ANDERS, Andrew (1787)
ANDERS, Judith (1807)
ANDREAS, Jacob
ANSON, James (1804-09, *New Jersey*)

BACHMAN, Christian (1798)
BANDEL, Frederick (c.1809, *Ohio*)
BARD, Johannes (1824-32)
BAUER, Andreas B. (1832)
BAUMAN, August (c.1900)
BECKER, J. M. (1829)
BEIDLER, C. Y. (1847)
BERGEY, Joseph K. (1803)
BICKSLER, Jacob S. (1829)
BIXLER, David (1828-48, also 1862)
BRECHALL, Martin *(ac.1783-1823)*
BRUBACHER, Hans Jacob *(HIBB)* (1789-1801)
BUSGAEGER, J. George (1815-25)

CASSEL, Christian (1771-72)
CASSEL, Huppert (1763-73)
CASSEL, Joel D. (1841-46)
CLEMENS, Johannes (1816)
CORDIER, David (1815)
CRECELIUS, Ludwig (1830)

DENLINGER, David (1830)
DETWEILER, John H.
DETWEILER, Martin M. (1765)
DIRDORFF, Abraham (1780-81)
DITMARS, Peter (1838)
DOCK, Christopher *(died 1771)*
DRESSLER, S. O. (1852)
DULHEUER, Henrich *(ac.1786)*

EGELMANN, Carl Friederich (1821-31)
EISENHAUER, Jacob

F., C. (1765)
FABER, Wilhelmus Antonius (1811-18)
FORRER, Johann
FRIES, Isaac (1825)
FROMFIELD, William (1821)

GAHMAN, John (1806)
GEISTWEITE, Rev. George (1801)
GISE, Henry (1846)
GODSHALK, Enos (1820)
GODSHALL, M. (1835)
GRIMES, William
GROSS, Isaac (1830)
GROSS, Jacob

HARTMAN, Christian B. (1846)
HARTZEL, John Jr. (1815)
HEEBNER, David (1817-18)
HEEBNER, John (1831)
HEEBNER, Maria (1842-43)
HERR, David
HEYDRICH, Baltzer (1784)
HEYDRICH, Balzer *(BH)* (1845)
HILL, Henry
HILLEGAS, Jacob (1811)
HOFFMAN, Johan S. (1811)
HUEBNER, Abraham (1772-74, also 1818)
HUEBNER, Henrich (1843)
HUEBNER, Susanna (1806-10, also 1828)
HUTH, Abraham (1816-1825)

JAECKEL, Christoph (1772)
JAMISON, J. S. (1843)

K., A.
K., H. (1769)
K., J. (1805)
KASSEL, Georg (1800)
KEEPER, Heinrich
KEHM, Anthony (1824)
KIEHN, David (1847)
KINSEY, Abraham K. (1864)
KLENK, Ferdinand (1875)
KRAUSS, Regina (1815)
KREBS, Friedrich *(ac.1790-1815)*
KRIEBEL, David (1803-05)
KRIEBEL, Hanna
KRIEBEL, Job (1825)
KRIEBEL, Maria (1843)
KRIEBEL, Sara (1842-45)
KRIEBLE, Abraham (1782)

## APPENDIX A *(Continued)*

LANDES, Rudolph (1814-16)
LANDIS, Catharine L. (1846-50)
LANDIS, John (1826-1829)
LANDIS, John A. (1852)
LAPP, Christian (1819)
LAPP, Henry *(c.1822-1913)*
LEHN, Henry (1843)
LEVAN, Francis D. (c.1820-50)
LIMBACH, Christian (1795)
LUECKIN, C. (1772)

M., C. (1793-96)
MEYER, Martin J. (1835)
MIESSE, Gabriel *(1807-1886)*
MILLER, John G (1831)
MOFFLY, Samuel (1805)
MOSTELLER, Johannes (1820)
MOYER, Martin (1835)
MUENCH, Karl C. (1799-1817)
MURRAY, William (1806-19, *New York*)

OBERHOLTZER, Jacob *(ac.1773-1810)*
OTTO, [Johann] Henrich *(ac.1772-1788)*

PETERMAN, Daniel *(ac.1819-1857)*
PETERS, Christian (1777)
PILE, John (1853)
PLANK, J. L. (1883)
PORTZLINE, Francis *(ac.1801-1848)*
PUWELLE, Arnold

RENNINGER, Johannes (1841-47)
RUDY, Durs (1804-42)

S., J. (1827)
SCHANTZ, Rev. Joseph
SCHERICH, C. (1851)
SCHNEIDER, Christian (1784)
SCHULLER, Johann Valentin *(ac.1800-1813)*
SCHULTZ, Lidia (1826)
SCHULTZ, Regina (1806 and 1848)
SCHULTZ, Salamon (1836)
SCHULTZ, Sara (1827)
SCHUMACHER, Rev. Daniel (1761-81)
SEILER, H. (1795)
SEUTER, John
SEYBERT, Abraham (1812)
SEYBOLD, Carl Frid· (1843)
SHINDEL, J. P. (1855)
SIEGFRIED, Samuel (1810)
SPANGLER, Samuel (1828-31)
SPEYER, [Georg] Friederich *(ac.1785-1800)*
STOBER, John (1852)
STRENGE, Christian (1794-1814)

TAYLOR, Alexander (1829, *Ohio*)
TEIBEL, [Johann] Georg (1763-79)

W., A. (1827-36)
W., I. T. (Wanner?)
WEBER, Isaac (1822)
WEIDNER, Heinrich (1832)
WEISS, Anna (1793)
WEISS, Henrich (1791)

ZINCK, John (1834)
ZUG, Johan (1788)

### *Identified by Style*

1780  SUSSEL-WASHINGTON artist
*(fig.230)*
YORK, Co. "GENERAL" artist *(fig.84)*
SOLY DEO GLORIA artist
LEACOCK TWP. artist (1788-92)

1790  HUBER artist (1790-99) *(fig.35)*
EARL TWP. artist (1790-1809)
MOON artist (1793-98)
SUSSEL UNICORN artist (1798-99)
EASTON BIBLE artist *(fig 46, 49, 208)*
READING-BERKS artist *(fig.203)*
FLYING ANGEL artist *(fig.207)*
PSEUDO-OTTO artist *(fig.239)*

1800  ADAMS Co. artist (1802) *(fig.77)*
WETZEL-GEOMETRIC artist
*(fig.62, 205)*
ENGRAVER artist *(fig.54)*
CROSS-LEGGED ANGEL artist *(fig.204)*
SPRINGING DEER artist *(fig.214)*
EHRE VATER artist *(fig.206)*
BALTIMORE Co. artist *(fig.293)*

1810  FLAT PARROT artist *(fig 210)*
WEAK artist *(fig.209)*
FLAT TULIP artist *(figs.67, 213)*
NORTHUMBERLAND COUNTY artist
*(fig.41)*
COPULIERT artist (1810-1818)
SPATTER TULIP artist
EARLY HYMNAL artist (1811-13)

1820  DURHAM-BUCKS COUNTY artist
(1820-24)
URN AND TULIP artist (1824-27)
DAUPHIN COUNTY artist (1825)
MT. PLEASANT artist (1825-37)
*(figs.220, 222)*

1830  HAUS-SEGEN artist (1828-31)
*(fig.235)*
HOSTETTER-WENGER artist (1830-32)
LATE HYMNAL artist (1833-48)
EARLY CENTRE COUNTY artist
*(figs 224, 225, 226)*

1840  LATE LADIES WITH ANCHOR artist
LATE CENTRE Co. artist *(fig.227)*

# APPENDIX B

## B: FRAKTUR PRINTING CENTERS

| *Pennsylvania* (24) | *Non-Pennsylvania* (11) |
|---|---|
| Allentown | Baltimore, Maryland |
| Annville | Canton, Ohio |
| Bath | Columbus, Ohio |
| Carlisle | Elkhart, Indiana |
| Chambersburg | Frederick, Maryland |
| Easton | Germantown, Ohio |
| Ephrata | Hagerstown, Maryland |
| Greensburg | Lancaster, Ohio |
| Hanover | New Market, Virginia |
| Harrisburg | New York, New York |
| Lancaster | Wooster, Ohio |
| Lancaster County, | |
|     Brecknock Taunschip | |
| Lebanon | |
| Millgrove | |
| Milton | |
| New Berlin | |
| Northampton County, Zion's Church | |
|     (Kreidersville) | |
| Orwigsburg | |
| Philadelphia | |
| Pottsville | |
| Reading | |
| Stroudsburg | |
| Sumneytown | |
| York | |

# APPENDIX C

## C: FRAKTUR PRINTERS

Note: Except where indicated, entry refers to Birth and Baptismal Certificate. Stipple-engraved and lithographed items are so marked.

1. ALLENTOWN (ALLENTAUN)
    Henrich Ebner (1817, 1818, 1820, 1821)
        H. Ebner und Comp.
    G. A. Sage                 (See G. Adolph Sage, *Reading)*
    Grater und Blumer
        Graeter & Blumer
    A. und W. Blumer (1835, 1836, 1837, 1838, 1839, 1840, 1843)
        A. & W. Blumer (1836)
        A. Blumer und Gebruder (1841, 1842)
        A. Blumer & Brothers (1842)
    Guth, Ruhe und Young
    Blumer und Busch (1844, 1845, 1846, 1847, 1848)
        Blumer & Busch (1845)
        Blumer, Busch und Co. (1849)
        Blumer, Busch & Co.
        Blumer, Bush & Co.
    Blumer und Leisenring (1860)
        Leisenring, Blumer und Co. (1861)
    Saeger & Leisenring (1863, 1864)
        Saeger und Leisenring (1861, 1862, 1863, 1864, 1865)
    E. D. Leisenring und Co.
        E. D. Leisenring & Co.
    Leisenring, Trexler und Co. ("Welt-Bote" Druckerei)
        Leisenring, Trexler & Co.
    "Welt-Bote" Druckerei
    R. Bright (Confirmation)
    Brobst, Diehl & Co. (*lith*)
    Trexler & Hartzell (*lith*)

2. ANNVILLE
    J. G. Struphar ("Way to Eternal Life," 1924)

3. BALTIMORE, MARYLAND
    Dulheuer, Henrich (1786)
    J. T. Hanzsche
        Joh. T. Hanzsche
    Joh. T. Hanzsche und bey J. G. Hanzsche
        J. G. Hanzsche
    A. Hoen & Co. (*lith*)

4. BATH
    S. Siegfried (1838)
    John S. Dreisbach (1848, 1849, 1850)
        J. S. Dreisbach (1861)

5. CANTON, OHIO
    Salamon Sala

## APPENDIX C (*Continued*)

FRAKTUR PRINTERS (*Continued*)

6. CARLISLE
    F. Sanno (1809, 1810, 1812, 1813)
    Friederich Sanno
    Moser u. Peters (1825, 1826) (see Moser u. Peters, *Harrisburg,*
    1827, 1828)
        Moser und Peters (1826, 1827) ("Life and Ages of Man"):
            (see Peters, *Harrisburg,* 1829, 1830, 1831)

7. CHAMBERSBURG
    Johann Herschberger
    F. W. Schopflin
        F. Wilhelm Schöpflin
    John Dietz
    Heinrich Ruby (1828) (Geistlicher Irrgarten)

8. COLUMBUS, OHIO
    V. Kastner (184-)

9. EASTON
    C. J. Hütter
        C. J. Hutter und Sohn
    H. & W. Hutter
        H. und W. Hütter
    A. H. Senseman

10. ELKHART, INDIANA
    John F. Funk and Brud. (Geistlicher Irrgarten)

11. EPHRATA
    John Bauman (1801, 1802, 1807, 1808)
        J. Bauman (1803)
        J. Baumann
        Johann Baumann (1803)
    Baumann u. Ruth (1811, 1812)
    Samuel Baumann (1811, 1813) (also "Adam and Eva")
        S. Baumann

12. FREDERICK (FRIEDRICHTAUN), MARYLAND
    C. T. Melsheimer

13. GERMANTOWN, OHIO
    Wm. Gunckel

14. GREENSBURG (GRUENSBURG)
    Johannes Armbrust

15. HAGERSTOWN, MARYLAND
    Gruber und May (18—)

16. HANOVER (HANNOVER)
    Wilhelm Lepper
    W. Lepper und E. Stettinius (1798)
    Starck und Lange (1811, 1812)
        Starck & Lange
    Dan. Phil. Lange (1817, 1818, 1819, 1821, 1822)
        D. P. Lange (1825, 1826, 1927, 1928, 1929, 1937)
    Gutelius & Schwartz
    Printed at the *Friend Office,* Hanover, Pa.

# APPENDIX C (*Continued*)

## FRAKTUR PRINTERS (*Continued*)

17. HARRISBURG
    Gleim und Wiestling
    Johann S. Wiestling (1824, 1826)
        John S. Wiestling (1827)
                                    (see Baab und Villee, *Lancaster*)
        Jacob Baab                  (see Baab und Dobler, *Reading*)
        Moser u. Peters (1827, 1828)
        Gustav S. Peters (1829) ("Joseph and his Brethren")
            G. S. Peters (1829, 1830, 1831) ("Life and Ages of Man")
                                    (1832 Metamorphosis)
        Theo. F. Scheffer
            Th. F. Scheffer
        Lutz u. Scheffer
            Lutz & Scheffer

18. LANCASTER
    Chr. J. Hutter (1801)
    Benjamin Grimler (1803)
    H. W. Villee (also Adam and Eva, and "Way to Eternal Life")
    Baab und Villee ("Way to Eternal Life")
                                    (see Jacob Baab, *Harrisburg*)
                                    (see Baab and Dobler, *Reading*)

19. LANCASTER CO., BRECKNOCK TAUNSCHIP
    Isaac Palm (1860)

20. LANCASTER, OHIO
    Johann Herman

21. LEBANON (LIBANON)
    Joseph Schnee
    Jacob Stover
        J. Stover
    Joseph Hartman
        J. Hartman (1818)
    R. J. Boyer ("Letter from Heaven")

22. MILLGROVE (ALUTA)
    Sam. Siegfried
    S. & S. Siegfried's

23. MILTON
    H. W. Villee ("Way to Eternal Life")

24. NEW BERLIN, UNION COUNTY
    G. Miller

25. NEW MARKET, VIRGINIA
    Ambrosius Henkels (1811)

26. NEW YORK, NEW YORK
    N. Currier (1846) (*lith*)
    Currier & Ives (*lith*)
    Ernst Kaufman (*lith*)
    J. E. Stohlmann (*lith*)

PLATE VI. Carl F. Egelmann, Engraved Birth Certificate, c.1820
*Author's collection*

# APPENDIX C (*Continued*)

## FRAKTUR PRINTERS (*Continued*)

27. NORTHAMPTON COUNTY, ZION'S CHURCH
(KREIDERSVILLE)
> John S. Dreisbach (1848) (Haus-Segen)

28. ORWIGSBURG
> Jacob Thoma
> Grim und Thoma
> Thoma und May

29. PHILADELPHIA
> Henrich Miller (1762) (Geistlicher Irrgarten)
> Georg W. Mentz (*eng*)
> Mentz und Rovoudt (*eng*)
> Augs. Kollner (1849) (*lith*)
> A. Kollner (*lith*)
> Ig. Kohler (1855) (*lith*)
> J. Kohler (*lith*)
> Schafer & Koradi (*lith*)
> King und Baird (Himmelsbrief)
> M. Dahlem (Adam and Eve)
> C. I. Rademacher (*lith*)
> H. Sebald (Lutheran Publication Society—Marriage Certificate)
> Traubel & Co. (*lith*)
> J. D. Wollenweber (Heiraths-Schein)

30. POTTSVILLE
> John P. Bertram
> J. P. Bertram
> G. Ph. Lippe
> A. E. Snyder
> J. T. Werner

31. READING
> Barton und Jungmann (1790, 1791, 1792, 1793)
> Jungmann und Gruber (1793, 1794)
> Gottlob Jungman (1793, 1797, 1799, 1804, 1809)
> J. Schneider u. Co. (1797, 1798)
> Johann Ritter
> John Ritter
> Johann Ritter und Companie
> Johann Ritter und Comp. (1811, 1812)
> Johann Ritter u. Comp.
> John Ritter und Comp.
> John Ritter & Co.
> J. Ritter & Co.
> Ritter u. Co.
> Ritter und Co.
> Ritter und Comp.
> Ritter & Co.
> Ritter & Co. (at) Eagle Book Store
> "Eagle" Buchstohr
> Eagle Book Store

## APPENDIX C (*Continued*)

**FRAKTUR PRINTERS** (*Continued*)

G. Adolph Sage            (see G. A. Sage, *Allentown)*
Henrich B. Sage
    Heinrich B. Sage (1822) ("Adam und Eva")
    Henry B. Sage
Carl A. Bruckman
    C. A. Bruckman
Samuel Meyers
Meyers und Christian
Baab und Dobler               (see Jacob Baab, *Harrisburg)*
                          (see Baab und Villee, *Lancaster)*
Philip Hantsch
Carl Kessler
A. Puwelle
D. Rhoads
Daniel Roths
Johann Walter
Carl Friederich Egelmann (1821, 1831) (Copybook) *(eng)*
    C. F. Engelmann (also "Adam und Eva") *(eng)*
Gabriel Miesse *(eng)*
    G. Miesse *(eng)*
C. L. F. Miesse *(eng)*

32. STROUDSBURG
    The Monroe Democrat

33. SUMNEYTOWN (SUMNEYTAUN)
    E. Benner (1835, 1836)

34. WOOSTER, OHIO
    Johann Sala (1826)

35. YORK
    D. May *(lith)*
    D. W. Crider *(lith)*
    Crider & Bro. (1873) *(lith)*
    H. M. Crider (1887) *(lith)*

# IX. BIBLIOGRAPHY

A: EUROPEAN FOLK ART BACKGROUNDS
B: THE PENNSYLVANIA GERMANS
C: PENNSYLVANIA GERMAN ARTS AND CRAFTS
D: PENNSYLVANIA GERMAN FRAKTUR

## A. EUROPEAN FOLK ART BACKGROUNDS

Bossert, Helmuth T., *Volkskunst in Europa.* Berlin: E. Wasmuth, 1926.
Second edition, 1938. Profusely illustrated.

——————, 'Volkskunst in Europa', *Geschichte des Kunstgewerbes*, VI
(1935), 339-416.

Duchartre, Pierre Louis, 'Arts populaires', *Cahiers de Belgique*, II (July, 1929),
323-338.

——————, *Art populaire* (2 vols.). Travaux artistiques et scientifiques du
ler congres international des arts populaires, Prag, 1928. Paris: Duchartre
Editions, 1931.

### AUSTRIA

Haberlandt, Michael, *Oesterreichische Volkskunst* (2 vols.). Wien: J. Löwy and
Friedrich Jasper, 1911.

——————, *Textile Volkskunst aus Oesterreich.* Wien: J. Löwy, 1912.

Holme, Charles, *Peasant Art in Austria and Hungary.* London, Paris, and New
York: 'The Studio' Ltd., 1911.

### FRANCE

Cases, Ph. de Las, *L'art rustique en France* (2 vols.). Paris: Librairie Ollen-
dorff, 1920.

Demeufve, Georges, *Les meubles regionaux et les collections d'art rustique au Musee
Lorrain.* Nancy: Arts Graphiques Modernes, 1932.

Duchartre, Pierre Louis, et Saulnier, Rene, *L'imagerie populaire.* Paris: Librairie
de France, 1925.

Gélis, Paul, *Le mobilier alsacien.* Paris: Ch. Massin & Cie, 1925. Collection de l'art
régional en France.

Riff, Adolphe, *L'art populaire en Alsace.* Strasbourg: A. und F. Kahn, 1921.

### SCANDINAVIA

Plath, Jona, *The Decorative Arts of Sweden.* New York: Charles Scribner's Sons,
1949. Profusely illustrated.

Wassenbergh, Vegter, and Bouma, *Fryske Folkskinst in Rige Printen.*

### SWITZERLAND

Baud-Bovy, Daniel, *Peasant Art in Switzerland.* London: 'The Studio' Ltd., 1924.

Lichtenhan, Lucas, and Burckhardt, Titus, *Schweizer Volkskunst.* Basel: Art
Populaire Suisse, Urs Graf Verlag, 1941.

Lutz, Max, *Alte Bürgerstuben der Schweiz.* Bern: Gezeichnet und Verlegt von
M. Lutz, 1946.

Ott, Margrith, *Das Ornament im bauerlichen Kunsthandwerk des Kantons Appensell.*
Zurich: Uto-Buchdruckerei, 1945. Good bibliography.

Weese, Artur et Maria, *L'ancienne Suisse.* Erlenbach-Zurich: Eugen Rentsch, 1925.

## BIBLIOGRAPHY A (*Continued*)

### GERMAN FOLK ART — GENERAL

Erich, Oswald A., und Beitl, Richard, *Wörterbuch der deutschen Volkskunde.* Leipzig: Alfred Kroner Verlag, 1936.

Hahm, Konrad, *Deutsche Volkskunst.* Berlin: Deutsche Buch-Gemeinschaft, 1928. First major work under the title "Volkskunst."

——————, *Deutsche Volkskunst.* Breslau: Jedermanns Bücherei, Ferdinand Hirt, 1932.

Karlinger, Hans, *Deutsche Volkskunst.* Berlin: Propylaen-Verlag, 1938. The most recent work in the field, profusely illustrated.

Lehmann, Otto, *Deutsches Volkstum in Volkskunst und Volkstracht.* Berlin: Walter de Gruyter & Co., 1938.

Ritz, J. M., *Süddeutsche Volkskunst.* München: Verlag Georg D. W. Callwey, 1938.

Schwindrazheim, Oskar, *Deutsche Bauernkunst.* Wien-Leipzig: Deutscher Verlag für Jugend und Volk, 1931.

Spamer, Adolf, *Die Deutsche Volkskunde* (2 vols.). Leipzig: Bibliographisches Institut, 1934-35.

Thiele, Ernst Otto, *Sinnbild und Brauchtum.* Potsdam: Voggenreiter Verlag, 1937.

Weigel, Karl Theodor, *Runen und Sinnbilder.* Berlin: Alfred Metzner Verlag, 1935.

Zaborsky, Oskar v., *Urvater-Erbe in deutscher Volkskunst.* Leipzig: Koehler & Amelang, 1936.

### GERMAN FOLK ART BY PROVINCES

Adler, Fritz, *Pommern.* Redslob 'Deutsche Volkskunst' Series, XI. Weimar: Verlag Bohlau, n.d.

Busse, H. E., *Baden.* Redslob 'Deutsche Volkskunst' Series, XIII. Weimar: Verlag Bohlau, n.d.

Clasen, Karl Heinz, *Ostpreussen.* Redslob 'Deutsche Volkskunst' Series, X. Weimar: Verlag Bohlau, n.d.

Creutz, Max, *Die Rheinlande,* Redslob 'Deutsche Volkskunst' Series, III. Weimar: Verlag Bohlau, 1924.

Gröber, Karl, *Schwaben.* Redslob 'Deutsche Volkskunst' Series, V. Weimar: Verlag Bohlau, 1925.

——————, *Alte Oberammergauer Hauskunst.* Augsburg: Dr. Benno Filser Verlag, 1930.

Grundmann, Gunther, und Hahm, Konrad, *Schlesien.* Redslob 'Deutsche Volkskunst' Series, VIII. Weimar: Verlag Bohlau, n.d.

Güthlein, Hans, und Ritz, J. M., *Das Feuchtwanger Heimatmuseum.* Augsburg: Dr. Benno Filser Verlag, 1929.

Jordan, Hans, und Grober, Karl, *Das Lindauer Heimatmuseum.* Augsburg: Dr. Benno Filser, Verlag, 1932.

Karlinger, Hans, *Bayern.* Redslob 'Deutsche Volkskunst' Series, IV. Weimar: Verlag Bohlau, 1925.

Lindner, Werner, *Mark Brandenburg.* Redslob 'Deutsche Volkskunst' Series, II. Weimar: Verlag Bohlau, 1924.

Orend, Misch, *Siebenburgen.* Redslob 'Deutsche Volkskunst' Series, supplement, Weimar: Verlag Bohlau, 1943.

Pessler, Wilhelm, *Niedersachsen.* Redslob 'Deutsche Volkskunst' Series, I. Weimar: Verlag Bohlau, 1923.

## BIBLIOGRAPHY A (*Continued*)

Polaczek, Ernst, *Volkskunst im Elsass.* Redslob 'Deutsche Volkskunst' Series, supplement. Weimar: Verlag Bohlau, n.d.

Redslob, Edwin, *Thüringen.* Redslob 'Deutsche Volkskunst' Series, VII. Weimar: Verlag Bohlau, 1926.

Ritz, Josef, *Franken.* Redslob 'Deutsche Volkskunst' Series, VI. Weimar: Verlag Bohlau, n.d.

Spamer, Adolf, *Hessische Volkskunst.* Jena: Eugen Diederichs Verlag, 1939.

Uebe, Rudolf, *Westfalen.* Redslob 'Deutsche Volkskunst' Series, IX. Weimar: Verlag Bohlau, 1927.

Weigel, Karl Theodor, *Sinnbilder in Bayern.* Berlin: Alfred Metzner Verlag, 1938.

Zink, Theodor, *Die Pfalz.* Redslob 'Deutsche Volkskunst' Series, XII. Weimar: Verlag Bohlau, n.d.

### GERMAN ARCHITECTURE

Thiede, Klaus, *Deutsche Bauernhäuser.* 'Die Blauen Bücher.' Leipzig: Karl Robert Langewiesche Verlag, 1937.

### GERMAN FURNITURE AND DECORATION

Feulner, Adolf, *Kunstgeschichte des Mobels seit dem Altertum.* Berlin: 1927.

Gephard, Torsten, *Mobelmalerei in Altbayern,* Munchen: Verlag Georg D. W. Callwey, 1937.

Hahm, Konrad, *Deutsche Bauernmöbel.* Jena: Eugen Diederichs Verlag, 1939.

Ritz, J. M., *Bauernmalerei.* Leipzig: Bibliographisches Institut, 1935. 15 illustrations including a "Patenbrief" aus Bayern.

——————, *Alte bemalte Bauernmobel.* Munchen: Verlag Georg D. W. Callwey, 1938.

Schöpp, Alexander, *Alte volkstümliche Mobel und Raumkunst aus Norddeutschland.* Elberfeld: Alexander Schopp Verlags-Buchhandlung, 1921.

——————, *Alte deutsche Bauernstuben Innenraume und Hausrat.* Berlin: Verlag Ernst Wasmuth, 1934.

Schröder, Albert, *Bemalter Hausrat in Nieder- und Ostdeutschland.* Leipzig: Schwarzhaupter-Verlag, 1939.

Sonner, Karl, *Bauernmalerei.* Munchen: Verlag Georg D. W. Callwey, 1937.

Uebe, F. Rudolf, *Deutsche Bauernmobel.* Berlin: Richard Carl Schmidt und Co., 1924.

### GERMAN IRONWORK

Hausen, Edmund, *Pfalzer Eisenguss.* Kaiserslautern: E. Lincks-Crusius Verlag, 1930.

Schroder, Dr. Albert, *Deutsche Ofenplatten.* Leipzig: Bibliographisches Institut, 1936.

### GERMAN TEXTILES

Lehmann, Siegfried, *Niedersàchische Stichmustertucher.* Hannover: Druck und Verlag Kusedruck, 1936.

Schmitz, Wilhelm, *Westfalischer Blaudruck in alter und neuer Zeit.* Münster: Westfalens Museen, 1935.

### GERMAN TOYS

Grober, Karl, 'Beginnings of the German Toy Industry', *American-German Review,* III, 1 (September, 1936), 36-40; 8 ill.

## BIBLIOGRAPHY B

### B. THE PENNSYLVANIA GERMANS

Appel, Mrs. T. Roberts, *Old Pennsylvania Recipes.* Lancaster, Pa.: 1933. Pp.16.

Aurand, A. M., *A Pennsylvania German Library.* Harrisburg, Pa.: The Aurand Press, 1930. Pp.61. A comprehensive listing of Pennsylvania titles.

Bachmair, J. J., *A German Grammar.* Carlisle, Pa.: Sanno and Loudon, 1813. Pp.457. Aimed at teaching the Germans to speak English.

Bartram, John, *Observations on the Inhabitants, Climate, Soil, Rivers, Productions, Animals, and Other Matters Worthy of Notice Made by Mr. John Bartram in his Travels from Pensilvania to Onondago, Oswego, and the Lake Ontario in Canada.* London: J. Whistler and B. White, 1751. Pp.94.

Beatty, Charles, *The Journal of a Two Months Tour: with a View of Promoting Religion among the Frontier Inhabitants of Pennsylvania.* London: Davenhill and Pearch, 1768. Pp.110.

Beckel, Clarence E., 'Early Marriage Customs of the Moravian Congregation in Bethlehem, Pennsylvania', Pennsylvania German Folklore Society *Publications*, III (1938), 1-32.

Bining, Arthur C., Brunhouse, Robert L., and Wilkinson, Norman B., compilers, *Writings on Pennsylvania History: A Bibliography: A List of Secondary Materials Compiled under the Auspices of the Pennsylvania Historical Commission.* Harrisburg, Pa.: Pennsylvania Historical and Museum Commission, 1946. See pp.47-74.

Bitner, Mrs. Mabel E., 'The Pennsylvania State Museum', Pennsylvania German Folklore Society *Publications*, VII (1942), 43-49; 5 ill.

Bittinger, L. F., *The Germans in Colonial Times.* Philadelphia, Pa.: J. B. Lippincott Company, 1901.

Brendle, Thomas R. and Unger, Claude W., *Folk Medicine of the Pennsylvania Germans: The Non-Occult Cures.* Pennsylvania German Society *Proceedings*, XLV (1935). Pp.303+18 ill.

Bruford, W. H., *Germany in the Eighteenth Century.* Cambridge, England: The Cambridge University Press, 1935. Pp.x+354.

Budd, Thomas, *Good Order Established in Pennsilvania & New Jersey.* Possibly London: Andrew Sowle, 1685. Pp.40. Extremely rare.

Buffington, Albert F.-Barba, Preston A. A Pennsylvania German Grammar. Schlechter's, Allentown, Pa., 1954.

Cadbury, Richard T., editor, *Cazenove Journal.* Haverford College Study, 13. Haverford, Pa.: The Pennsylvania History Press, 1922. Pp.xvii+103.

Clemens, Gurney W., 'The Berks County Historical Society', Pennsylvania German Folklore Society *Publications*, VII (1942), 53-80; 16 ill.

Cobb, Sanford Hoadly, *The Story of the Palatines—An Episode in Colonial History.* New York: G. P. Putnam's Sons, 1897.

David, Hans T., 'Background for Bethlehem', *Magazine of Art*, XXXII, 4 (April, 1939), 222-225, 254; 4 ill.

Day, Sherman, *Historical Collections of the State of Pennsylvania.* Philadelphia, Pa.: George W. Gorton, 1843.

DeChant, Alliene, *Of the Dutch I Sing.* Kutztown, Pa.: Published by the Author, 1951.

Diffenderfer, F. R., *The German Immigrations into Pennsylvania through the Port of Philadelphia, 1700-1775.* Lancaster, Pa.: The New Era Printing Company, 1900.

Donehoo, George P., *Pennsylvania, A History.* New York: Lewis Historical Publishing Co., Inc., 1926. 7 volumes. Book 3: Eastern Pennsylvania, 1680-1760.

BIBLIOGRAPHY B  (*Continued*)

Dorman, William K., and Davidow, L. S., *Pennsylvania Dutch Cook Book of Fine Old Recipes*. Reading, Pa.: Culinary Arts Press, 1934. Pp.vii+48.

Dunaway, Wayland Fuller, *A History of Pennsylvania*. New York: Prentice-Hall Company, 1935. Pp.xxiii+828.

Dundore, M. Walter, 'The Saga of the Pennsylvania Germans in Wisconsin', Pennsylvania German Folklore Society *Publications*, XIX (1954), 33-166; 2 maps and 13 ill.

Egle, William H., *History of the Commonwealth of Pennsylvania*. Philadelphia, Pa.: E. M. Gardner, 1883. Pp.xii+1204.

Eshelman, H. Frank, *Historic Background and Annals of the Swiss and German Pioneer Settlers of South Eastern Pennsylvania*. Lancaster, Pa.: 1917.

Evangelisch-Lutherischen Gemein, *Nachrichten von dem vereinigten Deutschen Evangelisch-Lutherischen Gemeinen in Nord-America, absonderlich in Pennsylvanien*. Halle: 1787. Pp.1518.

Eyster, Anita L., 'Notices by German and Swiss Settlers in the *Pennsylvanische Berichte* (1742-1761) and in the *Pennsylvanische Staatsbote* (1762-1779)', Pennsylvania German Folklore Society *Publications*, III (1938), 1-41.

Falkner, Daniel, *Curieuse Nachricht in Norden America*. Franckfurt und Leipzig: Andreas Otto, 1702. Pp.ii+58.

Faust, A. B., *The German Element in the United States*. Boston: The Houghton Mifflin Company, 1909. 2 volumes. Pp.xxviii+730. A full historical treatment. Second edition, Steuben Society of America, 1927.

Fisher, Sydney G., *The Making of Pennsylvania*. Philadelphia, Pa.: J. B. Lippincott Company, 1896.

Flory, John S., *Literary Activity of the German Baptist Brethren in the Eighteenth Century*. Elgin, Ill.: Brethren Publishing House, 1908. Pp.xii+335.

Fogel, Edwin M., *Beliefs and Superstitions of the Pennsylvania Germans*. Philadelphia, Pa.: Americana Germanica Press, 1915.

————, 'Proverbs of the Pennsylvania Germans', Pennsylvania German Society *Proceedings*, XXXVI (1929). Pp. 221. The most important book in its field.

————, 'Of Months and Days', Pennsylvania German Folklore Society *Publications*, V (1940), 1-23.

————, 'Twelvetide', Pennsylvania German Folklore Society *Publications*, VI (1941), 1-22.

Frederick, J. George, *The Pennsylvania Dutch and Their Cookery*. New York: The Business Bourse, 1935. Pp.275. Informative and readable; their background and character, list of artists, and bibliography.

Frey, J. William, *Pennsylvania Dutch Grammar*. Clinton, S.C.: The Jacobs Press, 1942. Pp.xi+140. Invaluable for newcomers to the dialect.

Fuller, Raymond Tifft, 'Domain of Abundance', *Travel*, LXVI, 1 (November, 1935), 14-17, 49-50; 7 ill.

Gerstacker, Frederick, *The Wanderings and Fortunes of Some German Emigrants*. New York: D. Appleton & Co., 1848. Pp.270.

Gibbons, Phebe Earle, *'Pennsylvania Dutch' and Other Essays*. Philadelphia, Pa.: J. B. Lippincott & Company, 1882. Pp.318.

Gilbert, Russell Wieder, *A Picture of the Pennsylvania Germans*. Gettysburg, Pa.: The Pennsylvania Historical Association, 1947. Pp.ii+65. A good concise treatment.

Graeff, Arthur D., 'Cake Baking Recipes from Pennsylvania German Almanacs', *American-German Review*, VII, 2 (December, 1940), 25-29; 4 ill.

## BIBLIOGRAPHY B (*Continued*)

————, 'Conrad Weiser, Pennsylvania Peacemaker', Pennsylvania German Folklore Society *Publications,* VIII (1943). Pp.xiii+392.

————, *The History of Pennsylvania.* Philadelphia, Pa.: John C. Winston Co., 1944. Pp.320. Illustrated.

————, *The Pennsylvania Germans.* Keyser 'Home Craft Course' Series, 20. Plymouth Meeting, Pa.: Mrs. C. Naaman Keyser, 1945.

————, 'The Pennsylvania Germans in Ontario', Pennsylvania German Folklore Society *Publications,* XI (1946), 1-80.

————, 'Renascence of History', *The Dutchman,* VI, 5 (Summer, 1955), 36-38.

Graydon, Alexander, *Memoirs of a Life Chiefly Passed in Pennsylvania.* Harrisburg, Pa.: John Wyeth, 1811. Pp.378.

Haldeman, S. S., *Pennsylvania Dutch, a Dialect of South Germany with an Infusion of English.* London: Trubner & Co., 1872. Pp.viii+69. Good treatise on the language.

Hark, Ann, *Hex Marks the Spot.* Philadelphia and New York: J. B. Lippincott Co., 1938. Pp.316. A collection of sketches popularly written.

————, 'Who are the Pennsylvania Dutch?', *House and Garden,* LXXIX, 6 (June, 1941), 21, 64.

Hark, Ann, and Barba, Preston A., *Pennsylvania German Cookery.* Allentown, Pa.: Schlechter's, 1949.

Hark, Ann, and DeWitt, C. H., *The Story of the Pennsylvania Dutch.* New York: Harper & Bros., 1943. Pp.32 (unpaged). A juvenile with excellent lithographs.

Hark, J. Max, *Chronicon Ephratense: A History of the Community of Seventh Day Baptists at Ephrata, Lancaster County, Penn'a.* Lancaster, Pa.: S. H. Zahm & Co., 1889.

Heckman, Oliver S., *What to Read about Pennsylvania.* Harrisburg, Pa.: Pennsylvania Historical Commission, 1942. Pp vi+97. Good.

Hinke, William J., and Stoudt, John B., editors, 'A List of German Immigrants to the American Colonies from Zweibruecken in the Palatinate, 1728-1749', Pennsylvania German Folklore Society *Publications,* I (1936), 101-124.

Hoffman, William J., ' "Palatine" Emigrants to America from the Principality of Nassau-Dillenburg', *National Genealogical Society Quarterly,* XXIX, 2 (June, 1941).

Hohman, John George, *Albertus Magnus, der lang verborgenen Schatz und Haus-Freund.* Reading, Pa.: 1820. Pp.100. The original "hex" book. New edition, Harrisburg, Pa.: The Aurand Press, 1930. Pp.94.

Holme, John, *A True Relation of the Flourishing State of Pennsylvania,* 1686. Original unpaged manuscript in the Historical Society of Pennsylvania, Philadelphia.

Horne, A. R., *A Pennsylvania German Manual.* Kutztown, Pa.. Urick & Gehring, 1875. Pp.172. Basic grammar, a key work.

*House and Garden,* 'Pennsylvania Dutch Issue', LXXIX, 6 (June, 1941), 21-41; profusely illustrated.

Jackson, M. Katherine, *Outlines of the Literary History of Colonial Pennsylvania.* Lancaster, Pa.: The New Era Printing Co., 1906. Pp vii+177.

Johnson, Elmer E. S., 'The Schwenkfelder Historical Library', Pennsylvania German Folklore Society *Publications,* VII (1942), 31-40; 6 ill.

Jones, Dorothy Bovee, *The Herb Garden.* Keyser 'Home Craft Course' Series, 23. Plymouth Meeting, Pa.: Mrs. C. Naaman Keyser, 1947.

BIBLIOGRAPHY B (*Continued*)

Kalm, Peter, *Travels into North America*, trans. John Reinhold Forster (3 vols.).
Vol. I. Warrington: Wm. Eyres, 1770. Pp.xvi+8+400. Vol. II. London:
T. Lowndes, 1771. Pp.352. Vol. III. London: T. Lowndes, 1771. Pp.viii
+310+14.

Kapp, Friedrich, *Franz Daniel Pastorius' Beschreibung von Pennsylvanien.* Crefeld:
Kramer & Baum, 1884. Pp.6+140.

Klees, Frederic, *The Pennsylvania Dutch.* New York: The Macmillan Co., 1951.

Klosz, Heinz, *Lewendiche Schtimme aus Pennsilveni.* Stuttgart und New York: B.
Westerman, 1929. Pp.153. A collection of dialect works.

————, *Die pennsylvaniadeutsche Literatur.* München: Der Deutsche Akad-
emie, 1931. Heft IV, 230-272.

Knauss, James O., Jr., 'Social Conditions among the Pennsylvania Germans in the
Eighteenth Century', Pennsylvania German Society *Proceedings*, XXIX
(1922). Pp.217.

Knittle, Walter Allen, *Early Eighteenth Century Palatine Emigrations.* Philadelphia, Pa.: Dorrance and Company, 1937.

Krebs, Friedrich, 'A List of German Immigrants to the American Colonies from
Zweibruecken in the Palatinate, 1750-1771', Pennsylvania German Folklore
Society *Publications*, XVI (1951), 171-183.

————, '18th Century Emigrants from Edenkoben in the Palatinate', *The
Pennsylvania Dutchman*, IV, 9 (January 1, 1953), 9.

————, 'Palatine Emigrants from the District of Neustadt—1750', *The Pennsylvania Dutchman*, V, 1 (May, 1953), 9.

————, 'Pennsylvania Pioneers from the Neckar Valley, 1749-1750', *The
Pennsylvania Dutchman*, V, 2 (June, 1953), 13.

Krebs, Friedrich, and Rubincam, Milton, 'Emigrants from the Palatinate to the
American Colonies in the 18th Century', Pennsylvania German Society, *Special Study*, I (1953). Pp.32.

Kuhns, Oscar, *The German and Swiss Settlements of Colonial Pennsylvania: A
Study of the So-Called Pennsylvania Dutch.* New York: Henry Holt,
1900. Pp.v+268. A good study, out of print.

Lambert, Marcus B., *A Dictionary of the Non-English Words of the Pennsylvania-
German Dialect.* Norristown, Pa.: The Pennsylvania German Society, 1924.
Pp.xxxi+193. The most comprehensive dictionary, invaluable for the be-
ginner.

Landis, H. K., 'Pennsylvania German Foods', *American-German Review*, V, 1 (September, 1938), 38-41, 53; 4 ill.

Langdon, William Chauncey, *Everyday Things in American Life.* New York:
Charles Scribner's Sons, 1939 Pp.xx+353. Good on Pennsylvania.

Lauer und Mattill, *Deutsche Amerikaner in Kirche und Staat.* Cleveland, Ohio:
Lauer und Mattill, 1892. Pp.316.

Learned, Marion Dexter, *The Pennsylvania-German Dialect.* Baltimore: Isaac
Friedenthal, 1889. Pp.114.

Lichtenthaler, Frank E., 'Storm Blown Seed of Schoharie', Pennsylvania German
Folklore Society *Publications*, IX (1944), 1-105.

Light, Richard, 'The Hershey Museum', Pennsylvania German Folklore Society
*Publications*, VII (1942), 83-90; 4 ill.

Lins, James C., *A Commonsense Pennsylvania German Dictionary.* Reading, Pa.:
James C. Lins, 1887.

Ludwig, G. M., 'The Influence of the Pennsylvania Dutch in the Middle West',
Pennsylvania German Folklore Society *Publications*, X (1945), 1-101.

## BIBLIOGRAPHY B (Continued)

Mann, Horace M., 'The Bucks County Historical Society', Pennsylvania German Folklore Society *Publications*, VII (1942), 7-28; 22 ill.

Meynen, Emil, *Bibliography on German Settlements in Colonial North America, Especially on the Pennsylvania Germans and their Descendants, 1683-1933*. Leipzig: Otto Harrassowitz, 1937. Pp.xxxvi+636.

Mittelberger, Gottlieb, *Reise nach Pennsylvanien im Jahr 1750 und Rückreise nach Teutschland im Jahr 1754*. Stuttgart: Gottlieb Friderich Jenisch, 1756. Pp.120.

Mortimer, Charlotte B., *Bethlehem and Bethlehem School*. New York: Stanford & Delisser, 1858. Pp.208.

—————————, *Marrying by Lot*. New York: Putnam & Sons, 1868. Pp.xi +405. An account of an early Moravian custom.

Musselman, G. Paul, 'Hook-and-Eye and Shoe-Fly Pie', *Saturday Evening Post*, CCXII, 40 (March 30, 1940), 12-13, 37-38, 40, 42-43.

Myers, Elizabeth L., *A Century of Moravian Sisters*. New York: Fleming H. Revell, 1918. Pp.243.

Myers, Richmond E., 'The Moravian Christmas Putz of the Pennsylvania Germans', Pennsylvania German Folklore Society *Publications*, VI (1941), 1-10.

Nitzsche, George E., 'The Christmas Putz', Pennsylvania German Folklore Society *Publications*, VI (1941), 1-28.

Nolan, J. Bennett, 'John Conrad Weiser the Elder', *American-German Review*, II, 3 (March, 1936), 42-45.

Nutting, Wallace, *Pennsylvania Beautiful*. Framingham, Mass.: Old America Company, 1924. First appearance in print of the word "hex."

Ogden, John C., *An Excursion into Bethlehem and Nazareth in the Year 1799*. Philadelphia, Pa.· Charles Cist, 1800. Pp.167.

Pastorius, Francis Daniel, *Kurtze Geographische Beschreibung der letzmals erfundenen Amerikanischen Landschaft Pensylvania*. Nurnberg: Christian Sigmund Froberg, 1692. Pp.32.

—————————, *Umstandige Geographische Beschreibung der zu allerletzt erfundenen Provintz Pennsylvania*. Frankfurt und Leipzig: Andreas Otto, 1704. Pp.vi+140.

Pearson, John, *Notes Made during a Journey in 1821 in the United States of America from Philadelphia to the Neighborhood of Lake Erie; through Lancaster, Harrisburg, Carlisle and Pittsburgh, and back to Philadelphia through Louistown, Huntingdon, & New Holland, in Search of a Settlement*. London: W. & S. Couchman, 1822. Pp.72.

Pennsylvania, *A Guide to the Keystone State*. American Guide Series. New York: Oxford University Press, c.1940. Pp.xxxii+660.

Pennsylvania German Folklore Society, Annual *Publications*. Fogelsville, Pa.: 1936 to date.

*Pennsylvania German Magazine, The*. An important periodical which suspended publication in 1914.

Pennsylvania German Society, Annual *Proceedings*. Norristown, Pa.: 1891 to date.

Pfund, Harry W., review, 'Pennsylvania German Pioneers' by Ralph Beayer Strassburger, *American-German Review*, II, 1 (September, 1935), 44-45.

Proud, Robert, *The History of Pennsylvania in North America*. Philadelphia, Pa.: Zachariah Poulson, Jr., 1797-98. Vol. I. Pp.508; Vol. II. Pp.373+146.

Raschen, J. F. L., 'Gleanings From a Travel Book', *American-German Review*, Part 1. XII, 1 (October, 1945), 15-18; Part 2. XII, 2 (December, 1945), 11-13.

## BIBLIOGRAPHY B *(Continued)*

Rauch, E. H., *A Pennsylvania Dutch Hand-Book.* Mauch Chunk, Pa.: E. H. Rauch, 1879. Pp.238.

*Record of Indentures of Individuals* not only Germans *Bound Out as Apprentices, Servants, Etc. in Philadelphia, October 3, 1771 to October 5, 1773.* Pennsylvania German Society *Proceedings,* XVI (1907). Pp.325. Gives date of arrival, term, amount, and occupation.

Reichard, Harry Hess, *Pennsylvania German Dialect Writings and Their Writers.* Pennsylvania German Society *Proceedings,* XXVI (1915). Pp.400. The basic work in this field, very comprehensive.

—————————, *Pennsylvania German Verse.* Pennsylvania German Society *Proceedings,* XLVIII (1940). Pp.299. Excellent anthology.

—————————, 'The Christmas Poetry of the Pennsylvania Dutch', Pennsylvania German Folklore Society *Publications,* VI (1941), 1-87.

Reichmann, Felix, 'The Landis Valley Museum', Pennsylvania German Folklore Society *Publications,* VII (1942), 93-102; 1 ill.

Reichmann, Felix, and Doll, Eugene E., 'Ephrata As Seen by Contemporaries', Pennsylvania German Folklore Society *Publications,* XVII (1952). Pp.xxi+206; 14 ill.

Richards, H. M. M., *The Pennsylvania-German in the Revolutionary War, 1775-1783.* Pennsylvania German Society *Proceedings,* XVII (1908). Pp.542.

Robacker, Earl F., *Pennsylvania German Literature: Changing Trends from 1683-1942.* Philadelphia, Pa.: The University of Pennsylvania Press, 1943. Pp.x+217. Covers dialect, German and English prose and verse.

Rominger, Charles H., 'Early Christmases in Bethlehem, Pennsylvania (1742-1756)', Pennsylvania German Folklore Society *Publications,* VI (1941), 1-35; 17 ill.

Rosenberry, M. Claude, 'The Pennsylvania German in Music', Pennyslvania German Society *Proceedings,* XLI (1933), 29-44.

Rubincam, Milton, 'On the Use of the Term Palatine', *American-German Review,* X, 1 (October, 1943), 15-16, 37.

Rupp, I. Daniel, *History of Lancaster County.* Lancaster, Pa.: G. Hills, 1844. Pp.531.

—————————, *History of Berks and Lebanon Counties.* Lancaster, Pa.: G. Hills, 1844. Pp.512.

—————————, *History of Northampton, Lehigh, Monroe, Carbon, and Schuylkill Counties.* Harrisburg, Pa: Hickok and Cantine, 1845. Pp.xiv+568.

—————————, *A Collection of Upwards of Thirty Thousand Names of German, Swiss, Dutch, French, and other Immigrants in Pennsylvania.* Philadelphia, Pa.: Ig. Kohler, 1876

Rush, Benjamin, *An Account of the Manners of the German Inhabitants of Pennsylvania,* as reprinted in Pennsylvania German Society *Proceedings,* XIX, 21 (1908), by Theodore E. Schmauk. Pp.128.

Sachse, Julius F., *The German Pietists of Provincial Pennsylvania.* Philadelphia, Pa.: P. C. Stockhausen, 1895. Pp.xviii+504.

—————————, *The Fatherland, 1450-1700.* Philadelphia, Pa.: The Pennsylvania German Society, 1897. Showing the part it bore in the discovery, exploration, and development of the Western continent.

—————————, *The German Sectarians of Pennsylvania.* Philadelphia, Pa.: P. C. Stockhausen, 1900. Pp.xvi+535. Basic source book.

—————————, *The Music of the Ephrata Cloister, also Conrad Beissel's Treatise on Music as Set Forth in a Preface to the 'Turtel Taube' of 1747.* Pennsylvania German Society Proceedings, XII, 9 (1903). Pp.108.

# BIBLIOGRAPHY B (Continued)

——————, trans. and ed., *Daniel Falckner's Curieuse Nachricht von Pensylvania in Norden-America.* Pennsylvania German Society *Proceedings*, XIV (1905). Pp.256.

Seidensticker, Oswald, *Die Erste Deutsche Einwanderung in Amerika.* Philadelphia, Pa.: Globe Printing House, 1883. Pp.94.

Seifert, Lester W. J., 'Lexical Differences between Four Pennsylvania German Regions', Pennsylvania German Folklore Society *Publications*, XI (1946), 155-169.

Shoemaker, Alfred L., 'Pennsylvania Dutch Canada', *The Dutchman*, VII, 4 (Spring, 1956), 8-14; 15 ill.

Shryock, Richard H., 'The Pennsylvania Germans in American History', *Pennsylvania Magazine of History and Biography*, LXIII, 3 (1939), 261-281.

Smith, Edward C., and Thompson, Virginia H., *Traditionally Pennsylvania Dutch.* New York: Hastings House, 1947. Pp.81. Beautifully illustrated.

'S Pennsylfawnisch Deitsch Eck, edited by Dr. Preston A. Barba. A weekly feature in the Allentown, Pa., *Morning Call.*

Stauffer, Elmer C., 'In the Pennsylvania Dutch Country', *National Geographic Magazine*, LXXX, 1 (July, 1941), 37-74; 43 ill.

Steineman, Ernst, 'A List of Eighteenth-Century Emigrants from the Canton of Schaffhausen to the American Colonies, 1734-1752', Pennsylvania German Folklore Society *Publications*, XVI (1953), 186-196.

Stoudt, John Baer, *The Folklore of the Pennsylvania-Germans.* Pennsylvania German Society *Proceedings*, XXIII (1915). Pp.155.

Stoudt, John Joseph, *The Pennsylvania Dutch, an Introduction to Their Life and Culture.* Allentown, Pa.: Schlechter's, 1950. Pp.32.

Strassburger, Ralph B., and Hinke, William J., editors, *Pennsylvania German Pioneers.* Pennsylvania German Society *Proceedings*, XLII, XLIII, XLIV (1934). Vol. I and II. 1727-1775; Vol. III, 1785-1808.

Thomas, Edith M., *Mary at the Farm and Book of Recipes.* Compiled during her visit among the "Pennsylvania Germans." Harrisburg, Pa.: Evangelical Press, 1915. Pp.423.

Thomas, Gabriel, *An Historical and Geographical Account of the Province and Country of Pensilvania and of West-New Jersey in America.* London: A. Baldwin, 1698. Pp 7+55.

Wertenbaker, Thomas J., *The Founding of American Civilization: The Middle Colonies.* New York: Charles Scribner's Sons, 1938. Pp.xiii+367. Chapters VII and IX, 'From Rhine to Susquehanna' and 'Volkskunst', are outstanding contributions in this field.

Weygandt, Cornelius, 'Our Pennsylvania Dutch', *Travel*, LXXV, 6 (October, 1940), 25-29, 38-39.

Wickersham, James Pyle, *A History of Education in Pennsylvania.* Lancaster, Pa.: The Inquirer Publishing Co., 1886. Pp.xxiii+683.

Wieand, Paul R., *Outdoor Games of the Pennsylvania Germans.* Keyser 'Home Craft Course' Series, 28. Plymouth Meeting, Pa.: Mrs. C. Naaman Keyser, 1950. Pp.34.

Wittke, Carl, *We Who Built America.* New York: Prentice-Hall, 1939. Pp.xviii+547. Comparative treatment of immigrant groups.

Wood, Ralph, editor, *The Pennsylvania Germans.* Princeton, N.J.: Princeton University Press, 1942. Pp.viii+299. An excellent series of articles by authorities in each field.

## BIBLIOGRAPHY B *(Continued)*

Yoder, Donald H., 'Emigrants from Wuerttemberg, The Adolf Gerber Lists', Pennsylvania German Folklore Society *Publications*, X (1945), 103-237.

——————, translator and editor, 'Pennsylvania German Pioneers from the County of Wertheim', by Otto Langguth, Pennsylvania German Folklore Society *Publications*, XII (1947), 147-289.

——————, 'Plain Dutch and Gay Dutch: Two Worlds in the Dutch Country', *The Pennsylvania Dutchman*, VIII, 1 (Summer, 1956), 34-55; 31 ill.

Yoder, Joseph W., *Rosanna of the Amish*. Huntingdon, Pa.: Yoder Publishing Co., 1940. Pp.319. Excellent for background study.

## C. PENNSYLVANIA GERMAN ARTS AND CRAFTS

Adams, Ruth, *Pennsylvania Dutch Art*. Cleveland and New York: World Publishing Co., 1950. Pp.64+27 ill., 9 color pl.

Allis, Mary, 'The Arts and Crafts of the Pennsylvania Germans', Service Bureau for International Education, New York: 1937.

Brazer, Esther Stevens, *Early American Decoration*. Springfield, Mass.: Pond-Ekberg Co., 1940. Pp.xiii+273.

Brinton '1704 House', *Antiques*, LXXI, 1 (January, 1957), 64-65; 3 ill.

Brooklyn Museum, *Popular Art in America*, exhibition catalogue. Brooklyn, N.Y.: Brooklyn Museum Press, 1939. Pp.39 and 14 plates.

Chew, Paul A., *Two Hundred and Fifty Years of Art in Pennsylvania*. Greensburg, Pa.: The Westmoreland County Museum of Art, 1959. Pp.xi+105; 211 ill.

Christensen, Erwin O., *Popular Art in the United States*. London: Penguin Books, 1948. Pp.30 and 32 ill.

——————, *The Index of American Design*. New York: Macmillan, for The National Gallery of Art, Washington, D.C., 1950. Pp.xviii+229; 378 plates in color and in black and white.

Dickson, Harold E., *A Working Bibliography of Art in Pennsylvania*. Harrisburg, Pa.: The Pennsylvania Historical and Museum Commission, 1948.

Downs, Joseph, *The House of the Miller at Millbach*. Philadelphia, Pa.: Pennsylvania Museum of Art, 1929. Pp.32; 26 pl., 4 figs. The architecture, arts and crafts, of the Pennsylvania Germans. Reprinted in the Pennsylvania German Folklore Society *Publications*, I (1936), 75-90; 12 ill.

——————, 'The DeForest Collection of Work by Pennsylvania German Craftsmen', Metropolitan Museum of Art *Bulletin*, XXIX, 10 (October, 1934), 163-169; 8 ill. and cover.

——————, *A Handbook of the Pennsylvania German Galleries in the American Wing*. New York: The Metropolitan Museum of Art, 1934. Pp.22 and 8 ill. Reprinted in the Pennsylvania German Folklore Society *Publications*, I (1936), 91-100; 4 ill.

——————, *Pennsylvania German Arts and Crafts, A Picture Book*. New York: The Metropolitan Museum of Art, 1942, 1943, 1946, 1949. Pp.4+30 plates.

Drepperd, Carl W., 'Origins of Pennsylvania Folk Art', *Antiques*, XXXVII, 2 (February, 1940), 64-68; numerous illustrations.

——————, *American Pioneer Arts and Artists*. Springfield, Mass.: The Pond-Ekberg Co., 1942. Pp.xiv+172. Chapter X on Folk Art.

Dyer, Walter A., *Early American Craftsmen*. New York: The Century Co., 1915.

## BIBLIOGRAPHY C (*Continued*)

Geesey Collection, Titus C., *Antiques*, LII, 4 (October, 1947), 255-259; 14 ill. Interiors and single pieces of unusual merit.

——————, 'Pennsylvania German Christmas', *Antiques*, LII, 6 (December, 1947), 426; 5 ill.

——————, 'Folklore,' The *Historical Review of Berks County*, XVII, 3 (April-June, 1952), 66-74; 4 ill.

——————, Titus C., and Others, *Pennsylvania Dutch Folk Arts* from the (by Lichten, Frances). Philadelphia, Pa.: Philadelphia Museum of Art, 1958. Pp.33+63 ill.

'High Folk Art Collection', Harry S. (by Zehner, Olive G.), *The Dutchman*, VI, 1 (June, 1954) 16-19; 11 ill.

'Himmelreich Collection', Walter, (by Kauffman, Henry J.), *The Dutchman*, VII, 3 (Winter, 1956), 18-29; 32 ill.

Kauffman, Henry, *Pennsylvania Dutch American Folk Art*. New York: Holme Press, 1946. Extensively illustrated, a key work.

Keyser, Mrs. C. Naaman, *Home Craft Course Series*. Plymouth Meeting, Pa.: Mrs. C. Naaman Keyser, 1943-1950. Some 28 booklets are listed in this bibliography according to subject.

Krick, Richard D., *Portfolio of Pennsylvania Dutch Art*. Philadelphia, Pa.: Carl Schurz Memorial Foundation, 1941.

'Landis Valley Museum', *American-German Review*, VII, 4 (April, 1941), 2-38. Entire issue devoted to Museum, fully illustrated.

Lefevre, Edwin, 'The Meaning of Pennsylvania Dutch Antiques', *The Saturday Evening Post*. Part 1. CCCVII (April 20, 1935), 16-17, 32, 35, 37; Part 2. CCCVII (April 27, 1935), 26, 31, 80, 82, 84, 87.

Lichten, Frances, *Folk Art of Rural Pennsylvania*. New York: Charles Scribner's Sons, 1946. Profusely illustrated, a key work.

——————, *Folk Art Motifs of Pennsylvania*. New York: Hastings House, 1954. Pp.96; profusely illustrated.

——————, see *Geesey Collection and Others* (1958).

——————, 'Pennsylvania-German Folk Art', *The Concise Encyclopedia of American Antiques*, II, 401-412; plates 249-256. New York: Hawthorn Books, Inc., 1958.

Lipman, Jean, and Meulendyke, Eve, *American Folk Decoration*. New York: Oxford University Press, 1951. Pp.xii+163; 181 ill., line drawings.

McClinton, Katharine Morrison, *A Handbook of Popular Antiques*. New York: Random House, 1945 and 1946.

'Metropolitan Museum Adds Two Pennsylvania German Rooms', *American Collector*, II, 9 (October 18, 1934), 1, 6.

Museum of Modern Art, exhibition catalogue, *American Folk Art: The Art of the Common Man in America, 1750-1900*. New York: The Museum of Modern Art, 1932. First major exhibition and catalogue.

Odenwelder Collection, Asher J., Jr., *Antiques*, LI, 4 (April, 1947), 246-249. Many illustrations.

——————, *The Collector's Art A and Z*. Keyser 'Home Craft Course' Series, 26. Kutztown, Pa.: The Kutztown Publishing Company, 1948.

'Pennsbury: Pennsylvania restores the manor house of its founder, William Penn', (by Cadzow, Donald A.), *American Heritage*, I, 4 (Summer, 1950), 50-51, 66-67, 5 ill.

## BIBLIOGRAPHY C (*Continued*)

*Pennsylvania Dutch Designs.* A Portfolio of ten plates in full color. The first of a series of silk screen prints by The Folk Art Press, Plymouth Meeting, Pa.: Mrs. C. Naaman Keyser, 1946.

'Pennsylvania German Arts' (The new Decorative Arts Wing at the Philadelphia Museum of Art), *Antiques,* LXXV, 3 (March, 1959), 264-271; 33 ill.

Pennsylvania German Design: *Primitive and Peasant Art.* Syracuse, N.Y.: Keramic Studio Publishing Company, 1932. Assembled from special issues of *Design,* XXXIII, 10 (March, 1932), 237-263.

*Pennsylvania German Designs.* A Portfolio of twenty silk screen prints. New York: The Index of American Design, Metropolitan Museum of Art, 1943.

Ramsay, John, 'Pennsylvania Dutch, a People whose Handicrafts merit wider Recognition', *House Beautiful,* LXVIII, 4 (October, 1930), 362-363, 394, 396-397, 398.

Rawson, Marion Nicholl, *Candleday Art.* New York: E. P. Dutton & Co., 1938. Pp.383.

Reichmann, Felix, 'On American Folk Art', *American-German Review,* X, 6 (August, 1943), 34-36. A review of Carl W. Drepperd's *American Pioneer Arts and Artists,* 1942. Excellent and sound.

Riccardi, Saro John, compiler, *Pennsylvania Dutch Folk Art and Architecture: A Selective Annotated Bibliography.* New York: New York Public Library *Bulletin,* XLVI, 6 (1942), 471-483.

Rice, William S., 'Early Pennsylvania Arts and Crafts', *School Arts Magazine,* XXXII, 7 (March, 1933), 395-400, 408-409.

Robacker, Earl F., *Pennsylvania Dutch Stuff: A Guide to Country Antiques.* Philadelphia, Pa.: The University of Pennsylvania Press, 1944.

————————, 'The Rise of Interest in Pennsylvania Dutch Antiques', *The Pennsylvania Dutchman,* VIII, 1 (Summer, 1956), 18-22; 8 ill.

————————, 'The Rise of Interest in Folk Art', X, 1 (Spring, 1959), 20-29; 17 ill.

Sales Catalogues of the American Art-Anderson and Parke-Bernet Galleries of New York City, Samuel T. Freeman & Co. of Philadelphia, and James G. Pennypacker of Reading, Pa.:

| | |
|---|---|
| Samuel W. Pennypacker, | 1905-09 (8 parts), and 1920 |
| Theodore Offerman | 1922 |
| Jacob Paxson Temple | 1922 |
| Howard Reifsnyder | 1929 |
| Schuyler B. Jackson | 1933 |
| George Horace Lorimer | 1944 (2 parts) |
| Mrs. A. K. Hostetter | 1946-47 (3 parts) |
| Mrs. Anna Maria Brix | 1946 and 1955 |
| Mr. and Mrs. Richard S. Quigley | 1947 |
| J. Stogdell Stokes | 1948 |
| Ira S. Reed | 1948 |
| William Keible | 1951 |
| Harry S. High | 1954 |
| Walter Himmelreich | 1958 |
| Mrs. Mabel I. Renner | 1958 |
| Arthur J. Sussel | 1958-59 (3 parts) |
| Charles C. Wolfe | 1959 |

Stokes Collection', *Antiques,* LXX, 5 (November, 1956), 468-471; 8 ill.

# BIBLIOGRAPHY C (*Continued*)

Stoudt, John Joseph, *Consider the Lilies How They Grow· An Interpretation of the Symbolism of Pennsylvania German Art.* Fogelsville, Pa.· The Pennsylvania German Folklore Society *Publications*, II (1937). Pp.333. Profusely illustrated.

——————, 'The Meaning of Pennsylvania German Art,' The *Historical Review of Berks County*, III, 1 (October, 1937), 3-8, and Frontispiece.

——————, *Pennsylvania Folk-Art: An Interpretation.* Allentown, Pa.: Schlechter's, 1948. Larger edition of *Consider the Lilies.* Pp.xix+43. More profusely illustrated.

Thomas, Wilbur K., 'The Landis Valley Museum, Another Step Forward', *American-German Review*, VI, 6 (August, 1940), 2-5, 20-23.

Trout, Walter C., 'A Community Where Art Flourished', *Design*, XLIII, 5 (January, 1942), 14-16; 7 ill.

'Trump Collection', (by Zehner, Olive G.), *The Dutchman*, VI, 3 (Winter, 1954-55), 10-12; 6 ill.

Wertenbaker, Thomas J., *The Founding of American Civilization: The Middle Colonies.* New York: Charles Scribner's Sons, 1938. Pp.xiii+367. Chapters VIII and IX, 'From Rhine to Susquehanna' and 'Volkskunst', are outstanding contributions in this field.

Weygandt, Cornelius, *The Red Hills.* Philadelphia, Pa.: The University of Pennsylvania Press, 1929.

——————, *The Dutch Country.* New York: Appleton-Century, 1939.

——————, *The Plenty of Pennsylvania.* New York: H. C. Kinsey & Co., 1942.

——————, 'Birds in Dutchland', *The Dutchman*, VI, 2 (Fall, 1954), 8-11; 14 ill.

——————, 'Beasts in Dutchland', *The Dutchman*, VI, 5 (Summer, 1955), 10-15; 22 ill.

Whitmore, Eleanore M., 'Origins of Pennsylvania Folk Art', *Antiques*, XXXVIII, 3 (September, 1940), 106-110. Interesting illustrations.

Williamsburg, Colonial, Inc., catalogue, *American Folk Art.* Williamsburg, Va.: Colonial Williamsburg, Inc., 1940. Pp.50+34 ill.

——————, *The Abby Aldrich Rockefeller Folk Art Collection,* (by Little, Nina Fletcher). Williamsburg, Va.: Colonial Williamsburg, Inc., 1957. Pp.402+165 color plates.

Williamson, Scott Graham, *The American Craftsman.* New York: Crown Publishers, 1940. Pp.xiv+239.

'Winterthur Museum', The Henry F. duPont, *Antiques*, LX, 5 (November, 1951), 443-446; 5 ill.

——————, New Rooms at (the Fractur Room), *Antiques, LXVII*, 2 (February, 1955), 135, 2 ill. and cover.

——————, 'New Pennsylvania Rooms at, (by Sweeney, John A. H.), *Antiques*, LXXV, 1 (January, 1959), 88-90; 7 ill.

Zerfass, S. G., *Souvenir Book of the Ephrata Cloister.* Lititz, Pa.: John G. Zook, 1921. Pp.84.

## ARCHITECTURE

Aurand, A. Monroe, Jr., *Historical Account of the Ephrata Cloister and the Seventh Day Baptist Society.* Harrisburg, Pa.: The Aurand Press, 1940.

Beck, Herbert H., 'Lititz', *The Pennsylvania Dutchman*, VIII, 1 (Summer, 1956), 24-27; 7 ill.

# BIBLIOGRAPHY C (Continued)

Brumbaugh, G. Edwin, 'Colonial Architecture of the Pennsylvania Germans', Pennsylvania German Society *Proceedings*, XLI (1930). Pp.60 and 105 ill. The basic work on this subject.

——————, 'Continental Influence on Early American Architecture', *American-German Review*, IX, 3 (February, 1943), 7-9, 37; 4 ill.

Dickson, Harold E., *A Hundred Pennsylvania Buildings*. State College, Pa.: Bald Eagle Press, 1954.

Dornbusch, Charles H., and Heyl, John K., 'Pennsylvania German Barns', Pennsylvania German Folklore Society *Publications*, XXI (1956), xxiv+299; 150 ill.

Downs, Joseph, 'A Pennsylvania-German House', Pennsylvania Museum of Art *Bulletin*, XXII, 108 (December, 1926), 265-275; 7 ill., 3 figs.

Earley, Israel B., 'Bindnagle's Church', *The Dutchman*, VI, 1 (June, 1954), 14-15; 5 ill.

Embury, Aymar, 'Pennsylvania Farmhouses: Examples of Rural Dwellings of a Hundred Years Ago', *Architectural Record*, XXX, 5 (November, 1911), 475-485.

Fegley, H. Winslow, 'Among Some of the Older Mills in Eastern Pennsylvania', Pennsylvania German Society *Proceedings*, XXXIX (1928). Pp.76 and 27 ill.

Heizmann, Louis J., 'Are Barn Signs Hex Marks?', *Historical Review of Berks County*, XII, 1 (October, 1946), 11-14.

Horwitz, Elizabeth Adams, 'Decorative Elements in the Domestic Architecture of Eastern Pennsylvania', *The Dutchman*, VII, 2 (Fall, 1955), 6-29; 20 ill.

Jayne, Horace H. F., 'Cloisters at Ephrata', *American Magazine of Art*, XXIX, 9 (September, 1936), 594-598, 620-622.

Kauffman, Henry J., 'Of Bells and Bell Towers', *The Dutchman*, VI, 1 (June, 1954), 24-25; 5 ill.

——————, 'The Riddle of Two Front Doors', *The Dutchman*, VI, 3 (Winter, 1954-55), 27; 1 ill.

——————, 'Moravian Architecture in Bethlehem', *The Dutchman*, VI, 4 (Spring, 1955), 12-19; 21 ill.

——————, 'Church Architecture in Lancaster', *The Dutchman*, VI, 5 (Summer, 1955), 16-27; 17 ill.

——————, 'Literature on Log Architecture: A Survey', *The Dutchman*, VII, 2 (Fall, 1955), 30-34; 4 ill.

——————, 'The Summer House', *The Pennsylvania Dutchman*, VIII, 1 (Summer, 1956), 2-7; 9 ill.

Kocher, Alfred Lawrence, 'The Early Architecture of Lancaster County, Pennsylvania', Lancaster County Historical Society *Papers*, XXIV, 5 (May 7, 1920), 91-106; 12 ill.

——————, 'Early Architecture of Pennsylvania', *Architectural Record*. Part 1. XLVIII, 6 (December, 1920), 512-530, 18 ill.; Part 2. XLIX, 1 (January, 1921), 31-47, 21 ill.

Landis, H. K., 'Hex Marks as Talismans', *Antiques*, XXX, 4 (October, 1936) 156-157; 5 ill.

——————, 'Early Kitchens of the Pennsylvania Germans', Pennsylvania German Society *Proceedings*, XLVII (1939). Pp.130 and 80 ill.

Mahr, August C., 'Origin and Significance of Pennsylvania Dutch Barn Symbols', *Ohio State Archaeological and Historical Quarterly*, LIV, 1 (January-March, 1945), 1-32.

Mercer, Henry C., 'The Origin of Log Houses in the United States', Bucks County Historical Society *Papers*, V (January 19, 1924), 568-583.

——————, 'An Eighteenth Century German House in Pennsylvania', *Architectural Record*, LXIII, 2 (February, 1928), 161-168; 7 fig.

# BIBLIOGRAPHY C (*Continued*)

Montgomery, Richard S., *Pennsylvania German Architecture.* Keyser 'Home Craft Course' Series, 19. Allentown, Pa.: Schlechter's, 1945.
————————, 'Houses of the Oley Valley', *The Dutchman*, VI, 3 (Winter, 1954-55), 16-26; 18 ill. and map.

Morrison, Hugh, *Early American Architecture, From the First Colonial Settlements to the National Period.* New York: Oxford University Press, 1952. See pp. 541-549 on "Pennsylvania Dutch Architecture."

Murtagh, William J., 'Half-Timbering in American Architecture', *Pennsylvania Folklife*, IX, 1 (Winter, 1957-58), 2-11; 9 ill.

Ormsbee, Thomas H., 'Pennsylvania Barns', *American Architect and Architecture,* CLI, 2661 (September, 1937), 43-50; 9 ill.

Raymond, Eleanor, *Early Domestic Architecture of Pennsylvania.* New York: William Helburn, Inc., 1931. Best work, 158 fine plates.

Sachse, Julius F., *The Kloster at Ephrata.* Leopard, Pa.: 1888-90. Manuscript with 50 excellent photographs, New York Public Library.
————————, 'Quaint Old Germantown in Pennsylvania', Pennsylvania German Society *Proceedings*, XXIII (1912), 1-7, 60 plates.
————————, *The Wayside Inns on the Lancaster Roadside Between Philadelphia and Lancaster.* Lancaster, Pa.: New Era Printing Co., 1912. Pp.vii +206.

Shoemaker, Alfred L., *Pennsylvania Dutch Hex Marks.* Lancaster, Pa.: The Pennsylvania Dutch Folklore Center, Inc., Franklin and Marshall College, 1950. Pp.32, many black and white illustrations.
————————, 'Somerset County Decorated Barns', *The Dutchman*, VI, 1 (June, 1954) 4-5; 6 ill.
————————, 'Dry House', *Pennsylvania Folklife*, IX, 4 (Fall, 1958), inside front cover; 1 ill.

Snyder, Karl H., *Moravian Architecture of Bethlehem, Pennsylvania.* New York: 1927. 24pp. (White Pine Series of architectural monographs, XIII, 4).

Stair, J. William, 'Brick-End Barns', *The Dutchman*, VI, 2 (Fall, 1954), 14-33; 35 ill., map, 3 diagrams.

Stauffer, Elmer C., 'Conewago Chapel', *The Dutchman*, VII, 4 (Spring, 1956), 28-33; 6 ill.
————————, 'The Trail of the Stone Arched Bridges in Berks County', *The Pennsylvania Dutchman*, VIII, 3 (Spring, 1957), 20-31; 38 ill. and map.

Stotz, Charles M., *The Early Architecture of Western Pennsylvania.* New York: William Helburn, Inc., 1936. Pp.290 plus more than a hundred photographs and diagrams.

Stoudt, John Joseph, *The Decorated Barns of Eastern Pennsylvania.* Keyser 'Home Craft Course' Series, 15. Allentown, Pa : Schlechter's, 1945.

Swope, Martha Ross, 'Lebanon Valley Date Stones', *The Dutchman*, VI, 1 (June, 1954), 20-22; 7 ill.

Tappert, Theodore G., 'Colonial Lutheran Churches', *American-German Review*, IX, 1 (October, 1942), 18-22.

'Two Pennsylvania German Rooms', *Pennsylvania Arts and Sciences*, I, 2 (Winter, 1936), 105-109.

Wallace, Philip B., *Colonial Churches and Meeting Houses.* New York: Architectural Book Publishing Co., 1931. Pp.xii+291.

Waterman, Thomas Tileston, *The Dwellings of Colonial America.* Chapel Hill, N C.· The University of North Carolina Press, 1950. See Chapter 2 on 'The Delaware Valley and Pennsylvania', pp.115-157.

Wertenbaker, Thomas J., *The Founding of American Civilization: The Middle Colonies.* New York Charles Scribner's Sons, 1938 Pp.xiii+367. Chapter IX, 'Volkskunst', 294-325, contains excellent architectural background.

# BIBLIOGRAPHY C (*Continued*)

FURNITURE AND DECORATION

Brazer, Clarence W., 'Primitive Hall and Its Furniture', *Antiques*, LIII, 1 (January, 1948), 55-57; 10 ill.
Brazer, Esther Stevens, *Early American Decoration*. Springfield, Mass.: Pond-Ekberg Co., 1940. Pp.xiii+273.
——————, see Fraser, Esther Stevens.
'Cabinets and Chests from the Middle Atlantic States' (Kernodle coll.), *Antiques*, LII, 1 (July, 1947), 34-35; 6 ill.
Cornelius, Charles Over, *Early American Furniture*. New York: The Century Company, 1926.
Cummings, John and Martha S., 'John Drissel and His Boxes', *Pennsylvania Folklife*, IX, 4 (Fall, 1958), 28-31; 7 ill.
Drepperd, Carl W., *American Clocks and Clockmakers*. Garden City, New York: Doubleday, 1947.
Dundore, Roy H., *Pennsylvania German Painted Furniture*. Keyser 'Home Craft Course' Series, 6. Allentown, Pa.: Schlechter's, 1944.
Eberlein, Harold D., 'Furniture Painting in Colonial America', *Arts and Decoration*, IV, 9 (July, 1914), 347-349; 4 ill.
——————, 'Bridal Furniture of the Pennsylvania Germans', *Antiquarian*, XIV, 5 (May, 1930), 35-37, 78; 10 ill.
Eberlein, Harold D., and Hubbard, C. V. D., 'Pennsylvania Dutch Furniture Combined Color and Vigor', *American Collector*, VI, 1 (February, 1937), 6-7, 10.
——————, 'Household Furniture of the Pennsylvania Germans', *American-German Review*. Part 1. III, 4 (June, 1937), 4-9, 9 ill.; Part 2. IV, 1 (September, 1937), 4-8, 8 ill.
——————, 'Pennsylvania Dutch', *Arts and Decoration*, LIV, 4 (December, 1941), 18, 27, 36; 6 ill.
Eckhardt, George H., *Pennsylvania Clocks and Clockmakers*. New York: The Devin-Adair Co., 1955.
Fraser, Esther Stevens, 'Pennsylvania Bride Boxes and Dower Chests', *Antiques*. Part 1. *Preliminaries*, VIII, 1 (July, 1925), 20-23, 4 ill.; Part 2. *County Types of Chests*, VIII, 2 (August, 1925), 79-84, 7 ill.
——————, 'Pennsylvania German Painted Chests', Pennsylvania Museum of Art *Bulletin*, XXI, 97 (November, 1925), 25-34, 40, and cover.
——————, 'A Lancaster Pennsylvania Chest', *Antiques*, X, 3 (September, 1926), 203-204; 4 ill.
——————, 'Pennsylvania German Dower Chests', *Antiques*. Part 1. XI, 2 (February, 1927), 119-123; 5 ill. Part 2. XI, 4 (April, 1927), 280-283 and cover; 5 ill. Part 3. XI, 6 (June, 1927), 474-476 and frontispiece; 14 ill.
——————, 'The American Rocking Chair', *Antiques*, XIII, 2 (February, 1928), 115-118; 9 ill.
——————, see Brazer, Esther Stevens.
James, Arthur E., *Chester County Clocks and Their Makers*. West Chester, Pa.: Chester County Historical Society, 1947.
Keyes, Homer Eaton, 'Introducing Stencilled Furniture', *Antiques*, I, 4 (April, 1922), 154-156; 6 ill.
——————, 'Some Pennsylvania Furniture', *Antiques*, V, 5 (May, 1924), 222-225; numerous illustrations of early chairs.
——————, 'A Pennsylvania Bride's Box', *American Collector*, IX, 9 (October, 1940), frontispiece.
Landis, D. H., 'Pennsylvania Decorated Boxes', *Antiques*, XXVII, 5 (May, 1935), 184-185; 5 ill
Lichten, Frances, *Pennsylvania German Chests*. Keyser 'Home Craft Course' Series, 11. Allentown, Pa.: Schlechter's, n.d.

# BIBLIOGRAPHY C (*Continued*)

Lipman, Jean, and Meulendyke, Eve, *American Folk Decoration*. New York: Oxford University Press, 1951. Pp.xii+163; 181 ill., and numerous line drawings.
Magee, D. F., 'Grandfather's Clocks: Their Making and Their Makers in Lancaster County', Lancaster County Historical Society *Papers*, XLIII, 5 (1939), 137-164; 9 ill.
Nutting, Wallace, *Furniture Treasury*. Framingham, Mass.: Old America Company, 1928. Second edition, New York: The Macmillan Company, 1948. 2 volumes, some 5000 illustrations with descriptions.
Palmer, Brooks, *The Book of American Clocks*. New York: Macmillan, 1950. Pp.viii+318; 312 ill.
'Pennsylvania Painted Dower Chest', *American Collector*, VII, 11 (Dec. 1938), cover.
Poole, Earl L., 'Joseph Lehn, Driven to Design', *American-German Review*, XV, 1 (October, 1948), 12-14; 3 ill.
Ramsay, John, 'Pennsylvania Dutch', *House Beautiful*, LXVIII, 4 (October, 1930), 362-363, 394, 396-398; 7 ill.
Reichmann, Felix, 'Pennsylvania-Dutch Furniture', Historical Society of Montgomery County *Bulletin*, III, 2 (April, 1942), 84-97; 1 ill.
Robacker, Earl F., 'Wooden Boxes of German Pennsylvania', *Antiques*, LXI, 2 (February, 1952), 171-173; 11 ill.

## CERAMICS

Barber, Edwin A., *Catalogue of American Potteries and Porcelains*. Philadelphia, Pa.: 1893.
————, *Tulip Ware of the Pennsylvania-German Potters*. Philadelphia, Pa.: The Pennsylvania Museum and School of Industrial Art, 1903. Still the basic work in this field.
————, *Lead Glazed Pottery*. Philadelphia, Pa.: Pennsylvania Museum of Art, 1907. Pp.32.
————, *The Pottery and Porcelain of the United States*. New York: G. P. Putnam, 1893, 1902, 1909. Pp. 65-88 about Pennsylvania slipware and sgraffito.
Billinger, R. D., 'Early Pennsylvania Pottery', *Journal of Chemical Engineering* (September, 1940). Good analysis of Pennsylvania clay.
Clarke, John M., *The Swiss Influence on the Early Pennsylvania Slip Decorated Majolica*. Albany, N. Y.: The New York State Museum, 1908. 8 ill.
Dyer, Walter A., *Early American Craftsmen*. New York: The Century Company, 1915. See Chapter XV, 387.
'Early Art Industries of the Pennsylvania Dutch', *Country Life in America*, XXX, 1 (May, 1916), 100, 102, 104, 106; 8 ill.
Eberlein, Harold D., 'The Decorated Pottery of the Pennsylvania Dutch', *Arts and Decoration*, IV, 4 (January, 1914), 109-112; 6 ill.
Haddon, Rawson W., 'Early Slip Decorated Canister', *Antiques*, IX, 3 (March, 1926), 166. Canister by Joseph Smith of Wrightstown, Bucks County, dated 1767.
Heckman, Albert W., 'Pennsylvania Slip Ware', *Design*, XXIII, 10 (March, 1922), 208-209; 8 ill.
Hettinger, E. L., 'Early Pennsylvania Potters', *American-German Review*, IX, 2 (December, 1942), 23-26; 6 ill.
James, A. E., *Potters & Potteries of Chester County, Pa.* West Chester, Pa.: Chester County Historical Society, 1945.
Jayne, H. H. F., 'Recent Purchase of Pennsylvania German Pottery', Pennsylvania Museum of Art *Bulletin*, XVII (May, 1922), 17-18, 26. Illustration on p. 26.
Keyes, Homer Eaton, 'Spatter', *Antiques*, XVII, 4 (April, 1930), 332-337.
Keyser, Mrs. C. Naaman, *Pottery*. Keyser 'Home Craft Course' Series, 1. Plymouth Meeting, Pa.: Mrs. C. Naaman Keyser, 1943.

## BIBLIOGRAPHY C (*Continued*)

——————————, *Pennsylvania German Pottery*. Keyser 'Home Craft Course' Series, 2. Plymouth Meeting, Pa.: Mrs. C. Naaman Keyser, 1943.

Kindig, Joe, Jr., 'A Note on Early North Carolina Pottery', *Antiques*, XXVII, 1 (January, 1935), 14-15; 4 ill.

Knittle, Rhea Mansfield, 'Henry McQuate, Pennsylvania Potter', *Antiques*, VIII (November, 1925), 286-287; 2 ill. Active in Lanacster County, 1826-1899.

Mercer, Henry C., 'The Pottery of the Pennsylvania-Germans', *The Pennsylvania German*, II (April, 1901), 86-88.

Nelson, Edna Deu Pree, 'Pennsylvania Pin-Decorated Slipware', *American Collector*, IX, 11 (December, 1940), 6-7; 7 ill.

Ormsbee, Thomas H., 'Persia, The Place Where the Blue Began', *American Collector*, II, 8 (October 4, 1934), 3-4.

——————————, 'The Chinese Conceit in Pennsylvania', *American Collector*, II, 10 (November 1, 1934), 3, 7.

Pennsylvania Museum of Arts *Bulletin*, 'The Collection of American Pottery', VI (April 1, 1904), 6.

——————————, 'Pennsylvania German Pottery', LXV (February, 1920), 25-29.

Pitkin, Albert Hastings, *Early American Folk Pottery*. Hartford, Conn.: The Case, Lockwood & Brainard Co., 1918. Pp 81-109.

Ramsay, John, 'Early American Pottery: A Résumé', *Antiques*, XX, 4 (October, 1931), 224-229; 19 ill.

——————————, *American Potters and Pottery*. Boston, Mass.: Hale, Cushman & Flint, 1939. Very good.

Reinert, Guy, 'Medinger, Last Pennsylvania Folk Potter', *American Collector*, III, 10 (May 2, 1935), 3, 9; 7 ill.

——————————, 'Slip Decorated Pottery of the Pennsylvania Germans', *American-German Review*, II, 3 (March, 1936), 12-14, 49, 12 ill.

——————————, 'Pennsylvania German Potteries of Berks County', *Historical Review of Berks County*, II, 2 (January, 1937), 42-49; 7 ill.

——————————, 'Johann Georg Buhler, Master Potter', *American-German Review*, V, 5 (June, 1939), 14-15.

Rice, A. H., and Stoudt, John Baer, *The Shenandoah Pottery*. Strasburg, Va.: Shenandoah Publishing House, Inc., 1929.

Riefstahl, R. M., 'Pennsylvania German Pottery in the Jacob Paxson Temple Collection', *Arts*, II, 2 (November, 1921), 76-80; 5 ill.

Robacker, Earl F., 'Spatterware', *The Dutchman*, VI, 2 (Fall, 1954), 2-4; 10 ill.

——————————, 'Pennsylvania Gaudyware', *The Dutchman*, VII, 4 (Spring, 1956), 2-7; 10 ill.

——————————, 'Pennsylvania Redware', *The Pennsylvania Dutchman*, VIII, 2 (Fall-Winter, 1956-57), 2-7; 14 ill.

Spargo, John, *Early American Pottery and China*. New York: The Century Company, 1926. Pp 121-156.

Stoudt, John Joseph, 'Inscriptions on the Pottery of the Pennsylvania Germans', Bucks County Historical Society *Papers*, IV (1917), 587-599.

Stow, Charles Messer, 'Pennsylvania Slip Ware', *Antiquarian*, XIII, 4 (November, 1929), 46-47, 82; 13 ill.

Thompson, Clara Belle, and Wise, Margaret Lukes, 'She Makes the Potter's Wheel Hum', *Woman's Day*, V, 7 (April, 1942), 12-13, 49-51. About Mrs. C. Naaman Keyser and her pottery.

Traux, William J., 'Early Pottery Lighting Devices of Pennsylvania', *Antiques*, XXXVII, 5 (May, 1940), 246-247; 8 ill.

Tulip Ware, 'Quaint Pottery Made in Pennsylvania', *Antiquarian*, III, 1 (August, 1924), 24-25; 1 ill.

Weygandt, Cornelius, 'The Last of the "Dutch" Potters', *General Magazine and Historical Chronicle*, XXXV, 1 (October, 1932), 12-20; 4 ill. on pages 78-79.

# BIBLIOGRAPHY C (*Continued*)

——————, 'A Maker of Pennsylvania Redware', *Antiques*, XLIX, 6 (June, 1946), 372-373; 6 ill. About Jacob Medinger and William J. McAlister, who assisted him.

## GLASS

Barber, Edwin A, *American Glassware Old and New*. Philadelphia, Pa.: Patterson and White Company, 1900. See Stiegel, pages 37-38.

——————, 'Some New Discoveries in Early American Glassware', Pennsylvania Museum of Art *Bulletin*, 13 (January, 1906), 1-7.

Brendle, Abraham S., 'Henry William Stiegel', Lebanon County Historical Society *Papers and Addresses*, VI, 3 (August, 1912), 59-76.

Dyer, Walter A., 'Baron Stiegel and His Glassware', *House Beautiful*, XXXVII, 1 (December, 1914), 24-28.

——————, *Early American Craftsmen*. New York: The Century Co., 1915.

Eberlein, Harold D., 'Baron Stiegel and His Manheim Glass', *Arts and Decoration*, IV, 7( May, 1914), 273-275

Eberlein, Harold D., and Hubbard, C. V. D., 'Baron Stiegel of Manheim', *American-German Review*, V, 5 (June, 1939), 4-9; 5 ill.

Heiges, George L., *Henry William Stiegel: The Life Story of a Famous American Glass-Maker*. Manheim, Pa.: The Author, 1937. New Edition, 1949.

Hostetter Sales Catalogues, I and II. Lancaster, Pa.: October and November, 1946.

Humphreys, Gregor Norman, 'Foreign Influences in American Glass', *Antiques*, XIV, 3 (September, 1928), 242-246; numerous illustrations.

Hunter, Frederick W, *Stiegel Glass*  Boston and New York· Houghton Mifflin Company, 1914  Revised edition with introduction by Helen McKearin, New York: Dover Publications, 1950. Pp.xxii+272; 159 halftones and 12 col. pl.

Knittle, Rhea Mansfield, *Early American Glass*. New York: The Century Co., 1927.

Law, Margaret L., 'Baron Stiegel and His Glass', *Antiquarian*, X, 5 (June, 1928), 41-43.

McKearin, George S., and Helen, *American Glass*. New York: Crown Publishers, 1941. Profusely illustrated, most comprehensive.

McKearin, Helen A, 'The Stiegel Blown Three-Mold Myth', *Antiques*, XVII, 4 (April, 1930), 338-341; 8 ill.

——————, Helen A. and George S., *Two Hundred Years of American Blown Glass*. Garden City, N.Y · Doubleday & Co, Inc., 1950. Pp.xvi+382; 114 plates of which 10 are in color. Excellent.

Moore, N. Hudson, *Old Glass· European and American*  New York: Frederick A. Stokes Company, 1924. Frontispiece and plates 129, 132, 134.

Northend, Mary Harrod, *American Glass*. New York: Dodd, Mead and Company, 1926. See page 37

Pyne, Francis Loring, 'Stiegel Glass', *Antiquarian* II (March, 1924), 18-21.

Quigley Sale Catalogue, Mr. and Mrs Richard S., Pennypacker Auction Centre, Kenhorst, Pa., April 24-25, 1947.

Riefstahl, Rudolf M, 'Early American Glass', *International Studio*, LXXVII, 311 (April, 1923), 8-11; 10 ill.

Siehng, J. H, 'Baron Henry William Stiegel', Lancaster County Historical Society *Papers*, I (1896), 44-65.

Watkins, Lura Woodside, *American Glass and Glassmaking*  New York: Chanticleer Press, 1950. Pp 104; 32 black and white plates, 4 color plates, plus line drawings

Wolfe Sale Catalogue, Charles C., Pennypacker Auction Centre, Kenhorst, Pa., October 19, 1959.

## BIBLIOGRAPHY C (*Continued*)

METALWORK: BRASS AND COPPER

Benson, Evelyn A., 'A Pennsylvania Dutch Colonial Button Mold', *The Pennsylvania Dutchman*, VIII, 4 (Summer-Fall, 1957), 34, 48; 3 ill.

Kauffman, Henry J., 'Coppersmithing in Pennsylvania', Pennsylvania German Folklore Society *Publications*, XI (1946), 83-153; 45 ill.

————————, *Early American Copper, Tin, and Brass*. New York: McBride, 1950. Pp.112 and 90 ill.

Kauffman, Henry J. and Zoe Elizabeth, *Pennsylvania German Copper and Brass*. Keyser 'Home Craft Course' Series, 25. Kutztown, Pa.: The Kutztown Publishing Company, 1947.

METALWORK. IRON

Abels, Robert, *Early American Firearms*. Cleveland and New York: World Publishing Co., 1950. Pp.63; 25 ill. and 9 col pl.

Allen, Philip Meredith, 'Old Iron', *Antiquarian*, XIII, 2 (March, 1927), 42-46; 6 ill.

Barber, Edwin A., 'American Iron Work of the Eighteenth Century', Pennsylvania Museum of Art *Bulletin*, XI, 40 (October, 1912), 59-62

————————, 'Cast Iron Stoves of the Pennsylvania Germans', Pennsylvania Museum of Art *Bulletin*, XIII, 5 (April, 1915), 19-23.

Dillin, Capt. John G. W., *The Kentucky Rifle*. Washington, D C.: National Rifle Association of America, 1924. Basic work. Third edition (New York: Ludlum and Beebe, 1946) contains additional chapter 'The Kentucky Pistol', by George N. Hyatt. 4th edition (York, Pa.: Trimmer Printing, Inc., 1959) new chapter on 'The Bedford County Rifle and Its Makers' by Calvin Hetrick.

Dyer, Walter A, 'American Fire Backs and Stove Plates', *Antiques*, XXV, 2 (February, 1934), 60-63; 13 ill.

Eberlein, Harold D., 'Decorative Cast Iron in Colonial America', *Arts and Decoration*, IV, 10 (August, 1914), 374-377, 7 ill

Fegley, H. Winslow, 'Historic Stove Plates', *House Beautiful*, XXXVII, 4 (March, 1915), 128-129; 11 ill.

Kauffman, Henry J, *Early American Gunsmiths, 1650-1850*. Harrisburg, Pa : The Stackpole Co., 1952. Pp.94; 70 ill.

————————, *The Pennsylvania Kentucky Rifle* Harrisburg, Pa.· The Stackpole Co., 1960. Pp. 376; 293 plates.

Kindig, Joe, Jr, *Thoughts On the Kentucky Rifle In Its Golden Age*. Wilmington, Del. George N. Hyatt, 1960. Pp. XII+561; 856 plates.

King, F. C, 'Early Pennsylvania German Iron Hinges', Pennsylvania Museum of Art *Bulletin*, XX, 92 (February, 1925), 82-88.

Landis, Henry K., and Landis, George Diller, 'Lancaster Rifles', Pennsylvania German Folklore Society *Publications*, VII (1942), 105-157; many illustrations.

————————, 'Lancaster Rifle Accessories', Pennsylvania German Folklore Society *Publications*, IX (1944). 107-184; 30 plates.

Mercer, Henry C., *The Decorated Stove Plates of the Pennsylvania Germans*. Bucks Co. Hist. Soc. *Contributions to American History*, 6. Doylestown, Pa.: 1899.

————————, *The Bible in Iron, or, the Pictured Stoves and Stove Plates of the Pennsylvania Germans*. Second edition, revised by Horace M. Mann. Doylestown, Pa.: Bucks County Historical Society, 1941.

National Society of the Colonial Dames of America, *Forges and Furnaces in the Province of Pennsylvania* Philadelphia, Pa.: Printed for the Society, 1914.

Nelson, Edna Deu Pree, 'Five Plate Stove Was First Here', *American Collector*, V, 2 (March, 1936), 1, 10-11.

Ormsbee, T. H., 'Stiegel as an Iron-Master', *American Collector*, I, 8 (April, 1934), 2.

Peirce, Josephine H., *Fire on the Hearth* Springfield, Mass.· The Pond-Ekberg Co., 1951. For list of Pennsylvania furnaces, see pages 233-34.

## BIBLIOGRAPHY C (*Continued*)

Robacker, Earl F., 'The Dutch Touch in Iron', *The Pennsylvania Dutchman*, VIII, 3 (Spring, 1957), 2-6; 12 ill.

Savage, Robert H., *Pennsylvania German Wrought Ironwork*. Keyser 'Home Craft Course' Series, 10. Kutztown, Pa.: The Kutztown Publishing Company, 1947.

Sonn, Albert H., *Early American Wrought Iron*. New York: Charles Scribner's Sons, 1923. 3 volumes fully illustrated

Stow, Charles M., 'A Portrait in Iron', *Antiquarian*, XIV (June, 1930), 29-31. Stiegel as a maker of stove-plates.

Thormin, Dorothy Miller, 'Types of Wrought Iron Hardware Applicable to Early American Architecture Treatment', *Antiques*. Part 1. XII, 4 (October 1927), 310-311, Part 2. XII, 5 (November, 1927), 400-401; and Part 3. XII, 6 (December, 1927), 500-501.

Thwing, Leroy, *Flickering Flames, A History of Domestic Lighting Through the Ages*. Rutland, Vermont: Charles E. Tuttle Co., 1958.

### METALWORK · PEWTER

Auman, Paul M., 'New Finds in Old Pewter by William Will: The Aaronsburg Communion Service', *Antiques*, LVII, 4 (April, 1950), 274-275; 5 ill.

Brinton, Francis D, 'New Light on Elisha Kirk', *Antiques*, LI, 4 (April, 1947), 253.

Downs, Joseph, *American Pewterers and Their Marks*. New York The Metropolitan Museum of Art, 1942.

Evans, John J., Jr., 'I. C. H., Lancaster Pewterer', *Antiques*, XX, 3 (September 1931), 150-153

———————, 'A Flat-Top Tankard', *Antiques*, LVII, 4 (April, 1950), 276-277; 4 ill.

———————, 'Some Pewter by William Will' (Hershey Museum), *Antiques*, LXI, 2 (February, 1952), 178-179; 5 ill.

———————, 'Lovebirds and lions: a pewter mystery solved', *Antiques*, LXXVI, 2 (August, 1959), 142-143; 4 ill.

Graham, John M., II, *American Pewter*. Brooklyn, N.Y.: The Brooklyn Museum Press, 1949. Pp.36, 31 ill.

Heyne, John Christoph, Pewterer, editorial note, *Antiques*, XXXIII, 1 (January, 1938), 13.

Jacobs, Carl, *Guide to American Pewter*. New York · The McBride Company, Inc., 1957.

Kauffman, Henry J., *Pennsylvania German Pewter*. Keyser 'Home Craft Course' Series, 8. Allentown, Pa. · Schlechter's, 1944.

Kerfoot, J. B., *American Pewter*. New York: Scribner, 1924, and New Edition by Crown Publishers, 1942.

Keyes, Homer Eaton, 'Pennsylvania Pewter', *Antiques*, XIII, 2 (February, 1928), 112-113; frontispiece and 4 ill.

———————, 'The German Strain in Pennsylvania Pewter', *Antiques*, XXVII, 1 (January, 1935), 23-25, 7 ill.

Laughlin, Ledlie I., *Pewter in America: Its Makers and Their Marks* (2 vols.). Houghton Mifflin Company, 1940. For 'The Pewterers of Pennsylvania', see Vol. II, pp.35-68 and plates LXV-LXVII.

Myers, Louis Guerineau, *Some Notes on American Pewterers*. Garden City, N.Y.: Country Life Press, 1926.

Nichols, Melville T., '"Trade Marks" on American Pewter', *Antiques*, LI, 6 (June, 1947), 394-396; 13 ill.

# BIBLIOGRAPHY C (*Continued*)

### METALWORK TIN

Heller, Edna Eby, 'Cookies Just for Nice', *The Dutchman*, VI, 3 (Winter, 1954-55), 8-9; 6 ill.

Hoke, Elizabeth S., *Pennsylvania German Painted Tin.* Keyser 'Home Craft Course' Series, 5. Allentown, Pa.: Schlechter's, 1943.

————, *The Painted Tray and Free Hand Bronzing.* Keyser 'Home Craft Course' Series, 29. Plymouth Meeting, Pa.: Mrs. C. Naaman Keyser, 1949.

Kauffman, Henry J., 'Punched Tinware', *The Pennsylvania Dutchman*, V, 10 (January 15, 1954), 3; 3 ill. and cover.

Keyes, Homer Eaton, 'Painted Tin Ware', *Antiques*, XIII, 3 (March, 1928), 197-198; frontispiece.

Nelson, Edna Deu Pree, 'Old Tin Pieces Are Friendly', *American Collector*, VI, 6 (July, 1937), 1 and 17-18.

Robacker, Earl F., 'Pennsylvania Cooky Cutters', *Antiques*, XXXIV, 6 (December, 1938), 304-307; 8 plates with numerous specimens

————, 'Folk Art in Pennsylvania Dutch Cooky Cutters', *American Collector*, X, 12 (January, 1942), 10-11; 5 ill

————, 'The Painted Toleware of Pennsylvania', Early American Industries Association *Chronicle*, II, 24 (September, 1943), 209

————, 'Christmas Cookies and Cutters' Keyser 'Home Craft Course' Series, 18. Kutztown, Pa.: The Kutztown Publishing Co., 1946.

————, 'The Case for Pennsylvania German Painted Tin', *Antiques*, LII, 4 (October, 1947), 263-265; 6 ill

————, 'Of Cookies and Cooky Cutters', *The Pennsylvania Dutchman*, IV, 8 (December, 1952), 4-5; 2 ill

————, 'Art in Christmas Cookies', *The Dutchman*, VI, 3 (Winter, 1954-55), 2-7; 12 ill.

————, 'Painted Tin or "Tole" ', *The Dutchman*, VI, 4 (Spring, 1955), 2-7; 14 ill.

Swan, Mabel M., 'The Village Tinsmith, *Antiques*, XIII, 3 (March, 1928), 211-214.

### PAINTING

Barba, Preston and Eleanor, 'Lewis Miller, Pennsylvania German Folk Artist', *American-German Review.* Part 1. 'Chronicler of York, Pa.', IV, 3 (March, 1938), 32-39, 50; 7 ill. Part 2. 'Traveler and Portraitist', IV, 4 (June, 1938), 11-19; 14 ill. Reprinted and enlarged in Pennsylvania German Folklore Society *Publications*, IV (1939). Pennsylvania sections printed in *Historical Review of Berks County*, III, 4 (July, 1938), 98-107; 13 ill and cover.

Bye, Arthur Edwin, 'Edward Hicks, Painter-Preacher', *Antiques*, XXIX, 1 (January, 1936), 13-16, 6 ill

Dickson, Harold E., *Pennsylvania Painters.* University Park, Pa.: The Pennsylvania State University, 1955.

Ford, Alice, *Pictorial Folk Art, New England to California* New York: The Studio Publications, Inc, 1949. Pp.172, 135 ill. and frontispiece.

————, *Edward Hicks, Painter of the Peaceable Kingdom.* Philadelphia, Pa.: University of Pennsylvania Press, 1952.

————, *Edward Hicks, 1780-1849.* Williamsburg, Va.· Abby Aldrich Rockefeller Folk Art Collection, 1960 Pp. 22; 7 ill.

*From Colony to Nation: An Exhibition of American Painting, Silver and Architecture from 1650 to the War of 1812.* Chicago, Ill.: The Art Institute of Chicago, 1949.

Hicks, Edward, *Memoirs of the Life and Religious Labors of E. Hicks· Written by Himself.* Philadelphia, Pa.: Merrihew and Thompson, 1851.

210

## BIBLIOGRAPHY C (*Continued*)

Hoke, Elizabeth S., *Pennsylvania German Reverse Painting on Glass*. Keyser 'Home Craft Course' Series, 12. Kutztown, Pa.: The Kutztown Publishing Company, 1946.

Kees, Ann, 'The Peaceable Painter', *Antiques*, LII, 4 (October, 1947), 254; frontispiece and 3 ill.

Lichten, Frances, 'John Landis, Author and Artist and Oriental Tourist', Philadelphia Museum of Art *Bulletin*, LIII, 257 (Spring, 1958), 51-53; 1 ill.

Lipman, Jean, and Winchester, Alice, *Primitive Painters in America*. New York: Dodd Mead, 1950. Pp 182; 72 ill. with 4 in color.

Poole, Earl L., 'Reverse Glass Paintings', *Historical Review of Berks County*, V, 1 (October, 1939), 2 and 3.

————, 'Artists and Painters of Reading', *Historical Review of Berks County*, IX, 2 (January, 1944), 34-38, 4 ill.

Price, Frederic Newlin, *Edward Hicks, 1780-1849*. New York: Printed for the Benjamin West Society of Swarthmore College and Ferargil Galleries, 1945.

Richardson, E. P., *Painting in America*. New York · Thomas Y. Crowell Co., 1956.

Shoemaker, Alfred L., 'Reading's First Artist, A Painter of Butterflies', *Historical Review of Berks County*, XIII, 3 (April, 1948), 89-90; 1 ill.

SCULPTURE

Allis, Mary, 'The Last of the American Folk Arts', *American Collector*, IX, 12 (January, 1941), 10-11, 14; 15 ill.

Barba, Preston A and Eleanor, 'Pennsylvania German Tombstones A Study in Folk Art', Pennsylvania German Folklore Society *Publications*, XVIII (1953). Pp.v+227; 98 ill.

Herricht, Fred, *The Putz, Carved Wood Figures*. Keyser 'Home Craft Course' Series, 17. Kutztown, Pa.: The Kutztown Publishing Company, 1946.

Hommel, Rudolf, 'Tavern Inscriptions', *American-German Review*, IX, 1 (October, 1942), 31-32; 2 illustrations with fraktur letters.

Kauffman, Henry J., 'Philadelphia Butter', *The Pennsylvania Dutchman*, VIII, 2 (Fall-Winter, 1956-57), 8-13; 15 ill.

Landis, H. K., 'Abbreviated Inscriptions in German Pennsylvania', *Antiques*, XXXII, 3 (September, 1937), 122-123; 5 ill.

Larsen, Peter, 'Butter Stamps and Molds', *Antiques*, XXXVI, 1 (July, 1939), 29-30; 5 ill

Lichten, Frances, '"Tramp Work": Penknife Plus Cigar Boxes', X, 1 (Spring, 1959), 2-7; 5 ill.

Lipman, Jean, *American Folk Art in Wood, Metal, and Stone*. New York: Pantheon Press, 1948. Pp.193; 183 ill, 4 col pl.

McAllister, W. J., *Pennsylvania German Wood Carving*. Keyser 'Home Craft Course' Series, 13. Allentown, Pa.. Schlechter's, 1945.

McKearin, Helen A., 'Schimmel, Carver of a Menagerie', *The New York Sun*, November 6, 1929. Page 35, columns 1-3.

Newark Museum, exhibition catalogue, *American Folk Sculpture*. Edited by Holger Cahill and Elinor Robinson, October 20, 1931 to January 31, 1932.

Ormsbee, Thomas H., 'Toy Banks Lured Children to Ways of Thrift', *American Collector*, I, 12 (May 31, 1934), 3, 6, 11.

Reichmann, Felix, 'Two Inscriptions from the Landis Valley Museum', *American-German Review*, VIII, 5 (June, 1942), 11-12, 38, 2 ill.

Robacker, Earl F., 'Pennsylvania German Wood Carvings', *Antiques*, XLIX, 6 (June, 1946), 369-371; 6 illustrations with numerous examples.

————, 'Butter Molds', *The Dutchman*, VI, 1 (June, 1954), 6-8; 5 ill.

# BIBLIOGRAPHY C (*Continued*)

TEXTILES

Atwater, Mary M., *The Shuttle-Craft Book of American Hand-Weaving*. New York: The Macmillan Co., 1951.

Bolton, Ethel Stanwood, and Coe, Eva Johnston, *American Samplers*. Boston: The Massachusetts Society of Colonial Dames of America, 1921.

————————, 'Five Contemporary Samplers', *Antiques*, XIV, 1 (July, 1928), 42-45. Three are from Pennsylvania, one dated 1785.

Carrick, Alice VanLeer, 'Eat Your Cake and Have It Too', *Ladies Home Journal*, XXXIX, 3 (March, 1922), 114, 116, 118; 18 ill.

Chapman, Etta Tyler, 'The Tyler Coverlets', *Antiques*, XIII, 3 (March, 1928), 215-218. Coverlet designs.

Colonial Coverlet Guild of America, *Heirlooms from Old Looms*. Chicago, Ill.: Privately printed, 1940 and 1955. Profusely illustrated.

Davidson, Marguerite P., *Pennsylvania German Home Weaving Patterns*. Keyser 'Home Craft Course' Series, 4. Allentown, Pa.: Schlechter's, 1943.

Frismuth, Sarah S., 'Old Samplers', Pennsylvania Museum of Art *Bulletin*, 15 (July, 1906), 37-41.

Graeff, Marie Knorr, *Pennsylvania German Quilts*. Keyser 'Home Craft Course' Series, 14. Kutztown, Pa.: The Kutztown Publishing Company, 1946.

Hall, Eliza Calvert, *A Book of Hand-Woven Coverlets*. Boston, Mass.: Little, Brown and Company, 1912. Frontispiece and pages 177, 188.

Harbeson, Georgianna Brown, *American Needlework*. New York: Coward-McCann Inc., 1938. Pp.xxxviii+232.

Hommel, Rudolf, 'About Spinning Wheels', *American-German Review*, IX, 6 (August, 1943), 4-7; 5 ill.

Huntley, Richmond, 'Door Panels Adhere to Oldest Sampler Form', *American Collecter*, II, 12 (November 29, 1934), 3 and 8.

Kelley, Hazel Reeder, *The ABC of Rug Making*. Keyser 'Home Craft Course' Series, 24. Kutztown, Pa.: The Kutztown Publishing Company, 1947.

Lichten, Frances, 'Pennsylvania Dutch Needlework: Where Did the Worker Find Her Patterns?', *The Dutchman*, VII, 4 (Spring, 1956), 18-21; 6 ill.

Little, Frances, 'Early Cotton Printing in America', *Antiques*, XIII, 1 (January, 1928), 38-42. Bird and tulip design in Pennsylvania resist prints.

————————, *Early American Textiles*. New York: The Century Company, 1931.

Maria Hocker's Sampler, Ephrata, 1768, Pennsylvania German Society *Proceedings*, XIX (1910), opposite page 98.

'Needle Work Ideas From Old American Designs', *Woman's Day*, V, 6 (March, 1942), 20-25.

Osburn, Bernice B., *Pennsylvania German Spinning and Dyeing*. Keyser 'Home Craft Course' Series, 16. Allentown, Pa.: Schlechter's, 1945.

Pennsylvania Appliquéd Bedspread, *Antiques*, XXI, 4 (April,1932), cover and 161.

Pennsylvania German Needlework, *American-German Review*, VII, 6 (June, 1941).

Peto, Florence, *American Quilts and Coverlets*. New York: Chanticleer Press, 1940. Well illustrated with new material.

Ramsay, John, 'A Note on the Geography of Hooked Rugs', *Antiques*, XVIII, 6 (December, 1930), 510-512.

Reinert, Guy F., *Pennsylvania German Coverlets*. Keyser 'Home Craft Course' Series, 9. Kutztown, Pa.: The Kutztown Publishing Company, 1947.

————————, *Coverlets of the Pennsylvania Germans*. Allentown, Pa.: Pennsylvania German Folklore Society *Publications*, XIII (1948). Pp.215+118 black and white ill.; also about books on dyeing, 170-215.

Robertson, Elizabeth Wells, *American Quilts*. New York: The Studio Publications, Inc., 1948. Profusely illustrated.

## BIBLIOGRAPHY C (*Continued*)

Specimen Pennsylvania German Sampler by Regina Huebner, 1794, Pennsylvania German Society *Proceedings*, XIII (1902), opposite p.200.
Wheeler, Candace, *The Development of Embroidery in America*. New York: Harper & Brothers, 1921. Pp.x+152.

### CONESTOGA WAGONS

Barba, Preston, 'Conestoga Wagons', *'S Pennsylfawnisch Deitsch Eck*, Allentown, Pa., "Morning Call" (November 25, and December 9, and 16, 1939).
Drachman, Albert I., 'The Conestoga Wagon', *The Dutchman*, VI, 4 (Spring, 1955), 24-29; 3 ill.
Frey, H. C., 'The Conestoga Wagon', Lancaster County Historical Society *Papers*, XXXIV, 13 (1930), 289-312.
————, 'The Conestoga Wagoners', *Pennsylvania Arts and Sciences*, III, 2 (July, 1938), 86-87, 114; 2 ill.
Landis, H. K., 'Conestoga Wagons and Their Ornamental Ironing', Pennsylvania German Folklore Society *Publications*, III (1938), 1-15; 7 ill.
Omwake, John, *The Conestoga Six-Horse Bell Teams of Eastern Pennsylvania*. Cincinnati, Ohio: Ebbert and Richardson, 1930.

### MISCELLANEOUS CRAFTS

Mercer, Henry C., *Light and Fire Making*. Bucks County Historical Society *Contributions to American History*, IV. Philadelphia, Pa.: MacCalla & Co., 1898.
Osburn, Burl N., *Bookbinding*. Keyser 'Home Craft Course' Series, 21. Allentown, Pa.: Schlechter's, 1945.
Reichmann, Felix, 'Pennsylvania Thrift—Some Old Time Penny Banks from the Landis Valley Museum', *American-German Review*, VII, 2 (December, 1940), 16-20, 15 ill.
Reinert, Guy F., 'Schiene- und Strohkorbe (Splint and Straw Baskets) An Old Pennsylvania Dutch Hand Craft', *American-German Review*, VII, 1 (October, 1940), 28-29; 7 ill.
————, *Pennsylvania German Splint and Straw Baskets*. Keyser 'Home Craft Course' Series, 22. Kutztown, Pa.· The Kutztown Publishing Co., 1946.
Robacker, Earl F., 'Antiques for Fancy and for Fun', *The Dutchman*, VI, 5 (Summer, 1955), 2-6; 12 ill.
————, 'Basketry: A Pennsylvania Dutch Art', *The Dutchman*, VII, 2 (Fall, 1955), 2-5, 10 ill.
Shoemaker, Alfred L., 'Scratch-Carved Easter Eggs!' (Fred Wichmann Collection), *The Dutchman*, VI, 4 (Spring, 1955), 20-23; 14 ill.
Zehner, Olive G., 'Hardly Bigger Than a Peanut' (antiques in miniature), *The Dutchman*, VI, 2 (Fall, 1954), 34-36; 11 ill.

## D. PENNSYLVANIA GERMAN FRAKTUR

### HANDWRITTEN FRAKTUR

Bender, Harold S., 'Christopher Dock, the Pious Schoolmaster on the Skippack', *American-German Review*, XI, 3 (February, 1945), 4-7, 36. See page 6.
Borneman, Henry S., 'Pennsylvania German Bookplates', *Colophon*, Il, 3 (July, 1937), 432-442; 3 col. pl.
————, *Pennsylvania German Illuminated Manuscripts* Norristown, Pa.: The Pennsylvania German Society *Proceedings*, XLVI, 1937. The basic work, with 36 color plates.

# BIBLIOGRAPHY D (Continued)

——————————, 'Fraktur-Schriften, Illuminated Manuscripts of the Pennsylvania Germans', *Pennsylvania Arts and Sciences*, III, 2 (July, 1938), 72-78, 116; 8 ill.

——————————, exhibition catalogue, *Pennsylvania German Fraktur*. Philadelphia: Carl Schurz Memorial Foundation, April 1 thru Sept. 1, 1943. Pp.4.

——————————, 'Exhibition of Pennsylvania German Fraktur', *American-German Review*, IX, 4 (April, 1943), 33-34; cover and 1 ill.

——————————, 'On the Illuminated Writings (Fraktur Schriften) of the Pennsylvania Germans', *American-German Review*, IX, 5 (June, 1943), 32-35; cover and 2 ill.

——————————, *Pennsylvania German Bookplates*. Philadelphia, Pa.: Pennsylvania German Society *Publications*, LIV, 1953. Pp iv+169; 24 color plates.

Boyer, Melville J., 'Specimens of Sacred Pictorial Poetry', Lehigh County Historical Society *Proceedings* (1944), 44-53. For Durs Rudy *Metamorphosis*, signed and dated 1832, see page 52.

Brooklyn Museum, exhibition catalogue, *Popular Art in America*. Brooklyn, N.Y.: Brooklyn Museum Press, 1939. Pp.2 and 3; ill. on p.19.

Brumbaugh, Martin G., *The Life and Works of Christopher Dock*. Philadelphia, Pa.: J. B. Lippincott & Co., 1903. Pp.272.

Chew, Paul A., *Two Hundred and Fifty Years of Art in Pennsylvania*. Greensburg, Pa.: The Westmoreland County Museum of Art, 1959. Pp.xi+105; 211 ill. See plates 148-151, 153-161.

David, Hans T., 'Hymns and Music of the Pennsylvania Seventh-Day Baptists', *American-German Review*, IX, 5 (June, 1943), 4-6; 1 ill.

——————————, 'Musical Composition at Ephrata', *American-German Review*, X, 5 (June, 1944), 4-5.

Downs, Joseph, *The House of the Miller at Millbach*. Philadelphia, Pa.: The Pennsylvania Museum of Art, 1929. Pp 27+32 pl.

——————————, *A Handbook of the Pennsylvania German Galleries in the American Wing*. New York: The Metropolitan Museum of Art, 1934. See page 8, figures 5 and 6.

——————————, *Pennsylvania German Arts and Crafts, A Picture Book*. New York: The Metropolitan Museum of Art, 1946. Introduction and 30 plates. For Fraktur, see plates 17-21.

Downtown Gallery, exhibition catalogue, *Vital Statistics*. New York: Downtown Gallery, 1936. Nos. 1-14.

——————————, *Children in American Folk Art*. New York: Downtown Gallery, 1937. Pages 8-9, numbers 26-31.

Drepperd, Carl W., *American Pioneer Arts and Artists*. Springfield, Mass.: The Pond-Ekberg Co., 1942.

Eberlein, Harold D., 'Pen and Brush Illuminations of the Pennsylvania Germans', *Arts and Decoration*, IV, 8 (June, 1914), 315-317, 327; 8 ill.

——————————, 'The Art of Fractur in Early Pennsylvania', *American Homes and Gardens*, XI, 11 (November, 1914), 390-391; 396; 6 ill.

——————————, 'What Early America Had On Its Walls', *International Studio*, LXXXVIII, 364 (September, 1927), 52-56.

Eberlein, Harold D., and Hubbard, C. V. D., 'Fractur Painting in Pennsylvania', *American-German Review*, III, 1 (September, 1936), 36-40; 8 ill.

——————————, 'Illuminated Monastic Manuscripts Were Origin of Fractur-Painting,' *American Collector*, V, 8 (September, 1936), 4-5, 10-11; 11 ill.

Eberlein, Harold D., and McClure, Abbot, *The Practical Book of Early American Arts and Crafts*. Philadelphia, Pa.: J. B. Lippincott Co., 1916. Pp.iii+339.

214

## BIBLIOGRAPHY D (*Continued*)

——————, *The Practical Book of American Antiques*. Philadelphia, Pa.: J. B. Lippincott Company, 1927. Chapter XII, 286-297, on 'The Art of Fractur or Pen-and-Brush Illuminations.'

Eckhardt, George H., 'The Henry S. Borneman collection of Pennsylvania-German fracturs', *Antiques*, LXXI, 6 (June, 1957), 538-540; 5 ill.

Edye, M. Louise, *Pennsylvania German Illuminated Manuscripts*. Keyser 'Home Craft Course' Ser. 7. Plymouth Meeting, Pa.: Mrs. C. Naaman Keyser, 1945.

Ford, Alice, *Pictorial American Folk Art, New England to California*. New York and London: The Studio Publications, Inc., 1949. Pp.30-33; illustrations on pages 146-147.

'Fractur, First Reference to Pennsylvania Dutch', in *Lancaster Examiner* of April 16, 1835, 'The Pennsylvania Dutchman', V, 10 (January 15, 1954), 16, 11. Reprinted by Alfred L. Shoemaker.

Frederick, J. George, *The Pennsylvania Dutch and Their Cookery*. New York: The Business Bourse, 1935.

Friedrich, Gerhard, 'The A. H. Cassel Collection at Juniata College', *American-German Review*, VII, 6 (August, 1941), 18-21; 4 ill.

——————, 'The Seven Rules of Wisdom', *American-German Review*, XI, 2 (December, 1944), 15-16; 2 ill.

Geesey Collection, Titus C., and Others, *Pennsylvania Dutch Folk Arts from the* (by Lichten, Frances). Philadelphia, Pa.: Philadelphia Museum of Art, 1958. Pp.12-13, 21-24; 6 Frakturs illustrated.

Gilbert, Russell Wieder, *A Picture of the Pennsylvania Germans*. Gettysburg, Pa.: The Pennsylvania Historical Association, 1947. Cover and pages 32-37.

Heilbron, Bertha L., 'Pennsylvania German Baptismal Certificates in Minnesota', *Minnesota History*, XXVII, 1 (March, 1946), 29-32.

'In the Museums' (Fraktur at the Brussels World's Fair), *Antiques*, LXXIII, 5 (May, 1958), 476.

Jackson, Schuyler B., sales catalogue, *Pennsylvania Furniture, Pen-Paintings and Other Objects, 1780-1850*. New York: American Art Association-Anderson Galleries, sale #4067, Nov. 29, 1933. Pp.59, with 27 fraktur illustrations.

Kauffman, Henry J., *Pennsylvania Dutch American Folk Art*. New York: American Studio Books, 1946. Pp.30-31, and many illustrations.

Keyes, Homer Eaton, 'A Pennsylvania German Bookplate', *Antiques*, XIV, 1 (July, 1928), 27; 1 ill.

——————, 'Valentine', (1812), *Antiques*, XV, 2 (February, 1929), 111-112; 1 ill.

Kieffer, Elizabeth C., 'Penmanship, The Art of the Scrivener', *The Pennsylvania Dutchman*, V, 13 (March 1, 1954), 3, 12, 15.

Kriebel, Lester K., 'A Brief History and Interpretation of Pennsylvania German Illuminated Writings (Fraktur-Schriften)', Historical Society of Montgomery County *Bulletin*, III, 1 (October, 1941), 20-31; 1 ill.

Lichten, Frances, *Folk Art of Rural Pennsylvania*. New York: Charles Scribner's Sons, 1946. See pages 190-223; many black and white, and colored plates.

——————, 'Fractur from the Hostetter Collection', *The Dutchman*, VI, 1 (June, 1954), 10-13; 6 ill.

——————, *Fraktur: The Illuminated Manuscripts of the Pennsylvania Dutch*. Philadelphia, Pa.: The Free Library of Philadelphia, 1958. Pp.26.

——————, see *Geesey Collection and Others* (1958).

Lipman, Jean, and Meulendyke, Eve, *American Folk Decoration*. New York: Oxford University Press, 1951. Pages 143-155.

BIBLIOGRAPHY D *(Continued)*

Mallory, Paul, 'Fractur Painting, A Medieval Survival', *Primitive and Peasant Art.* Syracuse, N.Y.: Keramic Studio Publishing Company, 1932. Assembled from special issues of *Design*, XXXIII, 10 (March, 1932), 254-255; 2 ill.

McClinton, Katharine Morrison, *A Handbook of Popular Antiques.* New York: Random House, 1945 and 1946. Chapter XVIII, 'Pennsylvania Dutch and Other Illuminated Manuscripts and Cutwork', pp.160-166.

Mercer, Henry C., 'The Survival of the Medieval Art of Illuminative Writing Among the Pennsylvania Germans.' Philadelphia, Pa.· American Philosophical Society *Proceedings*, XXXVI (September 17, 1897), 423-432. Reprinted for the Bucks County Historical Society *Contributions to American History*, II, 1897.

Miller, Elizabeth K., 'An Ephrata Hymnal', *Antiques*, LII, 4 (October, 1947), 260-262; 10 ill.

Museum of Modern Art, exhibition catalogue, *American Folk Art: The Art of the Common Man in America, 1750-1900.* New York: Museum of Modern Art, 1932. Pages 17-18, items 72-78.

Newark Museum, exhibition catalogue, *American Primitives.* Edited by Holger Cahill and Elinor Robinson. November 4, 1930 to February 1, 1931. P.69.

Ormsbee, Thomas H., 'Our Valentine First Handmade', *American Collector*, VI, 1 (February, 1937), 1, 12-13. History of American valentines.

Paul, Velma Mackay, 'Geburts und Taufschein', *American Antiques Journal*, III, 1 (January, 1948), 8-11; 8 ill.

Pennsylvania German Folklore Society *Publications*, I. Allentown, Pa.: Schlechter's, 1936. Fraktur listed under various museums.

'A Pennsylvania Illuminated Manuscript' 1801), *Antiques*, XLI, 2 (Feb., 1942), 117.

Pennypacker Sale Catalogue, Samuel W., Samuel T. Freeman & Co., Philadelphia, Pa., October 26 and 27, 1920. Especially items 1096-1138, 'Pennsylvania Dutch Art of Illumination—Taufschein and Early Prints', and items 1142-1215, 'Vorschrifften by Christopher Dock.'

Robacker, Earl F., *Pennsylvania Dutch Stuff: A Guide to Country Antiques.* Philadelphia, Pa.: University of Pennsylvania Press, 1944. Pages 57-58.

————, 'Major and Minor in Fractur', *The Dutchman*, VII, 3 (Winter, 1956), 2-7; 18 ill.

————, 'Paper for fancy', *Antiques*, LXXII, 6 (Dec., 1957), 543-545; 7 ill.

————, 'Books Not for Burning', *Pennsylvania Folklife*, IX, 1 (Winter, 1957-58), 44-52; 17 ill.

Schwartz, Esther I., 'New Jersey water colors', *Antiques*, LXXIV, 4 (October, 1958), 333; 4 ill.

Seip, Oswell J., 'Pennsylvania German Choral Books', Lehigh County Historical Society *Proceedings* (1944), 39-43. For Durs Rudy *Choral Buch*, 1814, and *Klavier Buch*, 1818, see page 42.

Shaffer, Ellen, 'Illuminators, Scribes and Printers: A Glimpse of the Free Library's Pennsylvania Dutch Collection', *Pennsylvania Folklife*, IX, 4 (Fall, 1958), 18-27; 12 ill.

Shelley, Donald A., 'An Unusual Valentine', The New York Historical Society *Quarterly Bulletin*, XXVII, 3 (July, 1943), 62-67; 2 ill.

————, 'Catalogue of Pennsylvania German Fraktur-Schrifften', Harry Shaw Newman Gallery (January, 1945). New York. Pp.8+5 ill.

————, 'Illuminated Birth Certificates, Regional Examples of an Early American Folk Art', The New-York Historical Society *Quarterly*, XXIX, 2 (April, 1945), 92-105; 9 ill.

————, 'American Primitive Painting: Illuminated Manuscripts', *Art in America*, XLII, 2 (May, 1954), 139-146, 165; 12 ill.

BIBLIOGRAPHY D (*Continued*)

Shoemaker, Alfred L., 'Reading's First Artist, A Painter of Butterflies', *Historical Review of Berks County*, XIII, 3 (April, 1948), 89-90; 1 ill.
————————, 'Johann Valentin Schuller—Fractur Artist and Author', *The Pennsylvania Dutchman*, III, 10 (October 15, 1951), 1; 1 ill.
————————, 'Notes on Frederick Krebs The Noted Fractur Artist', *The Pennsylvania Dutchman*, III, 11 (November 1, 1951), 3; 1 ill.
Stoudt, John Joseph, *Consider the Lilies How They Grow: An Interpretation of the Symbolism of Pennsylvania German Art*. Fogelsville, Pa.: The Pennsylvania German Folklore Society *Publications*, II (1937). See especially Parts 3 and 4, pages 133-174; several colored plates in text, and many black and white plates at back, including Ephrata work.
————————, *Pennsylvania Folk-Art: An Interpretation*. Allentown, Pa.: Schlechter's, 1948. Later edition of the above, with more plates.
'A Valentine in Fractur', *Antiques*, XLI, 2 (February, 1942), 144; 1 ill.
'Virginia Fractur' (at the Ohio Historical Society), *The Pennsylvania Dutchman*, IV, 9 (January 1, 1953), 1 ill. (1788/89).
Wertenbaker, Thomas J., *The Founding of American Civilization: The Middle Colonies*. New York: Charles Scribner's Sons, 1938. Pp.xiii+367.
Weygandt, Cornelius, *The Red Hills*. Philadelphia, Pa.: Univeristy of Pennsylvania Press, 1929. Several illustrations and discussion.
————————, *The Dutch Country*. New York: Appleton-Century, 1939. Pages 31-33, 106-108, 203-204; many illustrations.
————————, *The Plenty of Pennsylvania*. New York: H. C. Kinsey & Co., 1942.
Williamsburg, Colonial, Inc., exhibition catalogue, *American Folk Art*. Williamsburg, Va.: Colonial Williamsburg, Inc., 1940. Pp.33-34; items 138-144.
————————, *The Abby Aldrich Rockefeller Folk Art Collection* (by Little, Nina Fletcher). Williamsburg, Va.: Colonial Williamsburg, 1957. Pp.154, 265-275; 6 color plates.
Wood, T. Kenneth, 'Medieval Art Among the Pennsylvania Germans', *Antiques*, VII, 5 (May, 1925), 263-266; 7 ill.
Zehner, Olive G., 'Ohio Fractur', *The Dutchman*, VI, 3 (Winter, 1954-55), 13-15; 5 ill.

PRINTED FRAKTUR AND FRAKTUR PRINTERS

Bausman, Lottie M., *A Bibliography of Lancaster County, Pennsylvania, 1745-1912*. Philadelphia, Pa.: 1917.
Benson, Evelyn, 'Gilbert and Mason—Pennsylvania Wood Engravers', *The Dutchman*, VII, 3 (Winter, 1956), 8-13; 22 ill.
Bland, Jane Cooper, *Currier & Ives, A Manual for Collectors*. Garden City, N.Y.: Doubleday, Doran & Co., 1931.
Boyer, Walter E., 'Adam und Eva im Paradies,' *The Pennsylvania Dutchman*, VIII, 2 (Fall-Winter, 1956-57), 14-18, 3 ill.
————————, 'The German Broadside Songs of Pennsylvania,' *Pennsylvania Folklife*, X, 1 (Spring, 1959), 14-19; 4 ill.
Brigham, Clarence S., *History and Bibliography of American Newspapers, 1690-1820* (2 vols.). Worcester, Mass.: American Antiquarian Society, 1947.
Conningham, Frederick Arthur, *N. Currier and Currier & Ives Prints*. New York: Privately printed by F. A. and M. B. Conningham, 1930.
Crouse, Russel, *Mr. Currier and Mr. Ives*. Garden City, N.Y.: Doubleday, Doran & Co., Inc., 1930.
Doll, Eugene E., *The Ephrata Cloisters, History and Bibliography*. Philadelphia, Pa.: Carl Schurz Memorial Foundation, 1944.
Drepperd, Carl W., 'New Delvings in Old Fields; Found: A New Early American Engraver', *Antiques*, XLII, 4 (October, 1942), 204-205; illustrates 4 engravings and Miesse 'Familien Tafel'.

# BIBLIOGRAPHY D (*Continued*)

Evans, Charles, *American Bibliography. A Chronological Dictionary of All Books, Pamphlets, and Periodical Publications Printed in the United States of America* New York Privately printed, 1903-34 (volumes 1-12).

Fielding, Mantle, *American Engravers upon Copper and Steel.* Supplement to David McNeely Stauffer's *American Engravers.* Philadelphia, Pa.: Privately printed, 1917.

Friedrich, Gerhard, *A New Supplement to Seidensticker's American German Bibliography* Reprint from *Pennsylvania History* (October, 1940).

————, 'The A. H Cassel Collection at Juniata College', *American-German Review,* VII, 6 (August, 1941), 18-21; 4 ill

Fuhrmann, Otto W., 'Christopher Sauer, Colonial Printer', *American-German Review,* I, 4 (June, 1935), 39-44, 55; 2 ill plus 1 color.

Gerhard, Elmer Schultz, 'Lorenz Ibach. The Stargazing Blacksmith', *Historical Review of Berks County,* XIV, 2 (January, 1949), 45-47; for Eglemann see text and illustrations on page 46.

Hafer, E. E, *Charles F. Egleman* Paper read before The Historical Society of Berks County, 1912. Compare with Shoemaker's 'Notes' cited below.

Hildeburn, Charles S R., *A Century of Printing · The Issues of the Press in Pennsylvania, 1685-1784* Philadelphia, Pa.: 1885/6. Vol. I. 1685-1763; Vol. II. 1764-1784.

Hommel, Rudolf P, 'Gabriel Miesse, Coypist', *Antiques,* XLIII, 5 (May, 1943), 325. Illustrates two Haus-segens, one Johann Ritter and Comp

Keyes, Homer Eaton, 'Warmer, but not Fair', *Antiques,* XIV, 5 (November, 1928), 411-412, 1 illustration of 'Way to Eternal Life etc.'

McClinton, Katharine Morrison, *A Handbook of Popular Antiques.* New York: Random House, 1945 and 1946 Pp.160-166

McMurtrie, Douglas C., *A History of Printing in the United States* New York: R. R. Bowker Company, 1936

————, *The First Printers of York, Pennsylvania.* York, Pa.: The Maple Press Co, 1940

Metzger, Ethel Myra, *Supplement to Hildeburn's Century of Printing.* M A. Thesis (in typescript), Columbia University, New York, 1930.

Miller, Daniel, *Early German American Newspapers.* Pennsylvania German Society *Proceedings,* XIX, 22 (1911). Pp 107.

Nolan, J. Bennett, *The First Decade of Printing in Reading, Pennsylvania.* Reading, Pa.: Reading Eagle Press, 1930. Especially pages 4-13, illustrating Barton and Jungmann, and Schneider certificates.

Oda, Wilbur H, 'John Georg Hohman', *Historical Review of Berks County,* XIII, 3 (April, 1948), 66-71, 4 ill. See page 67

————, 'Gabriel Miesse—Doctor and Engraver', *The Pennsylvania Dutchman,* III, 11 (November 1, 1951). Page 1; 2 ill.

Oswald, John Clyde, *Printing in the Americas* New York: The Gregg Publishing Co., 1937.

Pennypacker, Hon. Samuel W., *Sales Catalogues of the Library (8 Parts).* Philadelphia, Pa.: Stan. V. Henkels, 1905-09
    Part V. *Publications from the Presses of the Early Inland Towns of Pennsylvania* November 26-27, 1907. Pp.102-151.
    Part VI *Early Pennsylvania Dutch Broadsides.* April 10, 1908.
    Part VII. *Ephrata, Pennsylvania Imprints* November 27-28, 1908. Pp 28-56.

Peters, Harry T., *Currier & Ives: Printmakers to the American People* Garden City, N Y Doubleday, Doran & Co., Inc Vol I. 1929; Vol. II, 1931. Special Edition for Book-of-the-Month Club, 1942

————, *America on Stone · The Other Printmakers to the American People.* New York · Doubleday, Doran & Co., Inc., 1931.

BIBLIOGRAPHY D (Continued)

Reichmann, Felix, Christopher Sower, Sr., 1694-1758, Printer in Germantown: An Annotated Bibliography. Philadelphia, Pa.: C. Schurz Foundation, Inc., 1943.
—————, 'Christopher Sower Exhibition', American-German Review, X, 3 (February, 1944), 8-10, 29; illustration of the Ephrata press.
Roorbach, Orville A., Catalogue of American Publications, Including Reprints and Original Works, from 1820 to 1852 Inclusive. New York · Orville A. Roorbach, 1852. 3 Supplements: I, 1852-55; II. 1855-58; and III, 1858-1860.
Sabin, Joseph, A Dictionary of Books Relating to America, From Its Discovery to the Present Time (29 vols.). New York: Sabin, 1862-92; Bibliographical Society of America, 1928-36.
Sargent, George H., 'A Press of the Pennsylvania Dutch,' Antiques, V, 3 (March, 1924), 136-138; 3 ill.
Seidensticker, Oswald, The First Century of German Printing in America, 1728-1830. Philadelphia, Pa.; Schaefer & Koradi, 1893.
Shaffer, Ellen, 'Illuminators, Scribes and Printers', see under Handwritten Fraktur.
Shoemaker, Alfred L., A Check List of Imprints of the German Press of Northampton County, Pennsylvania, 1766-1905. Northampton County Historical and Genealogical Society Publications, IV 1943). Pp.162; 4 ill.
—————, A Check List of Imprints of the German Press of Lehigh County, Pennsylvania, 1807-1900. Lehigh County Historical Society Proceedings, XVI (1947). Pp.240.
—————, 'Notes on Charles F. Egelman', Historical Review of Berks County, XIII, 4 (July, 1948), 99; 1 ill. (see Hafer, E. E., above).
—————, 'Peter Montelius—Printer and Teacher', The Pennsylvania Dutchman, III, 9 (October 1, 1951), 3.
—————, Check List of Pennsylvania Dutch Printer Taufscheins. Lancaster, Pa.: The Pennsylvania Dutch Folklore Center, Inc., 1952. Pp.48; 33 ill.
—————, 'Henry Dulheuer, The Old Traveler', The Pennsylvania Dutchman, III, 17 (February 1, 1952), 1, 3.
—————, 'Biographical Sketches of Montgomery County Publishers', The Pennsylvania Dutchman, III, 17 (February 1, 1952), 7.
—————, 'Biographical Sketches of Berks County Publishers', The Pennsylvania Dutchman, III, 18 (February 15, 1952), 6-8.
—————, 'Taufschein Scriveners', The Pennsylvania Dutchman, III, 19 (March 1, 1952), 6.
—————, 'Biographical Sketches of Lebanon County Publishers', The Pennsylvania Dutchman, III, 20 (March 15, 1952), 7.
—————, 'Biographical Sketches of Dauphin County Publishers', The Pennsylvania Dutchman, III, 21 (April 1, 1952), 7-8.
—————, 'More Taufschein Scriveners', The Pennsylvania Dutchman, III, 22 (April 15, 1952), 7.
—————, 'Adam and Eve Broadsides', The Pennsylvania Dutchman, IV, 6 (October, 1952), 4-5; 6 ill. and cover.
—————, 'Taufscheins', The Pennsylvania Dutchman IV, 7 (November, 1952), 14.
—————, 'The Ephrata Printers', The Pennsylvania Dutchman, IV, 9 (January 1, 1953), 11-13.
—————, 'Biographies of Hanover Publishers', The Pennsylvania Dutchman, IV, 22 (February 15, 1953), 15.
Stauffer, David McNeely, American Engravers upon Copper and Steel. (2 vols.). New York: The Grolier Club of the City of New York, 1907.
Thompson, D. W., 'Oldest American Printing Press', The Dutchman, VI, 3 (Winter, 1954-55), 28-33; 10 ill.
Unger, Claude W., 'Reading Dated Taufscheins Printed Before the Year 1800', The Pennsylvania Dutchman, III, 12 (November 15, 1951), 3.

BIBLIOGRAPHY D (*Continued*)

Wheeler, Joseph Towne, *The Maryland Press, 1777-1790*. Baltimore, Md.: The Maryland Historical Society, 1938.

Wroth, Lawrence C., *A History of Printing in Colonial Maryland, 1636-1776*. Baltimore, Md.: Typothetae of Baltimore, 1922.

——————, *The Colonial Printer*. New York: The Grolier Club, 1931; second edition, Portland, Maine, 1938.

Ziegler, Samuel H., 'The Ephrata Printing Press', Pennsylvania German Folklore Society *Publications*, V (1940), 1-12.

### FRAKTUR TYPE-FACE

Bauer, Konrad F., *Leonhard Wagner, der Schopfer der Fraktur*. Frankfurt-am-Main Bauersche Giesserei, 1936. Best account of Fraktur beginnings, Holbein portrait as frontispiece.

Crous, Ernst, und Kirchner, Joachim, *Die gotischen Schriftarten*. Leipzig: Klinkhardt & Biermann, 1938. Pp.46+64 facsims.

Johnson, J. A., *Type Designs, Their History and Development*. London: 1934.

McMurtrie, Douglas C., *Fraktur Type Design*. New York: Press of Arts Typographica, 1926. Pp.15.

Milchsack, Gustav, *Was ist Fraktur?* Braunschweig: E. Applehaus & Comp., 1925.

Mori, Gustav, *Das Schriftgiessergewerbe in Frankfurt am Main und Offenbach*. Frankfurt-am-Main; D. Stempel 1926. See examples 1717, 1727, and 1740.

Morison, Stanley, *Type Designs of the Past and Present*. London: The Fleuron Ltd., 1926.

Nash, Ray, *Some Early American Writing Books and Masters*. Hanover, N.H.: Printed for the Author, 1942. Pp.25.

Nesbitt, Alexander, *Decorative Alphabets and Initials*. New York: Dover Publications, Inc., 1959. See especially Plates 68, 70, 104-106, and 109.

Pukánszky, Béla, *Ungarische Frakturdrucke im 16. Jahrhundert*. Gutenberg-Jahrbuch, 1935. Pp.164-171.

Tschichold, Jan, *Schatzkammer der Schreibkunst, Meisterwerke der Kalligraphie aus vier Jahrhunderten, auf Zweihundert Tafeln*. Basel: Verlag Birkhauser, 1945.

Updike, D. B., *Printing Types, their History, Forms, and Use* (2 vols.). Cambridge: Harvard University Press, 1937.

Zeitler, Julius, *Moderne Frakturschriften*. Festschrift Loubier. Buch und Bucheinband, 1923. Pp.69-76.

### APPLIED FRAKTUR DESIGNS

Loring, Rosemond B., *Marbled Papers*. Boston, Mass.: Club of Odd Volumes, 1933.

——————, *Decorated Book Papers, Being an Account of Their Designs and Fashions*. Cambridge, Mass.: Department of Painting and Graphic Arts, Harvard College Library, 1942.

Nash, Paul, introduction by, *A Specimen Book of Pattern Papers, Designed For and in Use at The Curwen Press*. London: Published for the Curwen Press by The Fleuron Limited, 1923.

### FRAKTUR PRICKING

Jones, Leslie Webber, 'Pricking Manuscripts: The Instruments and Their Significance', *Speculum, A Journal of Mediaeval Studies*, XXI, 4 (October, 1946), 389-403.

# X Illustrations

The author is deeply indebted to
Charles T Miller, of the Henry Ford Museum
and Greenfield Village, for valuable technical
photographic assistance in preparing the
illustrations for this volume.

❀   ❀   ❀   ❀   ❀

Because of the time lapse involved and the fact that there have been so many large-scale Fraktur dispersals, it has been necessary to list owners in the following captions as they were at the time of photography

In this way, permission for the author to photograph for publication 20 years ago is here gratefully acknowledged and the pedigree of each item he secured from some 65 important pioneer collections is fully recorded.

For example, although two key collections — Henry S. Borneman and Levi E. Yoder — were acquired intact by the Free Library of Philadelphia, the contents of a dozen or more important early collections were divided largely among the following

*Abby Aldrich Rockefeller Collection, Williamsburg, Va.*
*The Free Library of Philadelphia, Philadelphia, Pa*
*H. F. du Pont Winterthur Museum, Winterthur, Del*
*M and M Karolik Collection, Museum of Fine Arts, Boston, Mass.*
*The Schwenkfelder Historical Library, Pennsburg, Pa*
*Titus C Geesey Collection, Philadelphia Museum of Art, Phila , Pa.*

# European Sources of Fraktur

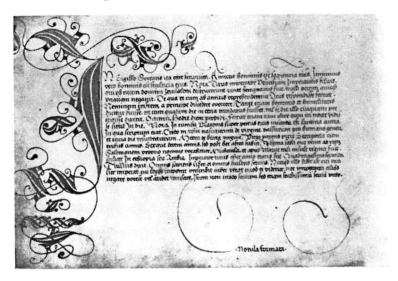

1. LEONHARD WAGNER, VORSCHRIFT, AUGSBURG, 1507

A page from his early Fraktur manuscript entitled "Hundert schriften von ainer hand der kaine ist wie die ander."
*Borneman, Pennsylvania German Illuminated Manuscripts, 1937, pl. 38*

2. VALENTINUM BOLTZEN VON RUFACH, ILLUMINIRBUCH, TITLE-PAGE, 1566

"Illuminir-Buch Kuenstlich alle Farben zumachen uund bereyten Allen Schreibern, Brieffmalern . . ."
*Borneman, Pennsylvania German Illuminated Manuscripts, 1937, pl. 1*

3. Antonio Neudoerffer, Schreibkunst, Title-Page, Nuremberg, 1601
Contains a whole series of Alphabets ranging from fairly simple
forms to highly complicated and ornamental forms as
shown in the following illustrations.
*Schatzki collection, New York, N. Y.*

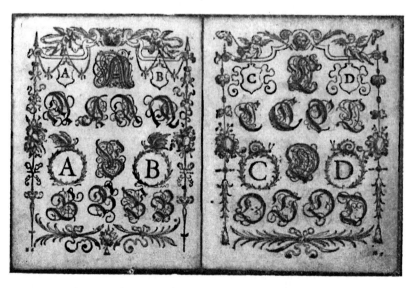

4. Antonio Neudoerffer, Schreibkunst, Nuremberg, 1601
Alphabet I, simple letter forms, simple borders.
*Schatzki collection, New York, N. Y.*

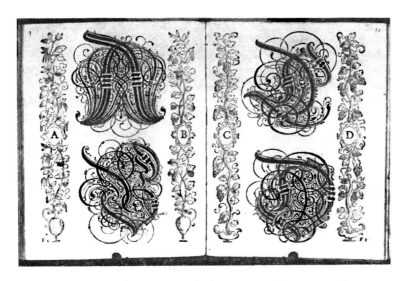

5. ANTONIO NEUDOERFFER, SCHREIBKUNST, NUREMBERG, 1601
Alphabet II, more complicated letters, fuller borders.
*Schatzki collection, New York, N. Y.*

6. ANTONIO NEUDOERFFER, SCHREIBKUNST, NUREMBERG, 1601
Alphabet IV, highly ornamental letters, human figures
in borders, little surface of page remains untouched.
*Schatzki collection, New York, N. Y.*

7. MICHAEL BAUERNFEIND, SCHREIB-KUNST, TITLE-PAGE, 1716
From early edition; many editions of this work were issued at Nuremberg,
extending through most of the 18th century; for example, see Figures 9 and 10.
*Schatzki collection, New York, N. Y.*

8. MICHAEL BAUERNFEIND, SCHREIB-KUNST, 1716
Fractur-Schrifft page from early edition, showing close relationship
to Pennsylvania works by Henrich Otto, especially as regards
the design of capital letters. See Figures 186 and 187.
*Schatzki collection, New York, N. Y.*

9. MICHAEL BAUERNFEIND, DER ZIERLICHEN SCHREIB-KUNST, NUREMBERG, 1737
Title-page of later edition of the preceding work.
*Schatzki collection, New York, N. Y.*

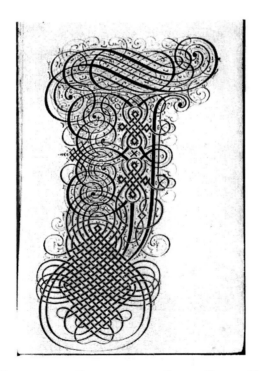

10. MICHAEL BAUERNFEIND, DER ZIERLICHEN SCHREIB-KUNST, NUREMBERG, 1737
Capital letter "F" from 1737 edition of preceding work.
*Schatzki collection, New York, N. Y.*

11. PRINTED LETTER OF APPRENTICESHIP, CREUTZENACH, c.1750

One of the richest sources for comparison with Pennsylvania Fraktur pieces is these Apprenticeship documents, both hand-written and printed. This specimen suggests the typography of the Ephrata, Pa. Cloister Press very strongly.

*Gewerbemuseum photo, Kaiserslautern, Germany*

12. HAND-WRITTEN LETTER OF APPRENTICESHIP, KUERN, 1751

This manuscript is particularly suggestive of the Mennonite work done in Montgomery County under the influence of Christopher Dock and his followers.

*Gewerbemuseum photo, Kaiserslautern, Germany*

13. HAND-WRITTEN LETTER OF APPRENTICESHIP, MEISENHEIM, LATE 18th C.
This German example again suggests the capital letters found so often in
Henrich Otto's earlier pieces, see Figures 186 and 187.
*Gewerbemuseum photo, Kaiserslautern, Germany*

14. HAND-WRITTEN LETTER OF APPRENTICESHIP, ROCKENHAUSEN, 1772
Like Figure 12, this calligraphy also shows closer relationships with Mennonite
work in Bucks and Montgomery Counties, which frequently employ
horizontal interlace or bandings to connect the letters in their main titles.
*Gewerbemuseum photo, Kaiserslautern, Germany*

15. Hand-Written Zierschrift, Graubuenden, 1744

This early Swiss manuscript is a perfect prototype for much of the work done
among the Swiss Mennonites of Lancaster County, especially a
group of manuscripts dating in the late 1760's.
*Lichtenhan, Schweizer, Volkskunst, 1941, p.33*

16. Hand-Written Probeschrift, Urnasch, 1771

Black-letter work suggesting Ephrata Cloister specimens such as
in Figure 110, and in the Wall Chart, Figure 124.
*Lichtenhan, Schweizer Volkskunst, 1941, p30*

17. HAND-WRITTEN PROBESCHRIFT, LANGWIES, 1805
Very similar to the more delicate Mennonite work here after 1800.
*Lichtenhan, Schweizer Volkskunst, 1941, p. 31*

18. HAND-WRITTEN GLUECKWUNSCH, GRAUBUENDEN, 1809
Concluding the group of four Swiss prototypes for Pennsylvania German
manuscripts, this could easily pass as an American one.
*Lichtenhahn, Schweizer Volkskunst, 1941, p.32*

19. HAND-WRITTEN CHRISTLICHER TAUFF-WUNSCH, 1737
A very early form of birth record, not unlike some of the first
Pennsylvania ones which followed this by several decades.
*American-German Review, August, 1935, p.35*

20. HAND-WRITTEN TAUFBRIEF, 1792.
The lion, crown, and panel-form of this piece correspond very
closely to the Pennsylvania ones of the same period.
*Gewerbemuseum photo, Kaiserslautern, Germany*

21. HAND-WRITTEN TAUFBRIEF, 1828
Just as motifs of the earlier pieces gave way in this country after 1800, so in this
German specimen, the order and composition of Figure 20 are now missing.
*Gewerbemuseum photo, Kaiserslautern, Germany*

22. PRINTED TAUF-ZEDEL, c.1815

These small printed birth-record forms were not only common abroad, but frequently turn up in collections in this country. They were apparently printed in Northern Alsace, and along the Palatinate, whence most of the Pennsylvania immigrants came.

*New-York Historical Society, New York, N. Y.*

23. HAND-WRITTEN LETTRE DE BAPTEME, 1814

This Alsatian example, brought to this country by a descendant, is a perfect counter-part of the Pennsylvania ones of the same era, especially some of the early 19th century Mennonite Vorschriften.

*Northrup collection, New York, N. Y.*

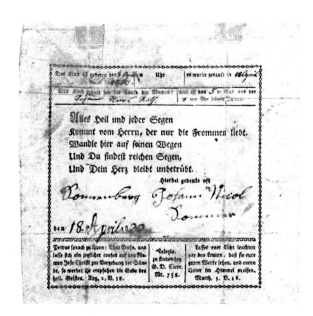

24-26.  PRINTED FOLD-UP TAUFF-WUNSCH, c.1830
Example of the later commercial productions developed in Europe, showing
front cover design, reverse view demonstrating "pin wheel"
fold, and interior text of the printed form.
*Author's collection*

27. HAND-WRITTEN SPIRITUAL LABYRINTH

Direct prototype of the Irrgartens printed at Ephrata in the mid-1780's,
and subsequently on many other Pennsylvania German presses
down into the first quarter of the 19th century.
*Landesmuseum photo, Darmstadt, Germany*

28. PRINTED HAUS-SEGEN, AUGSBURG, 19th C.

Although the author photographed this particular specimen here in Pennsylvania,
an identical Haus-Segen (minus the Augsburg imprint line) was found in the
Darmstadt Museum and a photograph brought back. Both are perfect prototypes
for Pennsylvania forms most of which were dated 1785 (Figs. 190 and 194).
*Troxell collection, Allentown, Pa.*

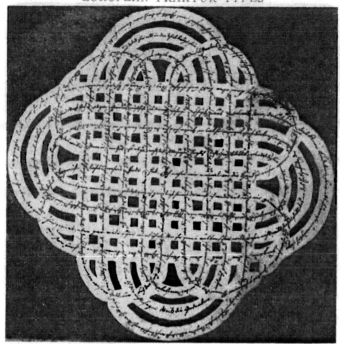

29. HAND-WRITTEN IRRGARTEN, IRENDSEE
Labyrinths and interlacing forms were apparently common abroad in many
forms. Just as in Pennsylvania, they sometimes remained uncolored.
*Gewerbemuseum photo, Kaiserslautern, Germany*

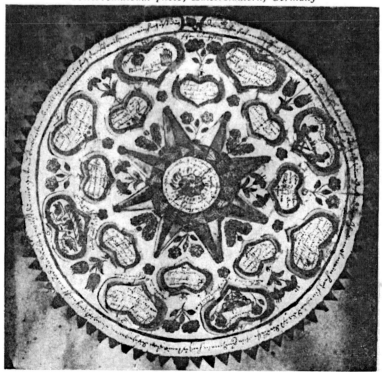

30. HAND-WRITTEN LIEBESBRIEF, BADEN
A perfect prototype for most Pennsylvania German examples, see Fig. 55.
*Gewerbemuseum photo, Kaiserslautern, Germany*

31. STUBENBERGER GEBETBUCH, BAYERN, 1832
Much more luxuriant in its treatment than most Pennsylvania ones, and
much more closely related to the Medieval manuscript tradition.
*Staatl. Museum für Deutsche Volkskunde photo, Berlin, Germany*

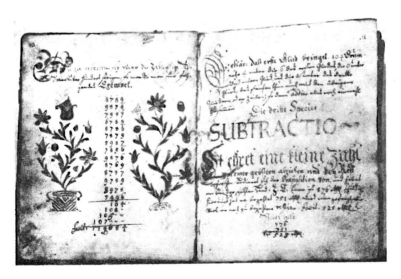

32. HAND-WRITTEN RECHENBUCH, MARK BRANDENBURG, 1745
Prototype for Pennsylvania German school and arithmetic books. in
which bits of Fraktur or other decoration also appear.
*Staatl. Museum für Deutsche Volkskunde photo, Berlin, Germany*

33. Henrich Dulheuer, Full-Size Birth and Baptismal Certificate

These measure roughly 13 x 16 inches, *half-size* 8 x 13 inches, and *quarter-size* 8 x 6½ inches, all of these being directly dependent upon the sheet-size of our early paper.
*Unger collection, Pottsville, Pa.*

34. Friedrich Krebs, Half-Size Birth and Baptismal Certificate

See caption above on paper sizes, also two following Frakturs.
*Odenwelder collection, Easton, Pa.*

35. Huber Artist, Full-Size Vorschrift, 1790

Vorschriften, like Birth and Baptismal certificates, follow certain prescribed sizes, as this illustration and the following one are calculated to show.
*Author's collection*

36. Earl Township Artist, Half-Size Vorschrift, 1809

Like many of these writing specimens, this one is made up of several component parts, each of which is more or less complete in itsel..
*Author's collection*

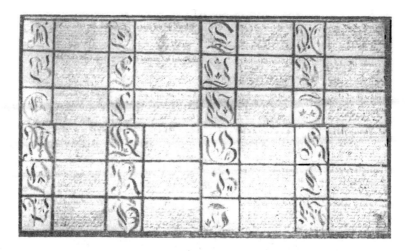

37. MENNONITE SCHOOL, GOLDENE ABC, 1808
Not a single piece, in this instance, but four separate pages.
*H. F. du Pont Winterthur Museum, Winterthur, Del.*

38. HENRICH OTTO, SPIRITUAL LABYRINTH, PRINTED 1785
One of the more popular religious broadside forms.
*Author's collection*

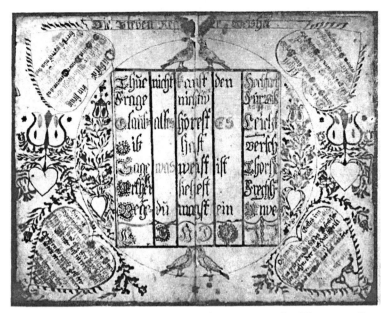

39. SCHWENKFELDER SCHOOL, THE SEVEN RULES OF WISDOM, 1785

One of the rarer religious forms, those which have turned up to date
are of Schwenkfelder origin, as is this one.
*Schwenkfelder Historical Library, Pennsburg, Pa.*

40. JACOB OBERHOLTZER, RELIGIOUS SPIRAL

Executed in alternating lines of red and black text.
*Lorimer collection, Philadelphia, Pa.*

41. Northumberland County Artist, Haus-Segen, Early 19th C.
House blessings, inscriptions over doors, or on date-stones, were
quite common, and go back to European customs.
*Author's collection*

42. Andreas B. Bauer, The Spiritual Wonder-Clock, 1832
A comparatively rare form, this example with the grandfather
clock is probably unique.
*Schwenkfelder Historical Library, Pennsburg, Pa.*

43. EPHRATA MARTYRBOOK, BOOKPLATE, 1748-49
This page is the hand-illuminated Bookplate, preceding the printed
Title-page, giving in large Fraktur letters the name of the owner.
For printed Title-pages see Figures 108 and 109.
*Geesey collection, Wilmington, Del.*

44. MENNONITE SCHOOL, SONGBOOK, BOOKPLATE, 1815
Typical of these small-size Fraktur gems for delicacy and color.
*Author's collection*

45. CHRISTIAN STRENGE, TESTAMENT, BOOKPLATE, c.1790
*American Antiquarian Society, Worcester, Mass.*

46. EASTON BIBLE ARTIST, BIBLE, BOOKPLATE, 1791
Only a few of these larger illuminated Bookplates have come to the
author's attention, there being many more in the smaller Songbooks
and Testaments, such as the two preceding examples.
*Troxell collection, Allentown, Pa.*

47. JACOB OBERHOLTZER, COPYBOOK, BOOKPLATE, 1786
Booklet contains, as usual, only four pages of writing samples threaded together
*Author's collection*

48. EPHRATA MS., THE CHRISTSIAN ABC BOOK, CAPITAL LETTERS "H", 1750
This volume, the great treasure of the Ephrata Cloister, contains many
alphabets of upper and lower case letters. The more usual ABC book
would be much plainer and undecorated, except for the letters.
*Stoudt Consider the Lilies. 1937. p.268*

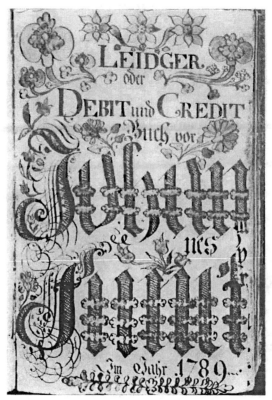

49. EASTON BIBLE ARTIST, LEDGER, BOOKPLATE, 1789
A rare form of book illumination for such a utilitarian object.
*Yoder collection, Silverdale, Pa.*

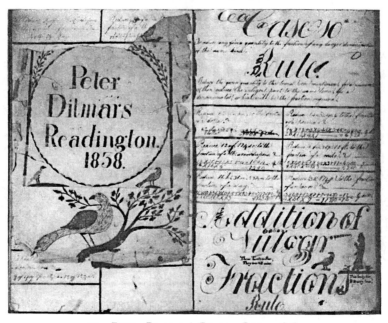

50. PETER DITMARS' SCHOOL BOOK, 1838
*Halpert collection, New York, N. Y.*

51. HAND-ILLUMINATED BOOKMARKS
While the simplicity of these might lead one to the assumption that they had been
drawn by children in school, further examination reveals that these Bookmarks
and other small Fraktur designs are more often the work of
those same artists who did the larger pieces.
*Yoder collection, Silverdale, Pa.*

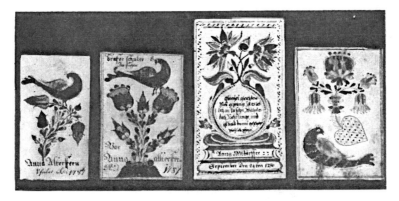

52. ANNA ALTDOERFFER'S REWARDS FOR MERIT, 1787-90
An unusual set of four small cards, all the work of one illuminator.
*Lorimer collection, Philadelphia, Pa.*

53. REGINA SCHULTZ, SMALL DESIGN, IN CLOTH FRAME, c.1806
A charming bit of Folk art, bound and framed with fragments of dresses.
*Reading Public Museum and Art Gallery, Reading, Pa.*

54. ENGRAVER ARTIST, SMALL DESIGN, IN PAPER-BOUND FRAME
The unknown artist who drew this tiny specimen about 2 x 3 inches, also decorated
quite a few Certificates, but unfortunately he never signed his name.
*H. F. du Pont Winterthur Museum, Winterthur, Del.*

55. CHRISTIAN STRENGE, LOVE-LETTER, c.1800
Cut out with a knife, and then decorated with Fraktur designs and verses.
*Metropolitan Museum of Art, New York, N. Y.*

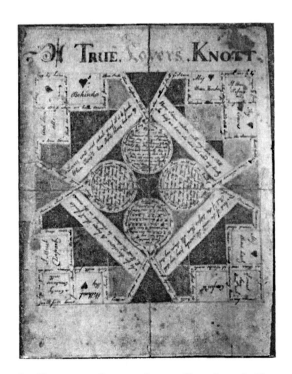

56. UNKNOWN QUAKER ARTIST, TRUE-LOVER'S KNOT
A variation of the more usual Love-letter or Valentine, but not a
fold-up piece. It has some Labyrinthian features.
*Bucks County Historical Society, Doylestown, Pa.*

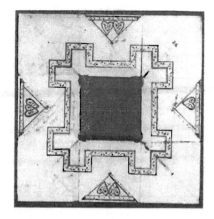

57. UNKNOWN QUAKER ARTIST, FOLD-UP VALENTINE, 1794
When folded in "pin wheel" fashion, it was quite small in size,
measuring about 5 inches square. A fine early example.
*Bucks County Historical Society, Doylestown, Pa.*

58. UNKNOWN QUAKER ARTIST, FOLD-UP VALENTINE, 1794
Constant folding and unfolding damaged the center part.
*Bucks County Historical Society, Doylestown, Pa.*

59. UNKNOWN ARTIST, THE AMPLE GROVE
*Kindig collection, York, Pa.*

60. FRAKTUR CHRISTMAS GREETING, 1786
Very tiny fragment, measures about 2 inches square; most unusual.
*American-German Review, December, 1942, cover*

61. C. F. ARTIST, LANCASTER COUNTY, NEW YEAR'S WISH, 1765
A large and very handsome early Fraktur piece with good color.
*H. F. du Pont Winterthur Museum, Winterthur, Del.*

62. WETZEL-GEOMETRIC ARTIST, ABSTRACT DESIGN
For a half-size Birth Certificate by this same artist, see Figure 205.
*Author's collection*

63. MENNONITE SCHOOL, ADAM AND EVE, 1835
*Yoder collection, Silverdale, Pa.*

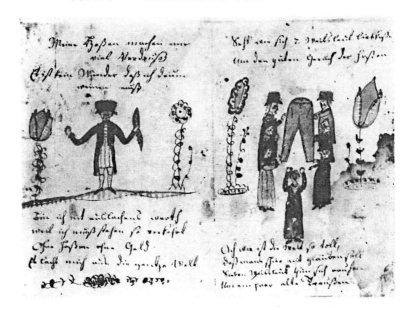

64. Friedrich Krebs, "Wedding Fable" Subject
Sometimes also called "The Maidens under the Tree," this theme has usually
been found on iron stoveplates. The above text fully identifies it here
as an earthy Folk-theme instead.
*Karolik collection, Museum of Fine Arts, Boston, Mass.*

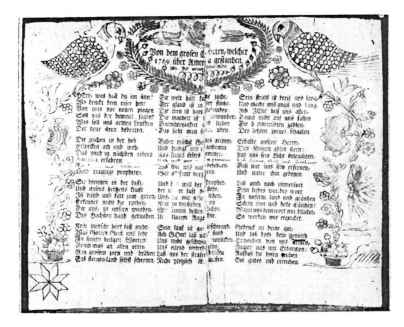

65. Henrich Otto, The Great Comet Of 1769
A Schwenkfelder representation of this theme may be found at the
Philadelphia Museum of Art, in the Millbach Rooms.
*Unger collection, Pottsville, Pa.*

66. SCHWENKFELDER SCHOOL, ARCHITECTURAL DESIGN
The detailed representation of a Pennsylvania house is unusual; see also Fig. 179.
*Lorimer collection, Philadelphia, Pa.*

67. FLAT TULIP ARTIST, RAMPANT LIONS, c.1810
See also Figure 213.
*Nadelman collection, Riverdale, N. Y.*

68. FRAKTUR STILL-LIFE, 1809
Similar treatment of floral forms may be found in illuminated Birth and
Baptismal Certificates occasionally, just after 1800.
*Lorimer collection, Philadelphia, Pa.*

69. FRAKTUR PORTRAIT AND BIRTH CERTIFICATE, 1823
Combination of Fraktur and Wash drawing.
*Pennsylvania State Museum, Harrisburg, Pa.*

70. CARL FRIEDERICH EGELMANN, ENGRAVED COPYBOOK, (2nd Ed.), 1831
Printed at Reading, it is the only such book on the subject, the remainder
being Mennonite manuscript Copybooks such as Figures 47 and 144-147.
*Sittig collection, Shawnee-on-Delaware, Pa.*

71. CARL FRIEDERICH EGELMANN, ENGRAVED COPYBOOK (1st Ed.), 1821
Detail of Frontispiece showing interior of scriptorium.
*Author's collection*

72. MERCER FRAKTUR PAINT BOX, c.1820
Dr. Henry C. Mercer's discovery of this original paint box instigated
his pioneer investigation of Fraktur in 1897.
*Mercer, The Survival of the Art of Illuminative Writing, 1897, p.424*

73. ABRAHAM K. KINSEY'S FRAKTUR BOX, 1864
Inscribed with artist's name and date on the lid, and filled with Vorschriften.
*Yoder collection, Silverdale, Pa.*

74a-d. CHRISTIAN PETERS, FOUR INCOMPLETE VORSCHRIFTEN, c.1777
Examples A to D show the manner in which Peters laid out his pieces. From
the traces of stitching along the left margins, it would appear that at
some time in the past they formed part of a book.
*Author's collection*

75. CHRISTIAN PETERS, COMPLETED VORSCHRIFT, c.1777
*Author's collection*

76. Rev. Daniel Schumacher, Certificate, c.1775
Shows early use of diagonal lines for shading and cross-hatching; see also
Figures 184 and 185.
*New-York Historical Society, New York, N. Y.*

77. Adams County Artist, Certificate, c.1802
The entire background of this Certificate has been stippled over with
small lines in pale yellow ink, an unusual technique form.
*Author's collection*

78. C. SCHERICH, PENMANSHIP HORSE, 1851
*Author's collection*

79. J. S. JAMISON, SPECIMENS OF DIFFERENT HANDS, 1843
Professional penmanship advertisement listing forms he could execute.
*Pennypacker collection, Kenhorst, Pa.*

80. FRAKTUR PORTRAIT OF BENJAMIN FRANKLIN
Penmanship and Fraktur applied to portraiture in odd fashion.
*Lorimer collection, Philadelphia, Pa.*

81. FRAKTUR AND WASH PORTRAIT OF CHRISTIAN HUNSICKER, 1850
Portraiture in combination with Fraktur Birth Record; unusual painted
and grained cardboard frame and hanger.
*Geesey collection, Wilmington, Del.*

82.  (GEORG) FRIEDERICH SPEYER, PART-PRINTED CERTIFICATE
Early rectangular text-block form with borders drawn or stamped.
*Pennsylvania State Museum, Harrisburg, Pa.*

83.  HENRICH OTTO CERTIFICATE, WITH BLOCK-PRINTED BORDERS, PRINTED 1784
Three large border blocks supply most of the decoration here.
*Unger collection, Pottsville, Pa.*

84. York County "General", Printed Certificate With Hand-Drawn Borders
Rectangular text-block remains with free-hand borders around it.
*Unger collection, Pottsville, Pa.*

85. Printed Certificate With Stamped Borders, 1793
Later "Heart Form" of Certificate with small design blocks stamped at random
around the borders, but no connecting elements to hold them together.
*Berks County Historical Society, Reading, Pa.*

86. J. Bauman, Two-Color Certificate
Treated as a unit, with large color-blocks in red or green around the borders.
*Newman collection, New York, N. Y.*

87. Isaac Palm, Haus-Segen with Color-Blocked Borders, Printed 1860
*Unger collection, Pottsville, Pa.*

88. Large Sheet Of Embossed Dutch Gilt Paper

With large Adam and Eve subject at center, surrounded by a multitude of
birds and wild fowl of every size and shape. Among these can
be recognized some of the identical forms found applied
to printed Certificates by Friedrich Krebs.
*Unger collection, Pottsville, Pa*

89. F. Krebs, Certificate With Large Applied Cutouts Of Religious Scenes
*Reformed Church Library, Lancaster, Pa.*

90. F. KREBS, CERTIFICATE, APPLIED CUTOUTS WITH COLORED BACKGROUND, 1792
Extraordinary assortment of animals here, including an elephant!
*Unger collection, Pottsville, Pa.*

91. F. KREBS, CERTIFICATE, APPLIED CUTOUTS WITH COLORED BACKGROUND, 1804
**Author's collection**

92. JOHANN RITTER, ALL-PRINTED CERTIFICATE, c.1814
One of the most common printed forms, with brilliant colors applied.
*New-York Historical Society, New York, N. Y.*

93. A. UND W. BLUMER, ALL-PRINTED CERTIFICATE, 1835
One of the later forms with rainbow striping, spotted aprons on
the angels, and late eagle woodcut at the top.
*Berks County Historical Society, Reading, Pa.*

94. Moser und Peters, Color-Blocked Certificate, 1825
Color applied with red and yellow color-blocks, no pattern on angels' skirts.
*Pennsylvania State Museum, Harrisburg, Pa.*

95. Moser und Peters, Color-Blocked Certificate With Patterns, 1826
Note floral patterns in two colors on angels' skirts.
*Philadelphia Museum of Art, Philadelphia, Pa.*

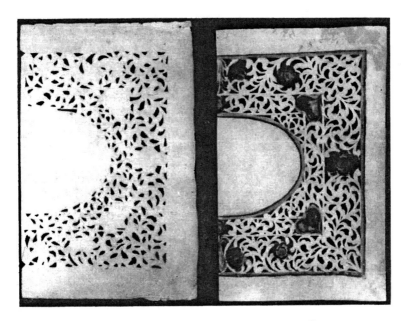

96. WILHELMUS ANTONIUS FABER, INCOMPLETE CUTOUTS
A pair of cutouts, folded; one plain and the other with color added, showing
the manner in which Faber worked. These can be fitted one over the
top of the other, thereby suggesting use of a pattern.
*Author's collection*

97. W. A. FABER, COMPLETED CUTOUT WITH COLOR ADDED, READY FOR TEXT
Faber usually featured a heart-shaped text paned as in Fig. 234, rather than oval
(as here) or octagonal, as in Figure 98.
*Author's collection*

98. W. A. FABER, CUTOUT HAUS-SEGEN, 1818
Fully signed and dated, it is a rich and ornamental design,
and no doubt constitutes his masterpiece.
*Brooklyn Museum, Brooklyn, N. Y.*

99. PINPRICK LOVE-LETTER
One of half a dozen seen by the author, and apparently not nearly
so common a technique here as it was in Europe.
*Troxell collection, Allentown, Pa.*

100. LOVE-TOKEN WITH RIBBON DRAWN-WORK
This is another European technique which did not catch hold here.
Note the date 1835, bordering the Victorian period.
*Yoder collection, Silverdale, Pa.*

101. C. F. EGELMANN, STIPPLE-ENGRAVED CERTIFICATE, FIRST STATE
Other examples in this technique may be seen in Figures 70-71, and 267-279.
*Pennsylvania State Archive, Harrisburg, Pa.*

102. N. CURRIER, LITHOGRAPHED CERTIFICATE
The latest printing technique employed in the production of
Birth and Baptismal Certificate forms; see also Figures 280-286.
*Unger collection, Pottsville, Pa.*

103. EPHRATA CLOISTER, EXTERIOR VIEW OF SARON
The later plaster shown on the walls in this view has since been removed under
the restoration program of the State Historical Commission.
*Raymond, Early Domestic Architecture of Pennsylvania, 1931, pl. 1*

104. EPHRATA CLOISTER, INTERIOR VIEW OF THE SAAL
Showing one of the large Fraktur Charts (c.1755) which adorn the walls.
*Raymond, Early Domestic Architecture of Pennsylvania, 1931, pl.5*

105. EPHRATA MS., RULE-BOOK OF THE ROSE OF SHARON, TITLE-PAGE, 1745
Beautifully illuminated volume listing the names of the Sisters and
giving other pertinent information about their activities.
*Pennsylvania Historical Society, Philadelphia, Pa.*

106. Ephrata Ms., The Turteltaube, Title-Page, 1746

This is the magnificently illuminated copy of the great Ephrata hymnal
made for, and presented to, the leader Conrad Beissel.
*Stoudt, Pennsylvania Folk-Art, 1948, p.157*

107. Ephrata Ms., The Turteltaube, 1746
Showing typical interior pages of the hymnal.
*Pennsylvania Historical Society, Philadelphia, Pa.*

108. EPHRATA MARTYRBOOK, TITLE-PAGE OF VOLUME I, PRINTED 1748
Generally accepted as the most monumental volume printed in the American Colonies prior to the Revolution. Note elaborate Fraktur title.
*Author's collection*

109. EPHRATA MARTYRBOOK, TITLE-PAGE OF VOLUME II, PRINTED 1749
In contrast to the title of Vol. I, the Fraktur letters have here become much more simplified, closer to the Ephrata manuscripts.
*Author's collection*

110. EPHRATA MS., SINGLE PAGE ILLUMINATION, LETTERS "C" AND "G", c.1750
*Brooklyn Museum, Brooklyn, N. Y.*

111.  EPHRATA MS., TITLE-PAGE OF THE CHRISTIAN BOOK, 1750
The most ornate and highly embellished of all the Ephrata manuscripts.
*Stoudt, Pennsylvania Folk-Art, 1948, p.136*

112.  EPHRATA MS., FRONTISPIECE OF THE CHRISTIAN ABC BOOK, 1750
Baptism of Christ scene replaces alphabet letters and formal designs.
*Stoudt, Pennsylvania Folk-Art, 1948, p.138*

113. Great Lily Of Ephrata, From The Christian ABC Book, 1750
Showing stipple and etched work of the Ephrata Fraktur artists.
*Stoudt, Pennsylvania Folk-Art, 1948, p.141*

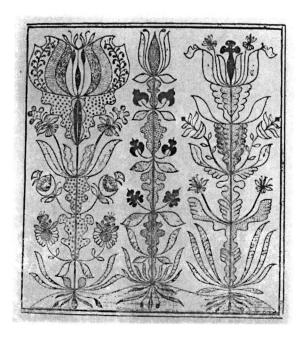

114. Lily Designs, From The Christian ABC Book, 1750
*Stoudt, Pennsylvania Folk-Art, 1948, p.140*

115-116. Ephrata Ms., The Christian ABC Book, 1750
Large alphabets with and without decorative borders.
*Stoudt, Pennsylvania Folk-Art, 1948, p.142*

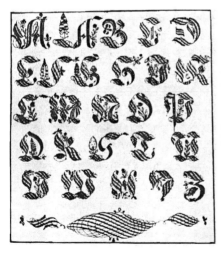

117. Ephrata Ms., The Christian ABC Book, 1750
Small capitals.
*Stoudt, Pennsylvania Folk-Art, 1948, p.150*

118. Ephrata Ms., The Christian ABC Book, 1750
Alphabets of large and small lower case letters.
*Stoudt, Pennsylvania Folk-Art, 1948, p.151*

119. Ephrata Ms., The Paradisisches Wunder-Spiel, Dedication Page, 1751
Detail of right-hand half of page with Dedication to Beissel; as
with the *Turteltaube*, this is the manuscript presentation copy
to Conrad Beissel which preceded the printed work.
*Stoudt, Pennsylvania Folk-Art, 1948, p.162*

120. The Paradisisches Wunder-Spiel, Printed 1754
Later Ephrata printed Hymnal, showing typical interior pages of the work.
*American Antiquarian Society, Worcester, Mass.*

121. FRAKTUR DETAIL FROM THE PARADISISCHES WUNDER-SPIEL, FIGURE 120
Showing one of the Ephrata Sisters in typical Cloister costume.
*American Antiquarian Society, Worcester, Mass.*

122. EPHRATA MS., TITLE-PAGE OF CHORAL BOOK, 1754
*Stoudt, Pennsylvania Folk-Art, 1948, p.169*

123. DETAIL FROM EPHRATA MANUSCRIPT
Showing Sister against stippled page.
*Sachse, Music of the Ephrata Cloister, 1901, p.32*

124. EPHRATA CLOISTER SAAL, FRAKTUR WALL CHART, c.1755
*Historic Records Survey photo, Washington, D. C.*

125. Ephrata Cloister Saal, Large Fraktur Irrgarten, c.1755
*Historic Records Survey photo, Washington, D. C.*

126. Ephrata Cloister Saal, Large Fraktur Chart, Dated 1755
*Historic Records Survey photo, Washington, D. C.*

127. FRONTISPIECE OF EPHRATA MANUSCRIPT
Note variety of stippling, dotting, hatching, and diaper patterns.
*Borneman, Pennsylvania Arts and Sciences, III, 2 (July, 1938), p.72*

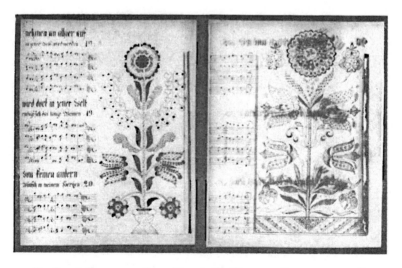

128. LATER SNOWHILL COPY (LEFT) OF EPHRATA TURTELTAUBE MS.,
1746 (RIGHT)
*Pennsylvania Historical Society, Philadelphia, Pa.*

129. INDENTURE FORM BEARING THE EPHRATA PRESS IMPRINT, c.1765
Initials perpetuate Fraktur letters of earlier Ephrata works.
*Pennsylvania Historical Society, Philadelphia, Pa.*

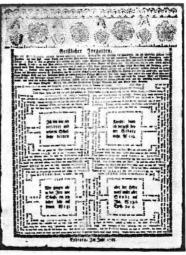

130. EPHRATA GOLDENE ABC, BEARING IMPRINT AND DATE 1772
One of the few broadsides from the later period of the Ephrata press.
*Unger collection, Pottsville, Pa.*

131. EPHRATA GEISTLICHER IRRGARTEN, PRINTED 1788
Unusual in that it bears at the top the textile block seen later, as well
as contemporaneously, in the Certificates of Henrich Otto.
*Unger collection, Pottsville, Pa.*

132. CHRISTOPHER DOCK, GOLDENE ABC
*Brumbaugh, Life and Works of Christopher Dock, 1908, p.240*

133. CHRISTOPHER DOCK, VORSCHRIFT
Pages such as this had tremendous influence in setting the pattern
for Fraktur writing for more than half a century.
*Brumbaugh, Life and Works of Christopher Dock, 1908, p.249*

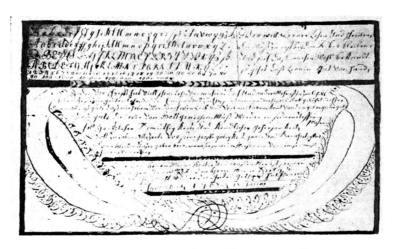

134. CHRISTOPHER DOCK, VORSCHRIFT, 1768
Note presence of penmanship flourishes which became so popular in
the Mennonite work done from 1780 onward.
*Brumbaugh, Life and Works of Christopher Dock, 1908, p.248*

135. MENNONITE VORSCHRIFT, 1786
Maintains almost literally the Christopher Dock composition above.
*Schwenkfelder Historical Library, Pennsburg, Pa.*

136. MENNONITE VORSCHRIFT, 1789
With interlace connecting letters of main title line; see Figure 14.
*Carlen collection, Philadelphia, Pa.*

137. MENNONITE VORSCHRIFT, 1792
Intricately designed capital "A" follows European
prototypes seen in Figures 5, 6, 10, 12, 14, 17 and 18.
*Brooklyn Museum, Brooklyn, N. Y.*

**138. Mennonite Vorschrift, 1794**
Horizontal bars connect letters of main title as in Europe; see Figures 13 and 14.
*Geesey collection, Wilmington, Del.*

**139. Mennonite Vorschrift, 1804**
Made up of several distinct component parts, one of them *on end!*
*Philadelphia Museum of Art, Philadelphia, Pa.*

140.  MENNONITE VORSCHRIFT, 1809
Characteristic Mennonite piece of the period from 1800 onwards.
*Borneman, Pennsylvania German Illuminated Manuscripts, 1937, pl.5*

141.  MENNONITE VORSCHRIFT, 1856
Demonstrates how tenacious designs such as the preceding one were.
*American-German Review, June, 1943, p.33*

142. JACOB OBERHOLTZER, BIBLE, BOOKPLATE, 1787
Illuminated Title-pages for books of all kinds were greatly favored by the
Mennonite illuminators. This one is also a Birth and Marriage Record.
*Stoudt, Pennsylvania Folk-Art, 1948, p.207*

143. JACOB OBERHOLTZER, SONGBOOK, BOOKPLATE, 1788
Illuminated Title-pages for small horizontal Songbooks and vertical Testaments,
or for quarter-size Copybooks (see Figures 47 and 144-147) are seen most often.
*Lorimer collection, Philadelphia, Pa.*

144. JACOB OBERHOLTZER, COPYBOOK, BOOKPLATE, 1782
Typical 4-page manuscript Fraktur booklet, as in Figure 47.
*Bucks County Historical Society, Doylestown, Pa.*

145. JACOB OBERHOLTZER, COPYBOOK, 1782
Page 2.
*Bucks County Historical Society, Doylestown, Pa.*

146. JACOB OBERHOLTZER, COPYBOOK, 1782
Page 3.
*Bucks County Historical Society, Doylestown, Pa.*

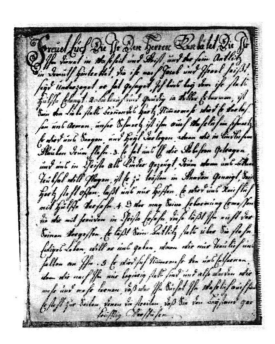

147. JACOB OBERHOLTZER, COPYBOOK, 1782
Page 4.
*Bucks County Historical Society, Doylestown, Pa.*

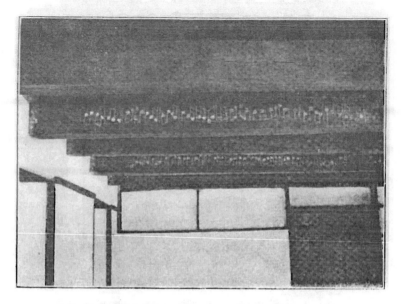

148. DEEP RUN SCHOOL, INTERIOR, BUCKS COUNTY, 1897
With bars of Mennonite music inscribed on the beams of the ceiling.
*Bucks County Historical Society Papers, II, 1909, p.72*

149. MENNONITE SONGBOOK, BOOKPLATE AND INTERIOR, 1810
*Yoder collection, Silverdale, Pa.*

150. MENNONITE SONGBOOK, BOOKPLATE, 1807
Vertical Songbooks and Testaments such as this were simply printed
volumes with a hand-illuminated Title-page at the front.
*Metropolitan Museum of Art, New York, N. Y.*

151. MENNONITE SONGBOOK, BOOKPLATE, 1835
Showing the late persistence of good quality Fraktur work.
*Author's collection*

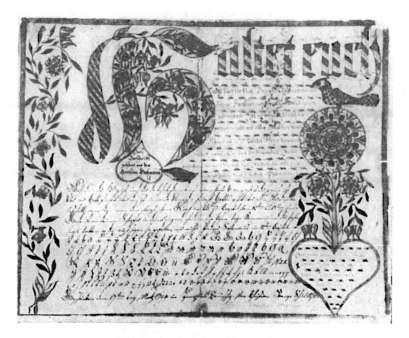

152. CHRISTIAN STRENGE, VORSCHRIFT, 1794
Strenge invariably signed himself as "Schoolmaster", as here; see also
Figures 45 and 55.
*Landis Valley Museum, Landis Valley, Pa.*

153. CHRISTIAN BACHMAN, VORSCHRIFT, 1798
*Landis Valley Museum, Landis Valley, Pa.*

154. HANS JACOB BRUBACHER *(HIBB)*, GOLDENE ABC, 1801
Typical of Brubacher's decorative form and geometric layout.
*Landis Valley Museum, Landis Valley, Pa.*

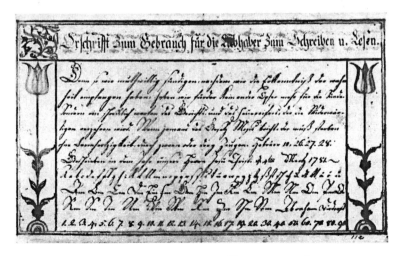

155. ABRAHAM DIRDORFF, VORSCHRIFT, 1781
Noted for these delicate Vorschrift pages entitled "For the use of
those who would love to write and read."
*Schwenkfelder Historical Library, Pennsburg, Pa.*

156. RUDOLPH LANDES, RELIGIOUS TEXT, 1816
*Lorimer collection, Philadelphia, Pa.*

157. JOHN LANDIS, VORSCHRIFT, 1828
Typical Lancaster County specimen of the 1820's and 30's.
*Hostetter collection, Lancaster, Pa.*

158. ABRAHAM HUEBNER, VORSCHRIFT, 1772
Typical early Schwenkfelder form.
*Schwenkfelder Historical Library, Pennsburg, Pa.*

159. ABRAHAM HUEBNER, VORSCHRIFT, 1773
The emphasis on the capital "J" almost suggests Mennonite influence.
*Lorimer collection, Philadelphia, Pa.*

160. DAVID KRIEBEL, VORSCHRIFT, 1805
Beautifully demonstrates the decorative flair of these
handsome Schwenkfelder pieces.
*Schwenkfelder Historical Library, Pennsburg, Pa.*

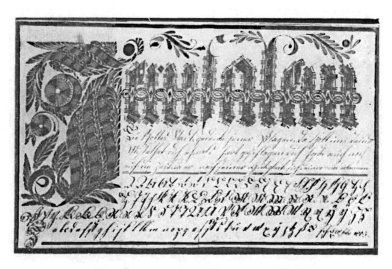

161. SCHWENKFELDER VORSCHRIFT, 1805
Demonstrates another Schwenkfelder technique, the feathering of letters.
*Unger collection, Pottsville, Pa.*

162. SCHWENKFELDER VORSCHRIFT, 1804
In the opinion of the author, one of the finest Schwenkfelder pieces.
*Schwenkfelder Historical Library, Pennsburg, Pa.*

163-164. SCHWENKFELDER DESIGNS, 1802 and 1806
Richness of forms and foliage points up Central European origins of these
people, who were perhaps the most cultured group to come to Pennsylvania.
*Schwenkfelder Historical Library, Pennsburg, Pa.*

165. SUSANNA HUEBNER, VORSCHRIFT, 1808
By perhaps the finest, and most varied, of all Schwenkfelder artists.
*Schwenkfelder Historical Library, Pennsburg, Pa.*

166. SUSANNA HUEBNER, SCHWENKFELDER HYMN, c.1808
*Schwenkfelder Historical Library, Pennsburg, Pa.*

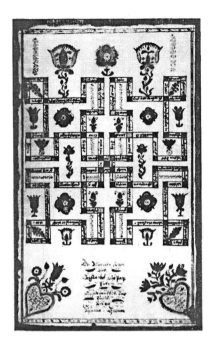

167. SUSANNA HUEBNER, GEISTLICHER, IRRGARTEN, 1808
*Schwenkfelder Historical Library, Pennsburg, Pa.*

168. SUSANNA HUEBNER, GOLDENE *ABC*, c.1808
*Schwenkfelder Historical Library, Pennsburg, Pa.*

169. SUSANNA HUEBNER, THE SEVEN RULES OF WISDOM, 1809
*Schwenkfelder Historical Library, Pennsburg, Pa.*

170. SCHWENKFELDER VORSCHRIFT, c.1803
Note the variety of treatments of the tulip motif in this one piece.
*Author's collection*

171. DAVID KRIEBEL, VORSCHRIFT, 1803
In the hands of a different decorator, the design of the previous
piece takes on a completely different character.
*Schwenkfelder Historical Library, Pennsburg, Pa.*

172. LATE SCHWENKFELDER CAPITAL LETTER "S"
Much weaker than the two preceding pieces.
*Yoder collection, Silverdale, Pa.*

173. LATE SCHWENKFELDER VORSCHRIFT, c.1840
As noted in the Mennonite work, the earlier compositions persist, but a
comparison of this with Fig. 171 demonstrates most effectively the
tremendous loss of vigor and character in the later period.
*Schwenkfelder Historical Library, Pennsburg, Pa.*

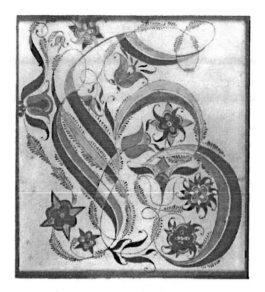

174. SCHWENKFELDER CAPITAL LETTER "H" FOR HEILIG
Not "B" for Beatus, as stated by Borneman, 1937, p.36 and Plate 17.
*Author's collection*

175. SCHWENKFELDER VORSCHRIFT, BEGINNING "SIEHE . . ."
Use of human figures in capital letters is unusual in this School.
*Schwenkfelder Historical Library, Pennsburg, Pa.*

176. SCHWENKFELDER BOOKPLATE, 1835
Shows the broad painting and blazing colors of later Schwenkfelder
work. See also the following illustration with the same
over-simplification of motifs, but absence of text.
*Yoder collection, Silverdale, Pa.*

177. SCHWENKFELDER DESIGN, LATER PERIOD, c.1835
*Lorimer collection, Philadelphia, Pa.*

178. SCHWENKFELDER FRAKTUR DESIGN, 1842
Typical of the Victorianizing of the earlier forms.
*Schwenkfelder Historical Library, Pennsburg, Pa.*

179. SCHWENKFELDER ARCHITECTURAL DESIGN, 1843
A later version of the same subject shown in Figure 66.
*Lorimer collection, Philadelphia, Pa.*

180. VERY LATE SCHWENKFELDER VORSCHRIFT, 1854
Compare Capital "I" with "J's" in Figures 159 (1773) and 161 (1805).
*Schwenkfelder Historical Library, Pennsburg, Pa.*

181-182. SCHWENKFELDER DESIGNS
Based on the use of the compass, but excellent nevertheless.
*Schwenkfelder Historical Library, Pennsburg, Pa.*

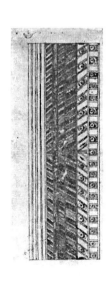

183. THREE SCHWENKFELDER BORDER DESIGNS
Typical themes found everywhere in Schwenkfelder Fraktur pieces.
*Schwenkfelder Historical Library, Pennsburg, Pa.*

184. REV. DANIEL SCHUMACHER, BIRTH CERTIFICATE, 1766
Black-and-white effect suggests Ephrata Fraktur pieces of early date.
*Author's collection*

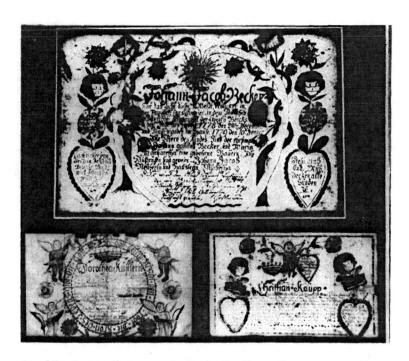

185. REV. DANIEL SCHUMACHER, GROUP OF BIRTH CERTIFICATES, 1768-1780
A comparative plate for checking characteristics of Schumacher's style.
*Pennsylvania Historical Society, Philadelphia, Pa.,*
*Berks County Historical Society, Reading, Pa., and*
*New-York Historical Society, New York, N. Y.*

186.  HENRICH OTTO, BIRTH CERTIFICATE, 1766
Note distinctive Capital "M".
*Hostetter collection, Lancaster, Pa.*

187.  HENRICH OTTO, CERTIFICATES AND DESIGNS, 1751-1788
A comparative plate for checking characteristics of Henrich Otto's style.
*Hostetter collection, Lancaster, Pa., Metropolitan Museum of Art,
New York, N. Y., same, and Private collection*

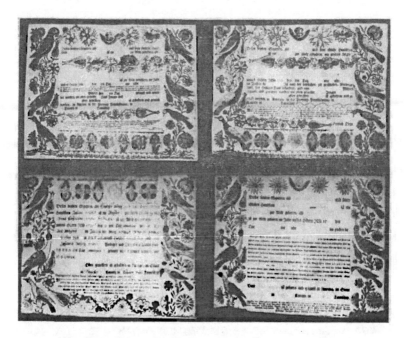

188. Four Types Of Henrich Otto Certificate Forms
Showing the development from the 1784 printed Certificate form onwards.
*Hostetter collection, Lancaster, Pa., Pennsylvania State Archive.
Harrisburg, Pa., Hostetter collection, Lancaster, Pa., and
Lancaster County Historical Society, Lancaster, Pa.*

189. Henrich Otto, Geistlicher Irrgarten, Printed 1784
*Hostetter collection, Lancaster, Pa.*

190. Henrich Otto, Christlicher Haus-Segen, Printed 1785
*Henry Ford Museum, Dearborn, Mich.*

191. FRIEDERICH SPEYER, BIRTH CERTIFICATE, c.1785
Signed in lower right corner of text-block.
*Kindig collection, York, Pa.*

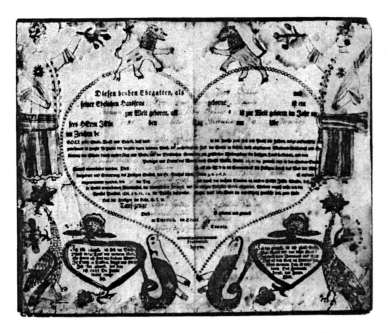

192. FRIEDERICH SPEYER, BIRTH CERTIFICATE, c.1788
*Kindig collection, York, Pa.*

193. FRIEDERICH SPEYER, FULLY-DEVELOPED BIRTH CERTIFICATE, PRINTED 1791
Whereas in Fig. 192 Speyer borrowed lion and bird motifs from
Henrich Otto, here he is borrowing mermaids from Friedrich
Krebs and angels from the Cross-legged Angel artist!
*Unger collection, Pottsville, Pa.*

194. FRIEDERICH SPEYER, CHRISTLICHER HAUS-SEGEN, PRINTED c.1785
In this instance, again, Speyer is following Otto, see Fig. 190.
*Hostetter collection, Lancaster, Pa.*

195. FRIEDRICH KREBS, EARLY CERTIFICATE — STYLE I
Demonstrates his simple, early, "line and dot" technique
*Pennsylvania State Archive, Harrisburg, Pa.*

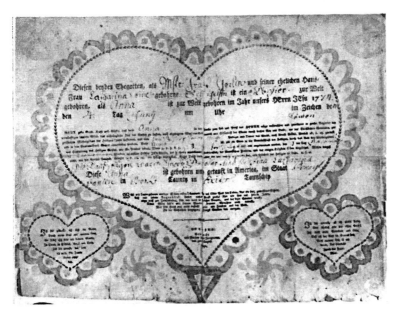

*New-York Historical Society, New York, N. Y.*
196. FRIEDRICH KREBS, CERTIFICATE, PRINTED 1790 — STYLE II
In this example he employed his later "wavy line" decoration.

197. FRIEDRICH KREBS, CERTIFICATE, PRINTED 1797 — STYLE III
This technique combines wavy lines or penmanship flourishes with small
design blocks stamped at random around the borders of the Certificate.
*Sittig collection, Shawnee-on-Delaware, Pa.*

198. FRIEDRICH KREBS, CERTIFICATE, PRINTED 1803 — STYLE IV
Here is Krebs' full-fledged style with great freedom of penmanship
and the parrots, crowns, and stars which he borrowed
from Otto and other Fraktur writers.
*Brazer collection, Flushing, N. Y.*

199. FRIEDRICH KREBS, HORSEMAN, c.1800
Drawn about the turn of the century, this free-hand Fraktur design
represents Krebs at his boldest and best as a decorator.
*Author's collection*

200. FRIEDRICH KREBS, CRUCIFIXION, c.1800
One of very few religious subjects attempted by Krebs, but
quite typical of his mature draftsmanship style.
*Landis Valley Museum, Landis Valley, Pa.*

201. C. M. Artist, Certificate, Dauphin County, Late 18th C.
*Metropolitan Museum of Art, New York, N. Y.*

202. H. Seiler, Certificate, Dauphin County, Late 18th C.
*Sussel collection, Philadelphia, Pa.*

203. READING-BERKS ARTIST, CERTIFICATE, BERKS COUNTY, LATE 18th C.
*Author's collection*

204. CROSS-LEGGED ANGEL ARTIST, CERTIFICATE, BERKS COUNTY, LATE 18th C.
*Lorimer collection, Philadelphia, Pa.*

205. Wetzel-Geometric Artist, Certificate, Berks County, Late 18th C.
See also Figure 62.
*Reading Public Museum and Art Gallery, Reading, Pa.*

206. Ehre Vater Artist, Certificate, Bucks County, Late 18th C.
*Author's collection*

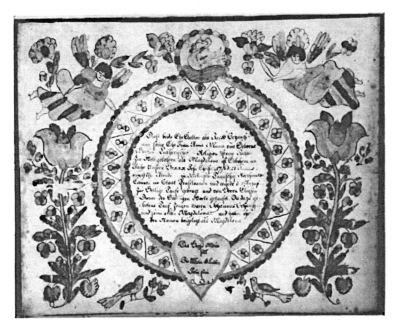

207. Flying Angel Artist, Certificate, Northampton County, Late 18th C.
*Stoudt collection, Allentown, Pa.*

208. Easton Bible Artist, Certificate, Northampton County, Late 18th C.
See also Figures 46 and 49.
*Author's collection*

209.  WEAK ARTIST, CERTIFICATE, DAUPHIN COUNTY, EARLY 19th C.
*Pennypacker collection, Kenhorst, Pa.*

210.  FLAT PARROT ARTIST, CERTIFICATE, LEBANON COUNTY, EARLY 19th C.
*Nadelman collection, Riverdale, N. Y.*

211. Martin Brechall, Certificate, Northampton County, Early 19th C.
Signed example.
*Sittig collection, Shawnee-on-Delaware, Pa.*

212. Abraham Huth, Certificate, Lebanon County, 1816
Signed and dated example.
*Unger collection, Pottsville, Pa.*

213. FLAT TULIP ARTIST, CERTIFICATE, UNION COUNTY, EARLY 19th C.
See also Figure 67.
*Reading Public Museum and Art Gallery, Reading, Pa.*

214. SPRINGING DEER ARTIST, CERTIFICATE, BERKS COUNTY, EARLY 19th C.
*Author's collection*

215. I.T.W. ARTIST. CERTIFICATE. BERKS COUNTY, EARLY 19th C.
Signed example.
*Sittig collection, Shawnee-on-Delaware, Pa.*

216. A. W. ARTIST. CERTIFICATE, YORK COUNTY, EARLY 19th C.
Signed example.
*Lorimer collection, Philadelphia, Pa.*

217. DANIEL PETERMAN, CERTIFICATE, YORK COUNTY, EARLY 19th C.
Signed example.
*Halpert collection, New York, N. Y.*

218. FRANCIS PORTZLINE, CERTIFICATE, NORTHUMBERLAND COUNTY, EARLY 19th C.
Signed example.
*Author's collection*

219. JOHANNES BARD, CERTIFICATE, ADAMS COUNTY, 1832
Signed and dated example.
*Geesey collection, Wilmington, Del.*

220. MOUNT PLEASANT ARTIST, CERTIFICATE, LANCASTER COUNTY, EARLY 19th C.
See also Figure 222.
*Author's collection*

221. HENRY LEHN, CERTIFICATE, LANCASTER COUNTY, 1843
Signed and dated example.
*Author's collection*

222. Mount Pleasant Artist, Certificate, Lancaster County, Early 19th C.
Showing not only the Fraktur, but a fine drawing on the wooden backboard.
*Author's collection*

223. John A. Landis, Spiral Labyrinth, Lancaster County, 1852
With interlacing text: "What is a gentleman?"
*Author's collection*

224. EARLY CENTRE COUNTY ARTIST, CERTIFICATE, 1823 — TYPE I
*Brazer collection, Flushing, N. Y.*

225. EARLY CENTRE COUNTY ARTIST, CERTIFICATE — TYPE II
*Author's collection*

226. EARLY CENTRE COUNTY ARTIST, CERTIFICATE — TYPE III
*Lorimer collection, Philadelphia, Pa.*

227. LATE CENTRE COUNTY ARTIST, CERTIFICATE — Type IV
*Stone collection, New York, N. Y.*

228. GEORG TEIBEL, VORSCHRIFT, 1763
Signed and dated example.
*Hostetter collection, Lancaster, Pa.*

229. CHRISTIAN PETERS, VORSCHRIFT, 1777
Signed and dated example.
*Brooklyn Museum, Brooklyn, N. Y.*

230. SUSSEL-WASHINGTON ARTIST, TAUFF-WUNSCH, c.1773
Lorimer collection, Philadelphia, Pa.

231. REV. GEORGE GEISTWEITE, VORSCHRIFT, 1801
Signed and dated example.
Lorimer collection, Philadelphia, Pa.

232. KARL C. MUENCH, CERTIFICATE, 1811
Signed and dated example.
*Lorimer collection, Philadelphia, Pa*

233. DURS RUDY, BAPTISMAL SCENE, n.d.
*Sittig collection, Shawnee-on-Delaware, Pa.*

234. Wilhelmus Antonius Faber, Certificate, c.1807
See also Figures 96-98.
*Author's collection*

235. Haus-Segen Artist, House Blessing, 1831
*Lorimer collection, Philadelphia, Pa.*

236. LUDWIG CRECELIUS, MIESSE FAMILIEN-TAFEL, 1830
Signed and dated example.
*Sussel collection, Philadelphia, Pa.*

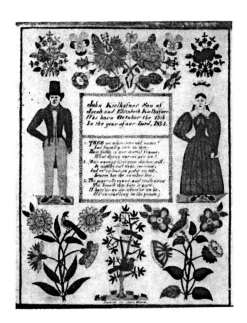

237. JOHN ZINCK, CERTIFICATE, 1834
Signed and dated example.
*Hostetter collection, Lancaster, Pa.*

238. HENRICH OTTO, CERTIFICATE, EARLY PRINTED FORM, LATE 18th C.
Imprinted with Otto's name in lower right corner.
*Allen collection, Philadelphia, Pa.*

239. PSEUDO-OTTO CERTIFICATE, LATER PRINTED FORM, c.1800
*New-York Historical Society, N. Y.*

240. F. Speyer, Horizontal Certificate, Early Block-Printed Form,
Late 18th C.
*Author's collection*

241. F. Speyer, Horizontal Certificate, Early Block-Printed Form,
Late 18th C.
*H. F. du Pont Winterthur Museum, Winterthur, Del.*

242. F. SANNO, HORIZONTAL, CERTIFICATE, CARLISLE, PRINTED 1812
*York County Historical Society, York, Pa.*

243. C. T. MELSHEIMER, HORIZONTAL CERTIFICATE, FRIEDRICHTAUN
(MARYLAND), n.d.
*Author's collection*

244. JOSEPH SCHNEE, HORIZONTAL CERTIFICATE, LIBANON, n.d.
*Unger collection, Pottsville, Pa.*

245. J. HARTMAN, HORIZONTAL CERTIFICATE, LIBANON, n.d.
*Sittig collection, Shawnee-on-Delaware, Pa.*

246. D. P. LANGE, HORIZONTAL CERTIFICATE, HANNOVER, PRINTED 1825
*Unger collection, Pottsville, Pa.*

247. WM. GUNCKEL, VERTICAL CERTIFICATE, GERMANTOWN (OHIO), n.d.
*Newman collection, New York, N. Y.*

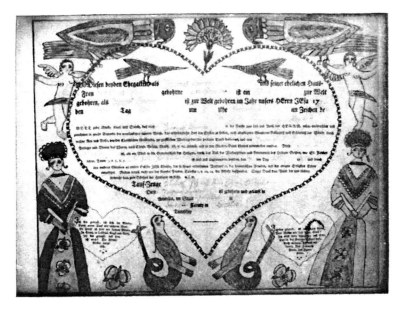

248. F. SPEYER, EARLY HEART — FORM CERTIFICATE, READING, LATE 18th C.
*Lancaster County Historical Society, Lancaster, Pa.*

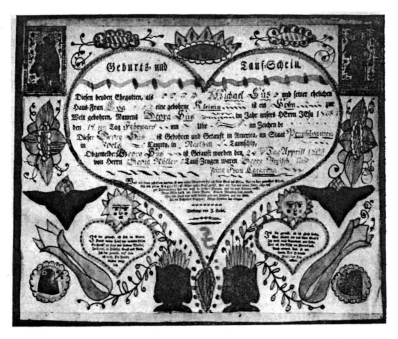

249. F. KREBS, LATER HEART — FORM CERTIFICATE, READING, POST 1800
*Sittig collection, Shawnee-on-Delaware, Pa.*

250. J. BAUMAN, CERTIFICATE, EPHRATA, n.d.
*Reading Public Museum and Art Gallery, Reading, Pa.*

251. LATER J. BAUMAN, CERTIFICATE, EPHRATA, n.d.
*Berks County Historical Society, Reading, Pa.*

252. LEPPER & STETTINIUS, CERTIFICATE, HANNOVER, PRINTED 1798
*New-York Historical Society, New York, N. Y.*

253. JACOB STOEVER, CERTIFICATE, LIBANON, n.d.
*Pennsylvania State Archive, Harrisburg, Pa.*

254. JOHANN RITTER, CERTIFICATE, READING, c.1814 — ANGEL I
*Nadelman collection, Riverdale, N. Y.*

255. DAN. PHIL. LANGE, CERTIFICATE, HANNOVER, PRINTED 1817 — ANGEL II
*Nadelman collection, Riverdale, N. Y.*

256. HEINRICH B. SAGE, CERTIFICATE, READING — ANGEL III
*Berks County Historical Society, Reading, Pa.*

257. G. S. PETERS, CERTIFICATE, HARRISBURG — ANGEL IV
*Berks County Historical Society, Reading, Pa.*

258. BAAB UND DOEBLER, CERTIFICATE, READING — ANGEL V
*Nadelman collection, Riverdale, N. Y.*

259. CARL KESSLER, CERTIFICATE, READING — ANGEL VI
*Berks County Historical Society, Reading, Pa.*

260. "WELT BOTE" PRESS, CERTIFICATE, ALLENTOWN — ANGEL VII
*Unger collection, Pottsville, Pa.*

261. H. W. VILLEE. CERTIFICATE, LANCASTER
*Unger collection, Pottsville, Pa.*

262. THEO. F. SCHEFFER, CERTIFICATE, HARRISBURG
*Pennsylvania State Museum, Harrisburg, Pa.*

263. SAMUEL MOFFLY, CERTIFICATE, 1805
Hand-drawn copy after Friedrich Krebs, Reading; see Fig. 198.
*Hostetter collection, Lancaster, Pa.*

264. UNKNOWN ARTIST, CERTIFICATE, c.1838
Hand-drawn copy after J. Bauman, Ephrata; see Fig. 86.
*Lorimer collection, Philadelphia, Pa.*

265. J. S. ARTIST, CERTIFICATE, MANHEIM, 1827
Hand-drawn copy after Johann Ritter, Reading, Angel I; see Fig. 254.
*Hostetter collection, Lancaster, Pa.*

266. S. O. DRESSLER, CERTIFICATE, 1852
Hand-drawn copy after G. S. Peters Harrisburg, Angel IV; see Fig. 257.
*Kindig collection, York, Pa.*

267. C. F. EGELMANN, ENGRAVED COPYBOOK. TITLE-PAGE (2nd Ed.), 1831
*Ruth collection, York, Pa.*

268. C. F. EGELMANN, ENGRAVED COPYBOOK, FRACTUR ALPHABET (2nd Ed.), 1831
*Author's collection*

269. C. F. Egelmann, Engraved Copybook, Vorschrift Page (2nd Ed.), 1831
*Author's collection*

270. Egelmann Early Certificate, Second State
With clouds in sky; for First State without clouds, see Fig. 101.
*Reformed Church Library, Lancaster, Pa.*

271. Egelmann Late Certificate, Second State
First State has plain tablecloth and other minor differences.
*Unger collection, Pottsville, Pa.*

272. GABRIEL MIESSE, ENGRAVED CERTIFICATE, COPY AFTER EGELMANN
See Fig. 270.
*Author's collection*

273. GABRIEL MIESSE, ENGRAVED CERTIFICATE, WITH TEXT IN ENGLISH
*Author's collection*

274. H. W. VILLEE, CERTIFICATE, LANCASTER
With wood blocks of putto and of two angels signed "G. Miesse."
*Unger collection, Pottsville, Pa.*

275-276. GABRIEL MIESSE'S BOOKPLATE
Obverse and reverse of the original engraved copper plate.
*Author's collection*

277. GABRIEL MIESSE, SWAN
Original engraved and signed copper plate.
*Author's collection*

278. GABRIEL MIESSE, COLUMBIA
Engraved on reverse of signed copper plate of Swan, Fig. 277.
*Author's collection*

279. G. MIESSE, GEORGE WASHINGTON (AFTER GILBERT STUART)
Original engraved and signed copper plate.
*Author's collection*

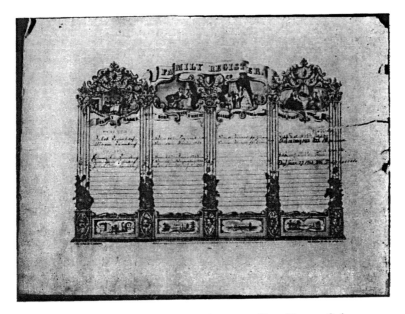

280. N. Currier, Family Register, New York, 1846
Lithograph.
*Berks County Historical Society, Reading, Pa.*

281. N. Currier, Certificate, New York, n.d.
Lithograph; see also Figure 102.
*Landis Valley Museum, Landis Valley, Pa.*

282. CURRIER & IVES, CERTIFICATE IN ENGLISH, NEW YORK, POST 1857
Lithograph.
*Berks County Historical Society, Reading, Pa.*

283. C. L. RADEMACHER, CERTIFICATE, PHILADELPHIA
Lithograph.
*Unger collection, Pottsville, Pa.*

284. AUGS. KOELLNER, CERTIFICATE, PHILADELPHIA, 1849
Lithograph.
*Unger collection, Pottsville, Pa.*

285. IG. KOHLER, CERTIFICATE, PHILADELPHIA, 1855
Lithograph.
*Landis Valley Museum, Landis Valley, Pa.*

286. SCHAEFER & KORADI, CERTIFICATE, PHILADELPHIA
Lithograph.
*Bucks County Historical Society, Doylestown, Pa.*

287. Decorated Berks County Blanket Chest
Typical Unicorn Chest with printed Fraktur pasted in lid.
*Brix collection, Philadelphia, Pa.*

288. Friederich Speyer, Adam & Eve Broadside
Detail of printed Fraktur in Blanket Chest shown above.
*Brix collection, Philadelphia, Pa.*

289. DECORATED LANCASTER COUNTY BLANKET CHEST, 1788
With Henrich Otto Drawing and Certificate, c.1788.
*Philadelphia Museum of Art, Philadelphia, Pa., Metropolitan Museum
of Art, New York, N. Y., and Private collection*

290. BRASS AND SILVER INLAID PENNSYLVANIA RIFLE, 1810-20
With J. Bauman printed Certificate. Ephrata, c.1803.
*Reading Public Museum and Art Gallery, and
Berks County Historical Society, both Reading, Pa.*

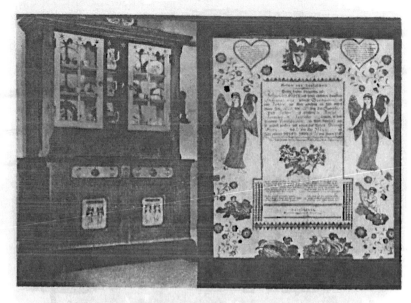

291. DECORATED MAHANTANGO VALLEY CHINA CUPBOARD, 1830
With J. Wiestling printed Certificate, Harrisburg, c.1824.
*Philadelphia Museum of Art, Philadelphia, Pa.,
and Author's collection*

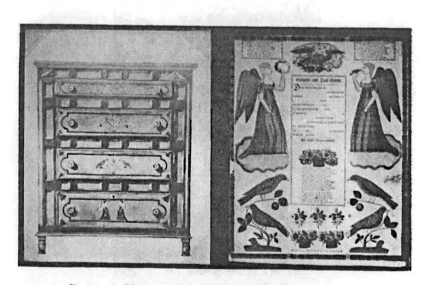

292. DECORATED MAHANTANGO VALLEY CHEST OF DRAWERS, 1830-35
With G. S. Peters printed Certificate, Harrisburg, 1829.
*Philadelphia Museum of Art, Philadelphia, Pa., and
Pennsylvania State Archive, Harrisburg, Pa.*

293. BERKS COUNTY, PA., AND BALTIMORE COUNTY, MD.,
BIRTH CERTIFICATES, c.1805
Both Taufscheins written and decorated by the same artist.
*Hofer collection, Cambridge, Mass., and
Halpert collection, New York, N. Y.*

294. FREDERICK, MARYLAND, BIRTH CERTIFICATE, 1809
Showing the transfer of Pennsylvania German motifs.
*New-York Historical Society, New York, N. Y.*

295. SHENANDOAH VALLEY, VIRGINIA, BIRTH CERTIFICATE, c.1787
Repeating motifs and layout of Pennsylvania German examples.
*Wichmann collection, New York, N. Y.*

296. SHENANDOAH VALLEY, VIRGINIA, BIRTH CERTIFICATE, c.1821
Continuing Pennsylvania German heart-form in new layout.
*New-York Historical Society, New York, N. Y.*

297. OHIO, BIRTH CERTIFICATE BY FRIEDRICK BANDEL, c.1809
The artist borrowed Otto's bird designs, as in Figure 188, for his borders.
*Trump collection, Medina, Ohio*

298. TRUMBULL COUNTY OHIO, BIRTH CERTIFICATE BY ALEXANDER TAYLOR, 1829
The designs and lettering closely resemble those of J. George Busgaeger,
active in Westmoreland County in Western Pennsylvania, 1815-1825.
*Trump collection, Medina, Ohio*

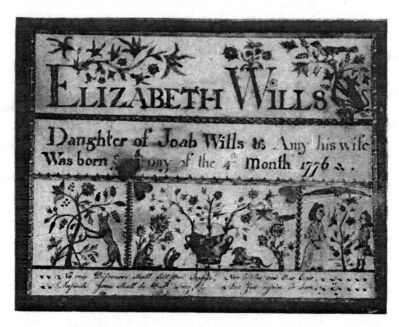

299. NEW JERSEY, ELIZABETH WILLS BIRTH CERTIFICATE, 1776
*Lorimer collection, Philadelphia, Pa.*

300. NEW JERSEY, FRANCIS STANGER MARRIAGE CERTIFICATE, 1803
Member of the family of glass blowers who started the second glass house
in New Jersey at Glassboro about 1780.
*Henry Ford Museum, Dearborn, Mich.*

301. New York State, Lipe Family Record, 1806
Drawn by William Murray.
*Sussel collection, Philadelphia, Pa.*

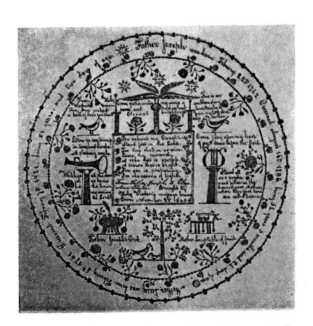

302. New York State, Shaker Spirit Drawing, 1845.
By Eliza Ann Taylor, New Lebanon eldress.
*Western Reserve Historical Society, Cleveland, Ohio.*

303. CONNECTICUT, FINCH FAMILY RECORD, c.1804
By William Holmes.
*Henry Ford Museum, Dearborn, Mich.*

304. NEW HAMPSHIRE, BUSWELL FAMILY RECORD, c.1799
*New-York Historical Society, New York, N. Y.*

305. VERMONT, TUCKER FAMILY REGISTER, c.1834
*New-York Historical Society, New York, N. Y.*

# XI Index

# Index

# OFFICERS
## OF THE
## PENNSYLVANIA GERMAN FOLKLORE SOCIETY
### 1959

### BOARD OF DIRECTORS

*President*............ ... ...... . .. ........ .. ARTHUR D. GRAEFF, Ed.D.
*Secretary*.. ... ..................... .... ... ..... ..... .. ........RALPH C. WOOD, Ph.D.
*Financial Secretary*................ .. .... ... ..... ... ... ...... .HARRY OXENREIDER
*Treasurer*...... ................... . ...... .... .. ... ...... ....... . ..... . . .EARL W. ROLLMAN
*Editor-in-Chief*.. ... ........ ... .. ....PRESTON A. BARBA, Ph D., Litt.D.

### *Vice-Presidents*

PRESTON A. BARBA  J. STEWART HEILMAN
JOHN Z. HARNER  RALPH W SCHLOSSER, Litt.D.

### *Honorary Vice-Presidents*

E. P FLANDES, M.D.  DONALD A. SHELLEY, Ph.D.
*DANIEL K. HOCH  PIERCE E. SWOPE, D.D.
ROBERT P. MORE, M.A.  JOHN W. WAYLAND, Ph.D.

### *Past-Presidents, Ex-Officio*

HENRY S. GEHMAN, Ph.D., S.T.D. *HIRAM H. KELLER, LL.D., P.J.
JAMES F. HENNINGER, LL.D., P.J. LEWIS C. SCHEFFY, M.D , Sc.D.

### *Directors, Elective*

| *(Term ending 1959)* | *(Term ending 1960)* |
|---|---|
| EARL T. ADAMS | HOWARD K. BEARD |
| ALBERT F. BUFFINGTON, Ph.D. | LUTHER BROSSMAN, Ph D. |
| MRS. GEORGE J. LERCH | OWEN L. FOX |
| GRANT M. STOLTZFUS | RALPH S. FUNK |
| CARL S SWARR | JOHN JOSEPH STOUDT, Ph D. |

### *(Term ending 1961)*

ROY H. DUNDORE
RUSSELL W. GILBERT, Ph.D.
GEORGE E NITZSCHE, Litt.D.
EDWARD W. SCHLECHTER
FREDERICK S. WEISER

* Deceased

CPSIA information can be obtained at www.ICGtesting.com
Printed in the USA
LVOW051935310512

283957LV00005BA/60/P